Building an Arsenal

BUILDING AN ARSENAL

The Evolution of Regional Power Force Structures

AMIT GUPTA

Westport, Connecticut
London

UA10
.G77
1997

Library of Congress Cataloging-in-Publication Data

Gupta, Amit, 1958–
    Building an arsenal : the evolution of regional power force
structures / Amit Gupta.
       p. cm.
    Includes bibliographical references and index.
    ISBN 0–275–95787–X (alk. paper)
    1. Arms race. 2. Arms transfers—India. 3. Arms transfers—
Israel. 4. Arms transfers—Brazil. 5. Defense industries—India.
6. Defense industries—Israel. 7. Defense industries—Brazil.
I. Title.
UA10.G77   1997
355.8′2—dc20   96–27453

British Library Cataloguing in Publication Data is available.

Library of Congress Catalog Card Number: 96–27453
ISBN: 0–275–95787–X

First published in 1997

Praeger Publishers, 88 Post Road West, Westport, CT 06881
An imprint of Greenwood Publishing Group, Inc.

Printed in the United States of America

The paper used in this book complies with the
Permanent Paper Standard issued by the National
Information Standards Organization (Z39.48–1984).

10 9 8 7 6 5 4 3 2 1

This book is dedicated to my parents,
Ambika and Sisir Gupta.

Contents

List of Tables

Acknowledgments

A number of people provided me with help, support, and encouragement in writing this book. Giri Deshingkar was both a friend and a mentor. I am also grateful to Marvin Weinbaum, Norm Graham, V. Arunachalam, Kota Harinarayana, and Kingshuk Nag for their insights into the international arms production and weapons acquisition process.

My wife, Susanne M. Birgerson, went through earlier drafts of the manuscript and made valuable suggestions. I would also like to acknowledge the help given to me by Ira Gupta, James Finlay, and Rupak Chattopadhyay. And, finally, I must acknowledge the indelible imprint left on this manuscript by Mabel van Basten.

1

The Analytical Framework

In the new world disorder, U.S. forces and military doctrine are being reconfigured to deal with the threat posed by regional powers. This change in military doctrine has resulted from the perceived intentions of various regional powers to build advanced conventional weapons and weapons of mass destruction. This book argues that such a strategy is based on examining the announced or supposed intentions of regional powers rather than their actual capabilities. In doing so, it follows the pathologies of the Cold War where the Soviet Union's military intentions were countered without taking into account its actual military capability. The result was an escalating arms race. In the post-Cold War context, continuing such Cold War pathologies not only sustains high defense spending but also leads to losing opportunities for co-opting regional powers into institutional and other mechanisms for creating a more peaceful and stable international system.

The purpose of this book, therefore, is to show how the weapons production and arms acquisition process of regional powers constrain their actual capabilities and subsequently determine their behavior in the emerging international system. The issue has significance because in an emerging multipolar system these states are seen to be on the threshold, because of their military buildups, of their potential for becoming major powers.

This book examines the weapons acquisition and arms production efforts of three regional powers—India, Israel, and Brazil. In the 1980s, all three countries had a major defense science base, all had programs to produce both advanced conventional weapons and unconventional weaponry, and all three had aspirations for achieving greater status in the international system. Studying this group of states, therefore, provides some indication of the possible successes and constraints other regional powers would face in their militarization process. It argues that, despite varying threat levels and different approaches to arms acquisition and production, this class of states faces similar constraints in the development of their force structures.

Such constraints emerge because the weapons acquisition process is determined by the interaction between demand and supply factors. The demand for weapons comes from the need to counter threats and the desire to fulfill the often competing bureaucratic agendas of the armed forces, the national leadership, and the defense industries. But the ability to achieve these force structures is dependent on the availability of external suppliers and the ability of a state to raise indigenous resources for weapons purchases. The interaction of these factors has led to unintended outcomes in weapons production and arms acquisition, specifically:

1. Regional powers tend to have incomplete force structures; some countries have good missile programs while others have good tanks or artillery but no country has a viable and complete military system as the major military powers in the world have had.
2. Military modernization efforts by this group of countries tends to have an on-again/off-again character, which is due to such constraints as the lack of financial resources, the unavailability of technology, and the infeasibility of producing particular weapons systems. Thus weapons programs may appear, disappear, and reappear due to the bureaucratic infighting between different groups.
3. The availability of resources leads to the opening and closing of military doctrine. When resources are available, a nation is able to build up its armed forces and pursue a more aggressive military doctrine. When resources are unavailable, a country is forced to pursue a more defensive posture.
4. It has been easier for a number of regional powers to produce weapons of mass destruction than advanced conventional weapons. Israel remains heavily dependent on external suppliers for conventional arms but it has been successful in developing a nuclear weapons and ballistic missile program. India's conventional programs have also run into time delays and cost escalations while its unconventional programs have succeeded.

Such constraints make it necessary for this class of states to continue to depend on external suppliers for building their military arsenals. It also makes it necessary for them to adopt a cooperative approach toward the major powers if they wish to achieve their quest for greater status in the international system.

The book concludes by discussing the implications that the rise of militarized regional powers has for U.S. national security policy in the emerging international system. As the remaining superpower, the United States has sought to create a new order in the emerging international system. Such attempts, however, have been limited by budgetary constraints and a domestic public opinion which is unwilling to commit American forces overseas for long periods of time. This has led the United States to seek multilateral means to achieve security in the new international system. So far such partners have been sought in the North but this volume argues that regional powers, due to the systemic and domestic constraints on the development of their force structures, may make potential allies in achieving peace and order in the emerging international system.

A CAVEAT

This study is not attempting to provide a theory about the efforts of regional powers to arm themselves. Instead it is an explanation of the trends that shape military force structures. The study, therefore, takes the approach suggested by Samuel Huntington is his book *The Third Wave*. Drawing the distinction between a theory and an explanation, Huntington writes: "A good theory is precise, austere, elegant, and highlights the relations among a few conceptual variables. Inevitably, no theory can explain fully a single event or group of events. An explanation, in contrast, is invariably complex, dense, messy, and intellectually unsatisfying. It succeeds not by being austere, but by being comprehensive."[1] This is a complex, dense, and messy study because it seeks to provide a more comprehensive and insightful explanation than theory provides. Theory, while simple and elegant, has the limitation of explaining less. In some theoretical approaches, as Susan Strange suggests, there is also a tendency to take common-senseical facts and place them in new categories or taxonomies. Strange suggests that international studies should be examining not what is apparent, but what are puzzles or even paradoxes.[2] Because this book seeks to explain less obvious or even paradoxical trends, it uses the more modest explanatory approach. The problem it seeks to examine arose from the transformation of the international system from a bipolar into a multipolar one.

THE PROBLEM

In the aftermath of the 1991 Gulf War and with the demise of communism, American security analysts began paying greater attention to the possibility of further North-South conflicts. The likely proliferation of high-tech weapons systems, particularly weapons of mass destruction, in the Southern countries created the fear that the West, led by the United States, would be increasingly engaged in combating such new military powers. This concern was reflected at the policymaking level by a shift in military strategy. US military strategy was reconfigured in the early 1990s to deal with a regional rather than a global threat. Discussing the nature of the threats to US security in the 1990s, the Pentagon argued that because of changes in the strategic environment, the threats it expected to face were regional rather than global, "We will, of course deter and defend against strategic nuclear attacks as we have for the past forty years. We will also retain the potential to defeat a global threat should one emerge. However, our plans and resources are primarily focused on deterring and fighting regional rather than global wars."[3]

The reason for such concern lay in the perceived growth in military capability of the regional powers of the Third World. It specifically came from three factors that had enhanced the military capability of these regional powers: the high level of conventional arms transfers to nations of the Third World in the 1980s; the fact that several Third World nations had embarked on ambitious arms production programs; and, on a related note, the move in some of these nations to acquire weapons of mass destruction and the means to deliver them.[4] As Michael Klare argues developing countries spent an estimated $341 billion (in constant 1988 dollars) on imported arms and military systems between 1981 and 1988. When this was coupled with their indigenous weapons production capability it gave these countries a "formidable war-making capability."[5] Klare concludes:

what makes this prospect especially worrisome, however, is the fact that more and more Third World countries are likely to acquire weapons of mass destruction in the years ahead, along with ballistic missiles of intercontinental or continental range. What this means, in effect, is that future regional conflict in the Third World will increasingly pose a threat of uncontrolled escalation, bringing the world closer to the brink of nuclear war.[6]

What emerges from Klare's description of the militarization of the Third World are two possible, and related, implications for the emerging post-Cold War international system. One is that unlimited transfers and the growing production of weapons of mass destruction make these nations into competitors for wealth and resources within the new international system. Further, it is implicit in this belief that these nations are non-status quo powers that are willing to use military power in this competition. The use of military power would include the willingness to use weapons of mass destruction such as nuclear, chemical and biological weapons. At another level, the rise of Third World arms producers removes the control imposed by the superpowers in the bipolar system on weapons transfers and instead we will see a new international system in which there is an uncontrolled flow of weapons thereby increasing conflict and tension levels.

The consequence of such thinking was the unveiling by the Clinton administration, in September 1993, of a Bottom-Up Review of the U.S. defense policy in a post-Cold War security environment. The review recommended the adoption of a force structure that would permit the United States, if necessary, to fight two simultaneous regional wars without allied support and achieve quick and decisive victories.[7] It was expected that such conflicts would be fought in an environment in which weapons of mass destruction would be used. The Department of Defense, therefore, recommended the establishment of a counterproliferation policy. It argued, "Weapons of mass destruction [WMD] may directly threaten U.S. forces in the field and, in a more perplexing way, threaten the effective force employment by requiring dispersal of those forces. Potential adversaries may use weapons of mass destruction to deter US power projection abroad."[8] Given the likelihood of facing an adversary armed with such weapons the Pentagon advocated a policy of counterproliferation which includes the detection and destruction of weapons of mass destruction from production through storage and deployment. It also calls for structuring forces to conduct military operations in a WMD environment.[9] Thus U.S. policy, in the face of systemic transformation, is being forced to move away from a global policy of containment to one of dealing with regional threats.

The apparent growth in Third World military capability could lead to a major shift from the days of bipolarity when the superpowers sought to control both the military capability of Third World countries as well as the level of conflict within different regions. Thus, in the Cold War era, the superpowers, in some cases, were able to impose less than perfect regional solutions in their attempts to counterbalance each other—the partition of Korea and the Arab-Israel conflict being instances to the point. Now, however, with the increase in military capability would seem to come immunity from superpower control and the likelihood of resolving outstanding disputes militarily. Countering such moves would require an expensive military commitment by the West—both in terms of the economic cost and the number of human lives lost.

At the very least it would mean the unrestricted flow of weapons, possibly weapons of mass destruction, in the international system. During the era of bipolarity the superpowers were fairly successful in controlling the global spread of weapons systems. Being the major suppliers of weaponry in the 1950s and 1960s, the superpowers were able to control both the quantity and quality of weapons sold—or given under grants—to the Third World. By the 1970s the level of control began to weaken as commercial considerations began to motivate arms sales—especially in the Middle East where the Western effort was to recycle petrodollars. Even then the United States was able to restrain the quality of weapons sold in critical areas like the Middle East. The Saudis, for example, were unable to get the complete weapons package they required for the F-15 from the United States because of Washington's concerns about preserving the military balance in the Middle East and due to the lobbying efforts of pro-Israeli groups.[10]

In the last decade of bipolarity, however, control over arms sales broke down. Other Western states as well as countries from the South, began to break superpower arrangements in a bid to gain exports and preserve their own arms industries. Thus when the Saudis were refused a more advanced version of the F-15 in the mid-1980s, they were able to buy a more capable aircraft from the British.[11] Another country to exploit the situation in the Middle East was France, which sold large quantities of weapons to Libya and, especially, Iraq. Similarly, the entire debate in the United States—in the late 1970s and early 1980s—on what arms to sell Pakistan without destabilizing the India-Pakistan military balance became irrelevant because of the massive arms transfers to India—from the Soviets and the West Europeans—in the early 1980s.

The ability to control the flow of arms transfers was further degraded by the entry of Third World countries like Brazil, Israel, and North Korea into the international market. Combined with the already strong Chinese presence, the entry of Third World countries into the arms market changed it from a seller's market into a buyer's one. Arms were readily available on the international market as the third-tier arms producers, driven by economic considerations, removed all restraints on weapons sales. This was particularly noticeable in the case of the Iran-Iraq war, where twenty-eight nations ended up selling weapons to both combatants.

What we see, therefore, is that in the new international system regional powers, due to their large scale purchase and domestic production of weaponry, are seen as the new threat. In defining this threat Western observers have looked not at the intentions of these nations but, instead, at the capabilities they are expected to have as a result of their acquisitions and weapons programs. Discussing this issue, a *New York Times* report stated, "Military planners often insist that they must address military capabilities of potential adversaries and not political trends that could be reversed."[12]

The problem with this approach, especially prominent in the United States, is that it focuses on intentions: it looks at what systems are being produced or acquired by a particular country; it then uses the likely existence of these systems to ascribe military capabilities to the possessor; and finally it presents this "capability" as a threat which has to be countered. This approach has limited value, as it does not take into consideration the complexity of the arms acquisition and weapons production process in Southern countries.

First, it does not explain why the military force structures emerge the way they do in Third World countries. The fact is that the force structures of Third World countries tend to be lopsided. Some countries have good missile programs while others have good tanks or artillery. But no country has a viable and complete military system as the major military powers in the world do. Second, the approach does not take into account the constraints that limit arms acquisition and weapons production in the Third World. Military modernization efforts of Third World countries tend to have an on-again off-again character which is due to such constraints as the lack of financial resources, the unavailability of technology, the feasibility of producing a particular weapons system, and the role organizational pressures play in shaping decisions on force expansion. Overlooking these factors has led to the United States painting an exaggerated picture of the capabilities of Third World countries and making them into larger threats than they actually are or are likely to become. Failure to recognize the impact of these factors also distorts attempts to understand the nature of the arms acquisition process in Third World countries and the future trends that may emerge in this process. These inadequacies become apparent when one examines the literature on militarization, as well as that of broader international relations, and applies it to the South.

The large body of literature on militarization in the South falls into two categories: one looks at global trends in arms production and acquisition, and the other concentrates on individual cases. The literature looking at global trends has sought to show what type of weapons have been transferred to the major nations of the South. It has also examined the degree to which these countries have been successful in their arms production efforts and the global impact of "Third World military industrialization." Such approaches are exemplified in two books by Thomas Ohlson and Michael Brzoska, who in the 1980s were at the Stockholm International Peace Research Institute.

Brzoska and Ohlson put together one book looking at arms production in the Third World and another looking at arms transfers to it. Their goal was to determine what sort of capabilities various countries had acquired to produce modern weaponry. In doing so they ignored how internal decisions and the external environment shaped production and acquisition outcomes.[13] The arms transfers volume, similarly, was more concerned with tabulating who got what from whom. As a consequence, it ignored the decision making process, the role played by resource availability, and individual choices.[14] More importantly neither volume provided a conceptual framework which could be applied across the Third World. James Everett Katz, similarly, edited two volumes in the mid-1980s looking at Third World arms production and militarization.[15] Both volumes essentially amounted to case studies of different nations again without an explanatory framework to provide a basis for comparison.

In the general literature on armament dynamics, Mary Kaldor argues that the transfer of weapons systems by the North leads to replication of military institutions and cultures around the world.[16] The existence of such structures in the Third World creates the continued demand for increasingly complex weapons systems as the military bureaucracies of the Southern countries seek to emulate those of the North. Kaldor 's argument is valid in that such replication creates a culture lag among Southern militaries as they aspire to become like their parent organizations. But there is a gap between aspirations and the eventual shape of force structures that cannot be explained using Kaldor's analysis. Instead one has to go within the decision making process to seek explanations to such outcomes.

There are several excellent efforts to explain the impact of organizational behavior and bureaucratic politics on arms production and military doctrine in the North. Edward Kolodziej has discussed the development of Military Industrial Scientific Technological complexes (MISTs), which are created to provide autonomy in weapons production but which, once in place, "tend to make claims on internal investment resources that progressively enlarge their impact on their national economies and the world economy."[17] Within the regional powers of the South, the MIST is divided into military and industrial-scientific camps, which often compete with each other for scarce resources. Barry Posen takes a different approach when he uses balance-of-power and organizational pressures as the determinants of military doctrine.[18] Although both categories are useful to explain the evolution of military forces, factors such as bureaucratic competition and the role of external suppliers need to be figured into a discussion of Southern regional powers. The latter point is particularly important because the military buildup of these countries has involved dependent militarization.

At the unit level of analysis, a number of substantive studies have been done on the security process of individual countries. Aaron Klieman and Stewart Reiser have both examined the Israeli case.[19] Reiser especially is useful because he examines the role of bureaucratic politics in determining weapons acquisition efforts in Israel. Raju Thomas, K. Subrahmanyam, and Ron Matthews have studied the politics of arms production and acquisition and security decision making in India.[20] Thomas's volume remains to date the only work done on the budgetary politics that shaped the development of the Indian armed forces from 1947 to 1971. In the Brazilian case, Patrice Franko-Jones has done an in-depth study of the economic, political, and technological factors impacting that country's decision to manufacture arms. Further, both Brzoska and Ohlson volumes as well as those by Katz are useful for garnering evidence on the national security process in different states. But no explanatory framework which can be applied across countries to analyze production and acquisition outcomes emerges from these studies.

Moving from the specific area of arms production and acquisition to general international relations literature, one finds two prevailing themes in the debate about the forces shaping the post-Cold War international system. One is the state-centric approach, which is best exemplified by post-Cold War Realism. The focus of post-Cold War Realism is on the diffusion of power caused by the shift from bipolarity to multipolarity and the challenges this transition poses for security management in the new international system. John Mearsheimer's writings, which are typical of this approach, discuss the challenges posed to systemic stability by the advent of multipolarity.[21] But Mearsheimer falls in the same trap as Brzoska and Ohlson in that he ascribes intentions and military power on the basis of the perceived capability to produce particular weapons systems. Mearsheimer's thinking runs along the following lines. Poland, as an example, sees itself faced with external threats which could endanger its survival. Poland has a civilian nuclear program, ergo Poland has the capability to make nuclear weapons. Poland therefore will address these threats by going nuclear or seeking allies who can provide a nuclear umbrella. Such deterministic thinking ignores the workings of the internal security process and therefore paints a worst case scenario that is both bad academics and a disastrous prescription for future policy. The other problem with post-Cold War Realism is that it ignores the role of non-Western regional powers.

With the death of the Cold War there is a belated recognition in the International Relations community that they have to examine the non-state centric issues (both internal and transnational) which drive international relations. Recognizing this problem, the agenda for the 1996 International

Studies Association conference states, "In our view, the new agenda should focus not only on the traditional concerns of international relations but also on the underlying social, economic, and political trends that were apparent before the end of the Cold War, contributed to that end, and continue to shape ideas, politics, and material life."[22] The agenda continues by calling for papers that "expand the existing boundaries of what has hitherto been understood as "international studies." In the past few years non-state literature has emerged on environmental disasters and international relations (Thomas Homer-Dixon), on the forces of integration and disintegration (Benjamin Barber), and on civilizational as opposed to ideological consciousness (Samuel Huntington).[23] All of these approaches view the South as a threat that needs to be contained. Thus there is scant literature which discusses the potential for North-South security cooperation in the new international system. One of the conclusions of this book, however, is that given military, political, and economic constraints in both the North and among some of the regional powers of the South such cooperation is both necessary and feasible. It therefore discusses international approaches, as opposed to simply great-power approaches, to maintaining security in the new international system.

THE SCOPE OF EXPLANATION

How then can the acquisition and production of arms by Third World states be explained? In order to do this one needs to first settle which states are to be included in this analysis. One of the most frequent criticisms of the term "Third World" is that it lumps together over a hundred economically, socially, and culturally diverse nations for the purpose of academic analyses. This criticism becomes all the more apparent when one examines the arms acquisition and weapons production processes in these countries. In the Third World the nature of the security dilemma varies considerably from nation to nation. High levels of disparity also exist in their military capabilities, their ability to acquire financial resources, their ability to procure arms, and their indigenous technological base. How then does one deal with the problem? One solution would be to do what Sir Humphery Appleby, the British Civil Service mandarin in the *Yes Minister* television series, suggested to his new minister, "Put the difficult part in the title and forget about it."[24] Not being able to take such a convenient step, however, one has to clearly define the scope of the following analysis. To do this one has to omit the bulk of the nations in the Third World.

There are only a few nations within the Third World which have the resources, or feel the threat, to maintain large military units. The bulk of Third World nations, due to resource constraints, have small armed forces and see themselves as facing largely internal threats. Sub-Saharan Africa as a region probably best brings out this distinction. If one omits South Africa, Angola, and Mozambique, the rest of the nations, although being of middling size, have fairly small armed forces. A country such as Cameroons, for instance, while having a population of approximately 10,000,000 has an army of only 6,000.[25] Second, very few of these countries have the indigenous capability, in terms of industrial infrastructure or scientific personnel, to produce or successfully absorb these weapons systems. One can therefore eliminate nations like El Salvador, Guatemala, or Botswana from this list. Third, the majority of the nations within the Third World do not face major external threats. This is reflected in the military force levels of most of the nations of Africa and Latin America where, despite large population levels, the actual armies are small and used primarily for counterinsurgency purposes.[26]

Fourth, one needs to eliminate nations for which the armed forces are not the primary defenders of security. Such nations, despite procuring and in some cases producing weaponry, lack the ability to become significant competitors in the quest for power and resources in the global arena. Within the international system exist states like Iceland and New Zealand which, while having military forces, do not have the capability to withstand an external attack. Within the Third World nations facing such a predicament also exist. Saudi Arabia is probably the best example of such a state which, despite have spent billions on upgrading its military forces, still lacks the capability to defend itself against a major regional rival.

Having eliminated these states what remains are a group of nations which not only have large standing military forces but have also invested in the development of a military-industrial-scientific base for the production of armaments. But this is not a sufficient form of delineation. There are a number of nations like Chile and Singapore who have built military-industrial complexes but are not seeking to become emerging powers within the international system. Thus what is produced or acquired also becomes important. The production and acquisition of weapons of mass destruction and of weapons of extraregional range, therefore, becomes the last condition in defining the scope of the study. It is nations with a significant conventional capability that are simultaneously trying to acquire nuclear, chemical, and biological weapons—in addition to ballistic missiles to deliver them—that are the focus of this study. Also included in this list of weapons are systems which have no relevance to the regional balance of power. Brazil's attempt to develop a nuclear submarine, for instance, is not generated by the threat posed by its principal regional rival Argentina. But the Brazilian acquisition of a nuclear submarine is viewed with concern outside the region since it is seen as giving the Brazilian Navy an extraregional capability. Similarly, the Indian Navy's nuclear submarine and aircraft carrier programs are not geared toward meeting regional threats. But it will give the Indian Navy a blue water capability which is viewed with concern in capitals as distant as Canberra and Djakarta.

One is thus looking at Third World countries that have the following factors operating within their national security system.

1. They have a scientific-industrial base that seeks to develop advanced weapons systems.

2. They have modern armed forces that feel the need to acquire advanced weapons systems and see themselves as part of a global military order.
3. They have or can acquire resources to procure advanced weapons from abroad.
4. They are seeking to develop or acquire weapons which give them an extra-regional capability (nuclear submarines, aircraft carriers, intermediate range ballistic missiles and long-range transport aircraft).
5. Are seeking to develop or acquire weapons of mass destruction and their associated delivery systems (ballistic missiles, long-range combat aircraft).

The number of Third World nations that fulfill these conditions are few. They include Brazil, India, Israel, Pakistan, Iraq (before the Gulf War), South Korea, North Korea and South Africa. Another nation that needs to be discussed in this context is China, which in terms of its developmental status ranks lower than some of the nations mentioned earlier. Yet China has built up a major military machine and has earlier faced some of the problems that this book proposes to discuss.

What we are discussing here is a small group of countries, and to call them Third World states, in the sense that term has been typically used, is erroneous. Their scientific base and their military capability put them in a different league than the vast number of other states that are lumped in this category. Instead, for the purpose of this book they are described as non-Western militarized regional powers. Militarization, as defined here, is a country's development of its military forces in order to assert its foreign policy and security interests (this has some elements of what Andreski calls militancy).[27]

ANALYTICAL FRAMEWORK

How does one move away from the examination-of-intentions approach to create a conceptual framework that explains the arms acquisition and weapons production process in the Third World? To answer this question this study develops a comparative framework and uses it to examine three comparable cases.

The cases we have chosen for this purpose are three emerging powers—Israel, India, and Brazil. They are similar in that all three are regional powers. All three view their principal threats as emanating from the region and all have sought the capacity to defend themselves against regional competitors. Each of them has a large scientific-industrial base, and each attempted to acquire weapons of mass destruction, albeit for differing purposes. Further, each of these states has sought, for differing reasons, to be perceived as a strong and influential state in the international arena. In order to do this each of these countries has tried to develop a military capability which is seen as part of the package of being an influential power. Thus, we are examining states which fall within the parameters established above to determine a militarized regional power. To construct a comparative framework and derive significant explanations from it, one needs to start by asking, what motivates the acquisition of weapons?

Broadly speaking, the motivation comes from two sets of imperatives—threats and organizational pressures. The rationale for armed forces is primarily to counter the external and, increasingly, internal threats faced by a nation. Within the context of the Third World, these threats emerge, generally, not from the broader international system but from the geographical region in which the state is located. Barry Buzan, in his classic work *People, States and Fear*, reintroduced the region as an intermediate level of analysis for discussing the security dilemma of states.[28] Buzan argued that regions occupied a central position in terms of determining the threat perceptions of Third World states. States saw other units within the region as the principal threats and the conflict dynamics of one region did not spill over into that of another. Thus in the Middle East there are rivalries between the Arabs and the Israelis, between the Arabs and Iran, and among the Arab states themselves. In South Asia it is between India and Pakistan. But the tensions of one region do not influence another, although states like India and Israel have used the potential of an extraregional threat to justify militarization efforts—particularly in the sphere of strategic weaponry. Since these rivalries have reached a situation where not dealing with regional threats may threaten the very survival of the state they are the ones that principally drive arms production and weapons acquisition.

Weapons acquisition to meet such threats is immediate and consistently funded. Further, the weapons acquired or produced are relevant to counter the threat. Thus the Israelis have consistently funded the acquisition and development of tanks because they play a central role in that nation's defensive preparations. The apartheid regime of South Africa, which in the 1970s and 1980s faced both external and internal threats to its remaining in power, produced and acquired weapons to meet the threats. A large portion of the weapons produced by Armscor, the South African arms company, are geared to meet the internal threat. India, whose principal enemy still remains Pakistan, has likewise concentrated on purchasing aircraft and tanks to counter that threat. Not only has there been an effort to maintain numbers in these crucial areas but continuous thinking goes into improving and eventually replacing these major weapons systems as well. The Israelis, therefore, seek to ensure that the air balance in the region remains in their favor and whenever an Arab nation attempts to acquire a new generation of aircraft the Israelis try either diplomatic maneuvers—as was the case with the Saudi purchase of the F-15—and failing that seek a comparable system (or an increase in numbers) to counter the threat.

ORGANIZATIONAL FACTORS

In contrast there is the acquisition of arms due to organizational reasons. Graham Allison, in his seminal study of the Cuban missile crisis, introduced two alternative models to the rational actor model that had dominated international relations. Model II, the organizational politics model, states that organizations are structured to carry out certain tasks and this structure imposes constraints on what an organization can do in the pursuit of actual policy. Nations, therefore, become the captives of the capabilities and limitations of their organizations in undertaking foreign policy actions. Allison cites, for example, how the World War I German army could only go in for full-scale mobilization which in turn automatically led to war.[29] Model III is the bureaucratic politics approach, which states that policies are the unintended outcome of the hauling and pulling between different groups within the system.[30] Barry Posen used both of these models in his explanation of French, British and German military doctrine—the first time it was used to deal with the military-strategic dimension.[31] While both of these models provide parsimonious tools with which to examine a nation's policy process, they need to be reshaped to discuss the arms acquisition and production process in the Third World context.

One limitation of the Allison model is that it does not explicitly state who the principal actors are and what their relationship to each other is. Further, it is not clear whether they operate as groups with equal power competing for limited resources, or whether the operate within an hierarchical framework with certain groups enjoying greater bargaining power. Finally, what are the forces which motivate these groups to act in a particular manner? Why, for example, do navies seek particular types of weapons rather than others?

Table 1.1
Organizational Dynamics of the National Security System

	Civil Leadership	Armed Forces	Arms Producers
Status within System	Superior	Superior	Subordinate
Motives that determine stance	Security	Security	Position in System
	Prestige	Perceived Missions	Technological Lags
	Development	Technological Lags	Technological Choice
	Ideology	Global Status	

This book suggests that there are three main actors within the defense decision making process of non-Western regional powers: the political leadership, the armed forces (the "users" of weapons systems), and the arms industries (the producers). Table 1.1 summarizes the characteristics of these actors and their motives driving their stand on weapons acquisitions and production.

The political leadership seeks to maintain a large armed force for reasons of security, prestige, and diplomacy. Various Third World leaders have sought to play a greater role within their regions and have used military buildups to promote this goal. Saddam Hussein's quest for Arab leadership, the Indian effort to be the predominant power in South Asia, and the Indonesian military buildup in the 1960s under Sukarno are examples of this. Political leaderships also play a key role in the weapons acquisition and production by opening and closing avenues for the procurement of weapons and technology from external suppliers. Pakistan's overtures in the 1950s to the United States and later China opened the avenues for a military relationship. Likewise, the decision of the then Pakistani prime minister, Liaquat Ali Khan, in 1948, to turn down an offer to visit the Soviet Union prevented the establishment of a military relationship with that country. In India, on the other hand, it was the Nehru's policy of nonalignment that allowed New Delhi, in the 1950s and 1960s, to receive military and economic aid from both the United States and the Soviet Union— with the Soviets emerging as India's principal suppliers in the 1960s.

Political leaders also have ideas regarding the development of their nation and see science and technology, in which defense science plays a significant role, as the engines to drive the development effort. Thus part of the rationale for establishing domestic arms production capabilities lies in the political leadership's belief that such industries could contribute to the overall development of the nation—a belief, as seen below, that is usually mistaken. India's defense minister in the early 1960s, Krishna Menon, argued that signing the agreement to license-produce the Soviet MiG-21 would allow India to build the foundation for a modern aircraft industry. As will be seen in the chapter on India, his hopes were not fulfilled.

The ideological leanings of the national leadership also influence their attitude toward the acquisition and production of arms. In the three cases to be discussed, arms production was either entirely run by the state or at least dominated by the state. State-driven industrialization took place because of the ideologies espoused by the national leadership. In India the "socialistic pattern of development," in Israel "Zionist economics," and in Brazil the doctrine of "Security and Development" all had self-sufficiency as a goal and called for state-led industrialization to achieve it.

The second actor in the organizational process is the armed forces—the users of weapons systems. The armed forces' stand on the procurement of weapons systems is determined by their demand for the best weapons systems to match the threat environment, their perceived mission, the existence of culture lags, and their position within the defense hierarchy of the nation. As the organizations charged with the primary responsibility to defend the nation, the armed forces demand the best weapons systems to fulfill the task. In practice this means that the armed forces demand the import of weaponry because the domestic arms industry is perceived as being unable to meet their quality demands. The inability of the arms industries to do this lies in the fact that they are playing a game of "catch up" vis-a-vis the more advanced arms industries of the North. As a consequence, they are unable to supply all the weapons systems that the users want. This, as is explained below, usually puts the armed forces into competition with the domestic arms producers for the available resources to procure or produce new systems.

Second, armed forces acquire weapons to fulfill their perceived missions. One obvious reason that armed forces require weapons is to handle the threat environment in which they are expected to operate. Another reason, which operates at times quite independently of threats, is the perceived role that an armed service sees itself as playing. All armed services see themselves assuming a military role commensurate with their status as well as the status of their country. Armed forces in the Third World are, by and large, the products of Western training and influence and as such borrow their perceived mission from Western doctrines. Air forces, for instance, would like to build up to the stage where they could carry out a strategic bombing role. Navies perceive themselves as having blue water fleets and Armies think in terms of building up large armored forces. What is interesting about such missions is that they are not grounded in threats but in the organization's desire to achieve a particular status for itself. Such organizational pressures for weapons procurement can be seen in the Brazilian and Indian Navies desires to have nuclear submarines although neither state faces a maritime threat which justifies such an investment. Similarly, the Chinese intention to build an aircraft carrier may emerge as a result of similar pressures because that nation's decision to build an aircraft carrier only came about in the 1980s—by which time both the Soviet and U.S. navies had major fleets operating in the Pacific. Under such circumstances the construction of one—or even a few—aircraft carriers was not going to change the naval balance of power in that ocean.

Another determinant in the weapons acquisition process is the presence of a technological lag. The notion of a technological lag first emerged in the US-USSR arms race. From the early 1960s, the Soviets, began copying whatever design trends the United States was currently pursuing with at times little regard for their own operational needs. Thus when the United States went in for variable geometry aircraft with the F-111, the Soviets responded with their own variable geometry aircraft—the Su-24, and the MiG-23 and MiG-27. The United States's B-1 bomber was a large variable geometry aircraft, so the Soviets built an even larger variable geometry aircraft, the Tu-160 Blackjack. Similarly, when the United States decided to produce a slow-flying ground attack aircraft in the A-10, the Soviets came up with their own counterpart in the Su-25 Frogfoot, which bore a striking resemblance to the Northrop A-9, an aircraft which had lost the U.S. Air Force competition to the A-10.

A similar situation exists in the Third World, where the domestic arms industries try to copy the latest technological breakthroughs in the West without taking into account their utility in their own combat environment or the technological feasibility of the project. Since these arms industries were established later, and do not have as large an R&D (research and development) budget as do Western arms industries, the game of intellectual catch-up seems inevitable. The situation is further aggravated by the armed forces' culture lag, which makes them demand that domestically produced weapons systems have the quality of weapons produced abroad. Since the armed forces are its principal customers, the domestic arms industry has no option but to comply. The best example of such a culture lag is that of the rash of combat aircraft projects that were launched in the Third World during the late 1970s and 1980s. Thus the specifications for aircraft like the Indian Light Combat Aircraft (LCA) and the Israeli Lavi bore a striking resemblance to the US Air Force's F-16 (as did Japan's FS-X program).

Fourthly, the ability of the armed forces to acquire weapons depends on their status within the national security hierarchy. In the West the term *military-industrial complex* is used to describe the fusion of interests of the armed forces, the defense industries, and the political leadership that allocates the resources. In the former Soviet Union, not only did a similar structure exist, but the national security concern was heightened and resources allocated to defense to the point that Christopher Donnelly—one of the most prominent European observers of the Soviet military—remarked that the Soviet Union did not *have* a war machine but it *was* a war machine.[32]

In Third World countries, however, the term *military-industrial complex* does not correctly explain the existing situation. In the superpower case the armed forces would—or could—only buy their weapons systems from the domestic arms industry and, therefore, worked in concert with the industry to produce the systems they required. In the Third World, however, the arms industry and the armed forces are not always collaborating with one another. Instead, they compete for the resources the state allocates for weapons procurement. This is because the armed forces can, and do, retain the option to procure weapons systems from external suppliers. In such a competition the armed forces, because of their role in maintaining internal and external security, tend to have an edge over the arms industries. As a consequence the armed forces try, when resources are available and suppliers are willing, to procure weapons from abroad.

Finally, we come to the producers. The arms industries of a number of Third World countries have been around for almost fifty years. In this time most of these arms industries have gone from overhauling weapons systems, to assembly and licensed production, to, finally, developing indigenous projects for weapons production. The variety and lethality of weapons produced have also increased substantially. Moreover, within these nations a substantial body of scientific-technocratic personnel has emerged and the industries themselves have become large entities. India, for example, has eight defense public sector undertakings, thirty-nine ordnance factories and fifty defense laboratories. Israel and Brazil, similarly, built up defense industries that cover the manufacture of weapons for all three branches of the armed forces.

The size of such industries, their longevity, and the cadre of trained scientific personnel that work in them create a constituency in these countries that is difficult for the political leadership to ignore. For along with the growth of these arms industries, their role within the national security system of the Third World states has also subtly changed. These industries are no longer content with license-producing weapons systems and instead want to develop complete systems within the country. This desire, therefore, has brought them in conflict with the armed forces, which seek to procure weapons systems from abroad. Five important facts have to be noted regarding the nature and consequences of the competition between users and producers for resources.

First, within the national security hierarchy the arms industry occupies a secondary position to the armed forces because the armed forces as protectors against external and internal aggression afford them greater status and bargaining power than the arms industries. In some cases, like Brazil, the military ran the country, thus adding to its bargaining power.

Second, although they are in a subordinate position, the arms producers have some bargaining power. The size of the arms industries, their longevity, and the fact that in most of these nations scientists have been able to develop personal ties with political leaders give the heads of these industries a bargaining strength in the resource allocation process. Further, technological restrictions also help increase the status of the arms industry. The growing Western constraints on the supply of sensitive technologies—particularly those which could be used for the production of weapons of mass destruction and their delivery systems—forces the users and the political leadership to depend on the domestic arms industry to deliver the goods. The lack of external suppliers has therefore led to the growth of select parts of the arms industry such as the nuclear and chemical programs and, more recently, ballistic missile endeavors. Indeed, such programs may be set up without the consent of the armed forces as the political leadership sees them as being priority items for procurement.

Third, arms industries, like the armed forces, are the victims of a technological lag. A technological lag is caused because on the one hand the arms industries are manned by talented outward-looking individuals who view themselves as competing on the larger stage of the global scientific arena. After all, different industries are producing similar systems and, therefore, comparison is inevitable. But on the other hand, Southern arms industries are also playing a game of technological catch-up. None of these nations, at least at present, has the lead in the development of major weapons systems because their R&D bases have yet to catch up with the West. As a consequence, their R&D efforts are largely geared toward trying to produce whatever is the latest idea in the West. Thus if Stealth technology was the buzzword in the Western arms industries in the late 1980s, it could be a driving slogan in the South in the mid-1990s.

It is important at this juncture to state what exactly is meant by high technology. There is a difference between true high technology and what is perceived to be high-technology in power political terms. Actual advanced technology is like high-speed computers where rapid changes take place. While such technology may be sought by Southern nations—both India and Israel sought American supercomputers to aid their scientific and, possibly, weapons endeavors—these are not the central technologies that these nations seek to acquire. Instead, high technology can be the most advanced, or most publicized, weapons available—with the label of advanced being a result of battlefield successes. Thus weapons which have not really been advanced, like the ZSU-23-4 Shilka, the Exocet missile, the General Dynamics F-16 fighter, and the Patriot missile have all been given that label (the Shilka got its reputation from the 1973 war, the Exocet from the Falklands War, the F-16 from the Osirak reactor raid, and the Patriot from the Gulf War). None of these systems was cutting edge technology. In fact the F-16 was the result of the U.S. Air Force's Light Weight Fighter project in the 1970s—which was meant to provide a cheap and technologically simple complement to the F-15 Eagle. Yet Southern nations sought to acquire these "advanced" systems or to produce comparable systems. Indeed the selling point of indigenously produced weapons has often been that they are better than their high-tech originals. Thus the Israeli Lavi was touted as being better than the F-16, and the Indian Akash antiaircraft missile is supposed to be better than the Patriot. High technology is also whatever makes a smaller power into a major power. WMD and strategic delivery systems like ballistic missiles and nuclear submarines fall in this category because they continue to serve as the currency of power in the international system. But in some cases, as with nuclear, biological, and chemical weapons, these are decades old technologies. Yet their possession continues to be viewed in these states as symbolic of having crossed a technological threshold and reached a certain political status within the international system. Thus what we will see in the three cases discussed is that the quest for technologically advanced weaponry is colored by the symbolic and power political aspects of these systems.

Fourth, technological choices are important in shaping production outcomes. If there was any lesson to be learned form the Gulf War it was that a missile program does not make a nation a military power. Iraq did not have the capability to produce a range of military systems across the board to counter both the U.S. forces and to avoid the impact of an arms embargo. Most Third World arms industries face similar problems. One of the reasons that developing systems across the board has not been possible is that some technologies are easier to absorb than others. Today, for example, there are twenty-four nations with ongoing missile programs but only two that have supersonic combat aircraft programs—India and Taiwan. The reason for this is that it is difficult to incorporate the technologies to build state-of-the-art combat aircraft. No Third World nation has been able to develop its own high performance jet engines or to develop the advanced radars and avionics that go into modern fighter jets (indeed very few First World states have been successful in this endeavor). On the other hand basic missile technology dates back to World War II and the German V-2 rocket and is, therefore, a lot easier to develop. A similar case can be made for chemical weapons, which were first used successfully in the First World War.

Further, much of Third World success in weapons production has not been based on the development of new systems but rather on the improvement of older ones. The Chinese F-6 is a reverse engineered copy of the Soviet MiG-19 and the Brazilian Xavante is an improvement of the Italian MB 326. Since improvement rather than invention is being followed it is even conceptually difficult to jump to the next technological step. No country can make the technological jump from producing piston engines to modern-day jet engines without going through the range of technologies that come between. As a consequence, no Third World nation has successfully developed follow-on systems to the weapons they have license-produced or reverse engineered. The Israelis, for example, stole the blueprints for the Mirage III from Switzerland and reverse engineered them to make the Kfir. But when it came to making a follow-on, the Lavi, the Israelis had to go to the United States for both critical technologies and design assistance. Similarly, India, despite license-producing the MiG-21 for nearly two decades and making improvements to the plane, was unable to build a follow-on. Instead it is now license-producing the MiG-27. What this means is that the most successful programs have been based on building what is feasible rather than what is state-of-the-art.

This situation is further complicated, however, by the fact that most Third World arms industries—some of the Latin American ones being major exceptions—have the domestic users as their principal customers. The fact is that in acquiring weapons systems the users tend to use the state of the art as the guidelines for procurement. Arms industries are therefore forced to commit themselves to developing systems that are fashionable rather than technologically feasible given their state of development.

One therefore sees in Third World national security systems three groups with different motives and varying bargaining capabilities engaged in shaping the weapons acquisition process. It is also clear that these groups face differing constraints and opportunities in their bid to shape the process in their favor. The question, therefore, arises, Is there any way to put these competing claims in a systematic framework of analysis?

To develop a systematic framework it is necessary to state that both threats and organizational ambitions serve as demand factors in the militarization process. While threats provide some of the justification for the acquisition of weapons they do not serve as a sufficient source of explanation. Nations can exist in a high-threat environment yet not seek to completely counter it. In the late 1960s, the Chinese faced a twin nuclear threat from the United States and the Soviet Union. Yet they did not build up their nuclear forces to comparable levels to those of the two superpowers. Even after the US threat had been dramatically reduced by the mid-1970s—with Washington going to the extent of agreeing to not fly SR-71 reconnaissance missions over mainland China—the Chinese did not turn their focus in a significant way toward achieving nuclear parity with the Soviets. India, similarly, has lived with Chinese nuclear superiority since 1974—and in the decade preceding that India did not even have a nuclear capability. Pakistan, also, has lived since 1971 with a conventional force disadvantage vis-a-vis its principal opponent, India.

Nor do organizational ambitions suffice as an explanation. While a desire to emulate other armed forces may exist, it does not account for the on-again off-again nature of programs or the lopsidedness of the force structure. It does not bring out why, for example, an air force ends up with only two squadrons of a high technology aircraft as Pakistan did with the F-16 in the 1980s. Nor does it explain why certain weapons programs are started, scrapped, and restarted at a later date. Thus, while threat perceptions and organizational imperatives may create the desire for weapons, it is supply factors that determine the acquisition process.

The supply factors that eventually shape the armament process in the regional powers of the South, are the availability of resources and the existence of an external supplier. The role of external suppliers in shaping regional power militarization has been threefold: to subsidize the military growth of these states; to ensure a continuous supply of weapons; and to transfer technology for licensed production and the eventual production of weaponry. Thus of the seventeen major arms importers of the Middle East and South Asia, only oil rich nations like Libya and Saudi Arabia could fund their military modernization programs with their internal resources. The majority of these nations have depended, instead, on an external supplier willing to provide weapons on favorable terms. Alternatively, these nations have been able to procure weapons only when their hard currency resources have been high enough to permit acquisitions.

Starting in the 1950s and then growing rapidly in the 1960s, the United States and the Soviet Union, in their effort to counter each other globally, provided weaponry on a subsidized basis—or even as grant aid—to nations around the world. The availability of such weaponry allowed nations like Turkey, Egypt, Israel, Pakistan, India, and the two Koreas to cheaply add weapons to their inventories and create what were for their regions large and impressive military forces. In the 1970s, however, the sources of cheap weaponry began to dry up and only a few nations continued to get arms on soft terms. The most prominent of these were Israel, Egypt, Syria, India, and the North Korea. Since most Third World states suffer from resource constraints the existence of an external supplier allows a nation to go in for a more affordable militarization program. Conversely, when the supplier is unwilling to provide new systems it puts major pressures on that nation's military expenditure.

External suppliers have also been seen as a measure ensuring a continuous supply of weapons, albeit with mixed results. Pakistan, for example, launched the 1965 war against India assuming that the United States would continue to provide it with weaponry during the conflict. Instead, Washington imposed an arms embargo that hurt the Pakistani war effort. India and Israel on the other hand would seem to have benefited from continuous weapons transfers by their respective suppliers—the former Soviet Union and the United States—especially in periods of conflict. But even in their case the external suppliers have denied weapons or constricted their flow in order to attain their own political objectives.

Finally, the external suppliers have served as the source for technology transfers for building up the arms industry. Thus the Indian arms industry—especially the aeronautics industry—was built up by the transfer of Soviet systems. The Chinese weapons industry was likewise built up by acquiring Soviet technology. The Israeli arms industry has developed largely due to the military connection with the Western Europe and the United States, and the North Korean arms industry has emerged as a result of Soviet and Chinese technical assistance. Without such technological assistance none of these arms industries would have been able to start licensed production and acquire the basic defense industrial infrastructure needed to set up a modern arms industry.

The second supply factor is the availability of financial resources. As mentioned earlier, only a few Third World nations have the internal resources to consistently fund their arms acquisition programs. Iran under the Shah and Libya and Saudi Arabia in recent times are the best examples of this (South Korea, in the future, may be another nation entering this category). For the rest of these nations, however, generating resources for weapons purchases has been a difficult process. The intermittent availability of such resources has led to weapons being procured only when the resources are available rather than when they are needed. Thus when internal resources are high the acquisition of weapons systems through hard currency takes place. When, on the other hand, such resources are unavailable, nations put their acquisition programs on hold, retaining existing forces and trying to develop the weapons systems indigenously. If these are the conditions that affect the acquisition and production process, how then does one use this framework to explain outcomes?

Given this framework the following facts emerge. First, in Third World national security systems procurement demands tend to fall into two categories—threats and organizational pressures. Funding for threats is generally immediate and consistent. Further, the weaponry procured to match such threats is based on the threat environment existing in the region. Organizational demands for weapons are generated from of the perceived role the armed forces and the weapons producers see for themselves. Second, given the nature of Third World security systems there is competition between the users and the producers for state resources. The users seek the resources to buy abroad and the producers want the resources to develop systems at home. Third, the struggle between the users and producers is slanted in favor of the users given the role they play within the national security system hierarchy. Fourth, the users greater bargaining power allows them to demand the procurement of the best weapons systems from abroad rather than depend on the domestic arms industry for them. Fifth, the arms industry is not without bargaining power within the national security system. Established for reasons of self-sufficiency and the need to increase national power and prestige, arms industries are large creatures hiring some of the best scientific personnel in the country. These personnel in turn have built political contacts and have thereby created a constituency for themselves in the political sphere. The competition between the two then is shaped by a group of other factors such as culture lags—both in the case of the users and the producers—technological feasibility, and the role of individuals. Such factors reshape the original demands but they in turn are acted upon by the two supply factors—resources and suppliers. Sixth, given the economic conditions of most of these nations and the level of their scientific-industrial base, the availability of resources and existence of a guaranteed external supplier become crucial to determining what shape the force structure will take. They also determine whether a systems will be purchased abroad or produced at home.

Given these facts one can suggest that the following generalizations are likely in the militarization processes of Southern nations:

1. Building a complete force structure depends on both the continued   availability of resources and the presence of an external supplier.
2. Resource availability and suppliers determine whether procurement or production will take place. When resources are available procurement takes place. Also resource availability may allow for both domestic production and weapons imports. When resources are unavailable, however, reliance is placed on the domestic arms industry.
3. Intermittent resources lead to the opening and closing of doctrine. When resources are available and it seems likely that force structures will develop so to does the doctrine to utilize them. On the other hand when resources are unavailable, force structures remain incomplete and with them doctrine closes. Thus China's decision not to build an aircraft carrier leads to reshaping a doctrine that would have stressed long-range maritime power projection.
4. Strategic weapons programs survive better than conventional ones. Strategic weapons—ballistic missiles, nuclear bombs, chemical and biological weapons—are expensive to produce and tend to destabilize regional balances. But, paradoxically, one can argue that it is easier to sustain such programs and bring them to fruition. The reason for this paradox lies in that conventional programs have to compete with external suppliers for markets within the country and, consequently, can easily be put on the backburner or even terminated. External suppliers will not provide strategic weapons. Nor are strategic systems easily prone to technological obsolescence.
5. As threats die, organizational pressures sustain weapons programs. Given the funding constraints on organizational programs, exports become a must. China's missile program, for example, has lacked a credible external threat since the late 1980s, and this perhaps explains the organizational pressure to export.

6. From an arms control perspective, organizational pressures to procure/produce are easier to control than those derived from threats. Israel, for example, sees its nuclear program as a response to the regional threat environment. Getting Israel to reduce or dismantle its nuclear arsenal could only be accomplished as part of a more comprehensive reduction of forces in the Middle East. The South African program was similarly driven by a regional threat. With the transition to majority rule in that country, however, the threat rationale died out and the nuclear weapons program was disbanded.

STRUCTURE

Chapters 2, 3, and 4, examine the Indian, Israeli, and Brazilian cases respectively. While these three countries are dissimilar cases in terms of threat levels and approaches to acquisition and production, they all sought autonomy in weapons production and moved to manufacture increasingly advanced technologies. These country studies show that similar structural constraints restricted these plans and left these nations with lopsided force structures and a continued dependence on external suppliers. Chapter 5 draws together the conclusions from the country cases and examines the extent to which the generalizations discussed above apply in these cases. Chapter 6 discusses the policy implications of this model of weapons acquisition and production for the future role of regional powers in the emerging international system, for U.S. policy toward the South, and for arms control efforts.

NOTES

1. Samuel P. Huntington, *The Third Wave: Democratization in the Late Twentieth Century* (Norman and London: University of Oklahoma Press, 1991), xiii.

2. Susan Strange, *States and Markets* (London: Pinter, 1988), 10-11.

3. *The National Military Strategy 1992* (Washington, D.C.: U.S. Department of Defense Publication, 1992), 11.

4. For a discussion of these three issues, see Martin Navias, "Ballistic Missile Proliferation in the Third World," *Adelphi Papers* No. 252 (London: IISS, 1990); and Janne Nolan, *Trappings of Power: Ballistic Missiles in the Third World* (Washington, D.C.: The Brookings Institution, 1991). Michael Klare, "Deadly Convergence: The Arms Trade, Nuclear/Chemical/Missile Proliferation, and Regional Conflicts in the 1990s," in World *Security: Trends and Challenges at Century's End* , Michael Klare and Daniel Thomas eds. (New York: St. Martin's Press, 1991); and Michael Klare, "The Next Great Arms Race," *Foreign Affairs*, 72, no. 3, (fall 1993): 136-152.

5. Klare, *Deadly Convergence*, 170-71.

6. Ibid., 171-72.

7. Les Aspin, *Report on the Bottom-Up Review*, (Washington, D.C.: Department of Defense, 1993), iii; and Andrew F. Krepinevich, *The Bottom-Up Review: An Assessment* (Washington D.C.: Defense Budget Project, 1994), i.

8. *Report on Nonproliferation and Counterproliferation Activities and Programs* (Washington, D.C.: Department of Defense, 1994), ES-1.

9. Ibid., 12.

10. Anthony Cordesman, "Defense Planning in Saudi Arabia," in *Defense Planning in Less Industrialized States* Stephanie G. Neumann ed. (Lexington, Mass.: Lexington Books, 1984), 84.

11. Paul Ferrari, Raul Madrid, and Jeff Knopf, *U.S. Arms Exports: Policies and Contractors* (Cambridge: Ballinger, 1988), 21.

12. *The New York Times*, 17 February 1992.

13. Michael Brzoska and Thomas Ohlson, eds., *Arms Production in the Third World* (London: Taylor and Francis, 1986).

14. Michael Brzoska and Thomas Ohlson, *Arms Transfers to the Third World, 1971-85* (Oxford: Oxford University Press, 1987).

15. James Everett Katz, ed., *Arms Production in Developing Countries: An Analysis of Decisionmaking* (Lexington, Mass.: Lexington Books, 1984); and James Everett Katz, ed., *The Implications of Third World Military Industrialization: Sowing the Serpent's Teeth* (Lexington, Mass.: Lexington Books, 1986).

16. Mary Kaldor and Asborn Eide, *The World Military Order: The Impact of Military Technology on the Third World* (London: Macmillan, 1979), 13-17.

17. Edward A. Kolodziej, "Whither Modernization and Militarisation: Implications for International Peace and Security," in *Peace, Defense and Economic Analysis*, Christian Schmidt ed. (London: Macmillan, 1987), 216-220.

18. Barry Posen, *The Sources of Military Doctrine: France, Britain, Germany between the World Wars* (Ithaca N.Y.: Cornell University Press, 1984).

19. Aaron Klieman, Israel's Global Reach: Arms Sales as Diplomacy (Washington, D.C.: Pergamon-Brassey's, 1985); and Stewart Reiser, *The Israeli Arms Industry* (New York: Holmes and Meier, 1989).

20. Raju G. C. Thomas, *The Defense of India: A Budgetary Perspective of Strategy and Politics* (New Delhi: Macmillan, 1978), K. Subrahmanyam, *Indian*

Security Perspectives (New Delhi: ABC, 1983), Ron Matthews, *Defense Production in India* (New Delhi: ABC, 1989).

21. John D. Mearsheimer, "Why We Will Miss the Cold War," *Atlantic Monthly*, August 1990, 35-47.

22. *International Studies Newsletter* 22, no. 4, (May 1995): 3.

23. Thomas F. Homer-Dixon, "On the Threshold: Environmental Changes as Causes of Acute Conflict," *International Security* 16, no. 2, (fall 1991); Benjamin R. Barber, Jihad v. McWorld, *Atlantic Monthly*, March 1992, 53-63. Samuel P. Huntington, "The Clash of Civilizations," *Foreign Affairs* 72, no. 2 (summer 1993): 22-49.

24. Anthony Jay and Jonathan Lynn, *The Yes Minister Diaries* (London: Andre Deutch, 1986), 11.

25. *The Military Balance, 1990-1991* (London: Brassey's, 1990).

26. For an excellent discussion about the insecurity dilemma of Third World states and the fact that they predominantly face internal threats see, Brian L. Job, "The Insecurity Dilemma: National, Regime, and State Securities in the Third World," in *The Insecurity Dilemma: National Security of Third World States*, Brian L. Job ed. (Boulder: Lynne Rienner, 1992), 11-35.

27. *Militarization* is a term which is used in a number of ways. Stanislav Andreski in a discussion of the world militarism covers the definitional aspects of this problem. One definition of militarism is the development of an aggressive foreign policy and the willingness to go to war—what Andreski calls *militancy*. A second interpretation is that of a society where the military has preponderance over the civilian organization. Andreski calls such a set-up a *militocracy*. Militarization, he argues, is where the military has control over social life and there is a subservience of society to the needs of the military. Andreski also suggests that militarism can mean an addiction to drills and ceremonies, an ideology propagating military ideals, and the use of military paraphernalia in social life e.g. the Salvation Army, Stanislav Andreski, *Military Organization and Society* [Berkeley and Los Angeles: University of California Press, 1968], 184-86.)

28. Barry Buzan, *People, States and Fear: The National Security Problem in International Relations* (Chapel Hill: University of North Carolina Press, 1983), 115-125.

29. Graham T. Allison, *Essence of Decision: Explaining the Cuban Missile Crisis* (Boston: Little, Brown and Company, 1971), 71-96.

30. Ibid., 162-182.

31. Posen, *The Sources of Military Doctrine*, 16.

32. Christopher Donnelly, *The Soviet Armed Forces: An Appraisal, Sandhurst Research Paper* (Soviet Studies Research Center, Sandhurst U.K., 1986).

2

Building an Arsenal: The Indian Experience

By the late 1980s, India possessed one of the largest and most advanced military forces in the developing world: its army had over 3000 tanks; its air force had 800 hundred airplanes, which included MiG-29s and Mirage 2000s; and the navy had a seventy-vessel fleet with plans to indigenously develop carriers and a nuclear submarine. Coupled with this large conventional force was India's venture into the area of ballistic and other missiles. It flight tested an intermediate range ballistic missile—Agni—and a short-range ballistic missile—Prithvi—with the latter now slated to enter service. The acquisition of these systems also led to shifts in military doctrine from a doctrine that was aimed at deterring an attack from Pakistan and China to one which called for the projection of Indian military power beyond the traditional confines of South Asia.

These developments prompted analysts to call India everything from the next superpower to a regional power with a very long extraregional arm. This chapter argues, instead, that despite acquiring an advanced military capability in the 1980s, India's ability to develop into a major power is constrained by the interaction between demand and supply factors which have been in existence since independence. The existence of threats and bureaucratic pressures have created demands for new weapons and for shifts in the doctrines of the three armed services, but the extent to which these demands have been met has been limited by the Indian government's ability to both mobilize hard currency resources, and find an external power willing to supply weapons to New Delhi. Consequently, these factors have shaped the evolution of force structures and military doctrine in several ways: force modernizations have, on occasion, taken place in low-threat periods; military doctrine has opened and closed with only a partial relation to changes in the external environment; and these factors have limited India's capacity to develop its indigenous weapons production capability. Due to the fact that the development of the Indian armed forces is still shaped by the interaction of these factors, the chapter concludes that it will be difficult for India to resolve these structural constraints and make the jump to great power status. The chapter examines the interaction of these factors in four historical periods: 1947–1961 which was considered to be one of low threats; 1962–1971 when India faced the highest level of external threats; 1972–1978, was again a low threat period; and 1979–1990 which was a period of considerable internal turmoil for India as well as one with major upheavals in the region. Additionally, it separates the discussion of conventional and nuclear programs in each of these periods in order to gain a better understanding of the forces that drove these programs and contributed to their success or failure.

THREATS AND BUREAUCRATIC PRESSURES

Since achieving independence in 1947, India has faced both internal and external challenges to its territorial integrity. The partition of British India into India and Pakistan transformed the Hindu-Muslim communal rivalry into an armed struggle between two nation-states. This rivalry was exacerbated by superpower support in the 1950s and 1960s, and later the 1980s, as both the United States and the Soviet Union provided weaponry to the two regional combatants. The Indian armed forces and the political leadership have, over the decades, used this rivalry to justify their demand for newer and more advanced weapons. The argument frequently made was that Pakistan's acquisition of a new weapons system had upset the regional military balance thereby forcing India to seek comparable weaponry. The external threat, however, was not restricted to Pakistan. Indian military planners continue to point out the presence of a Chinese nuclear force, and more recently the Chinese Navy, as also determining the Indian desire for new weapons systems. While threats provide a necessary component in explaining Indian weapons acquisition and doctrinal changes, they do not themselves constitute a sufficient explanation for it.

As Ravi Rikhye has shown, the action-reaction model is not particularly useful for explaining Indian weapons acquisition because in the vast majority of cases it was India that introduced a new weapons system into the South Asian region. Rikhye examines the induction of ninety-seven systems into the armed forces of India and Pakistan in the forty year period 1948–1988. His analysis concludes that on twenty-one occasions Pakistan was the first to introduce the system. India was the first to introduce the system on seventy-six occasions.[1] If one takes into account that some of the Pakistani "firsts" were due to Indian delays in procurement—as was the case with the 155 mm gun— and others were in such minuscule numbers that they could hardly alter the military balance between the two states, the number of Pakistani "firsts" in Rikhye's analysis actually goes down to six.[2] Further, action-reaction would mean matching the threat, however, the Indian philosophy has been to acquire two to three times the number of advanced weapons acquired by Pakistan. When Pakistan purchased the F-16 fighter in the early 1980s, India responded by purchasing both Mirage 2000s and MiG-29s (despite the war with China, India's primary conventional challenge is still perceived to be Pakistan). Thus, while threat environments are necessary in assessing Indian weapons procurement and doctrinal efforts, they do not provide a sufficient basis of analysis.

A more complex explanation of the demand for weapons acquisition and doctrinal shifts emerges when one examines the development of the Indian armed forces in terms of bureaucratic pressures. Three key groups comprise India's national security system—the national leadership, the armed forces, and the arms industry. Each of these groups exerts different bureaucratic pressures based on its goals and objectives. India's national leadership, for example, has always wanted India to be an important actor in international affairs and to have some degree of self-reliance in its defense capability. This view clashes with that of the armed forces, which have traditionally preferred to purchase weapons abroad. The third player in this bureaucratic game is the Indian arms industry which, over the years, has developed links with the political leadership of the country and has, therefore, been able to successfully press for the initiation of indigenous weapons programs.

SUPPLIERS AND RESOURCES

While threats and bureaucratic pressures may generate the demand for weaponry, the actual ability to acquire it and to subsequently shift doctrines rests on the availability of external suppliers and financial resources. External suppliers have played an important role in the Indian case because they provide qualitative upgrades and also allow for increasing India's weapons inventory at subsidized rates (such subsidies were provided because India was seen as fulfilling certain Cold War objectives of first the West and later the Soviet Union). Financial resources are important because often the internal demand for particular weapons systems has only been satisfied when hard currency resources have been available. When such resources have been unavailable, acquisitions have been put on hold and doctrinal changes have been stalled.

1947–1961: AN EMERGING SECURITY POLICY

The role of the Indian leadership has been crucial in determining the defense planning of the nation since independence. The early Indian leadership was bound by economic, political, technological, and foreign policy considerations in its attitude toward defense spending and the development of a sound military force structure for the nation. At the economic level, the early Indian nationalist leadership saw defense and development as competing claims and felt, therefore, that defense spending had to be restricted in order to promote developmental programs.[3] It was this economic consideration that saw the country's first prime minister, Jawaharlal Nehru, restrict military expenditure and, instead, use diplomatic initiatives to try and secure the nation's security. In fact military expenditure was raised dramatically only after India's defeat in the Sino-Indian war of 1962.[4]

At the foreign policy level, similarly, Nehru believed that a policy of non-alignment would not only keep India out of the emerging East-West conflict but also ensure its security from superpower intervention. Nehru believed that given India's size, potential importance, and nonaligned status, neither superpower would permit the other to conquer such a nation and both, therefore, would allow India to continue as an independent state along its perceived political path.[5] Thus, Indian diplomatic maneuvering was seen as compensating for the lack of defense spending.

But India's leadership also recognized that in order to remain nonaligned they would have to develop an indigenous military capability to withstand external pressures. To do this, Nehru and his most active defense minister, Krishna Menon, sought to create a domestic arms industry that would eventually satisfy all the requirements of the armed forces. It was with this in mind that the Indian government in the late 1940s contracted P.M.S. Blackett to suggest means to develop "defense science" in India.[6] In 1948 it also asked Willi Messerschmitt, the German aircraft designer who was then cooling his heels in Spain, to come to India, and write a report on the future of the Indian aircraft industry. Such early moves toward technological independence led the Indian government to initiate a trainer aircraft program in the late 1940s and later, in 1956, to recruit the German aircraft designer, Kurt Tank, to head a project for building a supersonic combat aircraft—the HF-24 Marut.

Political considerations also drove the decision to restrict military expenditure and with it the role of the military in affairs of the state. Nehru wanted to continue the British tradition of civilian control over the military and this meant restricting the strength of the military as a potential player in political affairs. Further, within the Indian National Congress, the ruling party, antimilitaristic sentiments prevailed for two reasons. An influential section of the party was Gandhian in its ideological leanings and therefore felt that the armed forces were an evil that should be eliminated from Indian society. Another section was suspicious of the armed forces because the latter had not participated in the freedom struggle but instead worked loyally for the British to crush the nationalist movement. The armed forces, like the bureaucracy, were seen as the remnants of the imperialist structure and therefore it was felt they should be disbanded and replaced by a new and nationalist force.

Nehru's reaction to these different pressures was to retain the military but maintain a strong civilian control over it. This was done by providing the civilian leadership and the bureaucracy with the power to deploy the armed forces for both internal and external crises.[7] Second, the finance ministry was made into one of the main decision makers in weapons acquisition. If the ministry declared that financial resources were unavailable for weapons purchases then the proposed procurement more likely than not was put on hold. But the most interesting step taken to ensure civilian control was to invite a civilian scientist, P.M.S. Blackett, to write a report on what likely threats India faced and what sort of force structure the armed forces should have to meet them.

The Blackett report addressed both the immediate threats to the nation as well as the need to provide India with the independent military production capability it required to maintain its nonaligned status. Blackett stressed that India's threats would emanate from within the region and devised force structures for each of these. The Navy, Blackett recommended, should get additional cruisers, destroyers, an escort carrier, submarines, and land-based and ship-based combat aircraft. The air force, in turn, was to obtain jet fighters and photo reconnaissance aircraft.[8]

In the sphere of defense production, Blackett stated that it would take some time for India to attain the capability to produce state-of-the-art weaponry and it should therefore concentrate on building noncompetitive systems— weapons where the relative quality of the system did not matter. Thus, India should try to build antiaircraft guns, transport vehicles, and set the grounds for an aircraft industry by designing and developing trainer aircraft. Due to the ideological orientation of the Indian leadership, the military industrialization became a state enterprise.

At the time of independence, India's leaders came from the Western-educated middle class. For this group, and particularly India's first prime minister, Jawaharlal Nehru, the West included the Soviet Union. Thus, there was a heavy dose of socialism in the ideas espoused by the new leadership. In practice this took the form of the state playing the major role in the development of industries. In the 1948 and 1956 industrial policies of the government of India, the future industrialization of the country was divided into three discrete categories: the public sector, the joint sector, and the private sector. All important industries, including the defense industry, were put under the purview of the public (state) sector; the feeling on the part of the national leadership being that the private sector, spurred by the profit motive, would not work to provide India with a strong defense capability.

THE ATTITUDE OF THE ARMED FORCES

The second set of bureaucratic pressures emerged from the armed forces themselves. The Indian armed forces had been raised, trained, and organized by the British, and the Indian army served the empire overseas in both the First and Second World Wars. The net result of such a heritage was twofold: a lasting impact on the organization and doctrine of the armed forces and an armed force that looked to the West for new ideas and weapons systems. Thus what existed, in effect, was a culture lag. The armed forces partially drew their ideas of force structure and doctrine from the West, thereby ignoring, at times, the threats on the ground. Combined with this culture lag was the perceived role that each service saw itself as playing.

The Indian armed forces saw themselves assuming a military role commensurate with their status as well as that of their country. The Indian Navy viewed itself as a blue water navy and from the late 1940s sought to include aircraft carriers in its fleet. Similarly, the Indian Air Force viewed itself as carrying out strategic bombing and interdiction missions and therefore requiring the aircraft to carry out these missions. This was despite the fact that the primary task of its predecessor, the Royal Indian Air Force, was to carry out operations against the Afghan tribes along British India's northwestern frontier.

The army, in contrast, was trained in British infantry tactics, and these traditions continued to dominate the Indian Army's thinking in the period immediately after independence. British doctrine advocated giving ground to the invader and then having the infantry launch a major counterattack. Major General Sukhwant Singh argues that such a strategy was easy for the British to carry out since they were fighting in alien lands and could therefore afford to trade ground for time.[9] Such a luxury was not available to the Indian Army after independence since nationalistic compulsions demanded that territory not be ceded to the invader. The primary mission of the army, therefore, was to defend the nation's territory from incursions by Pakistan and later China. The army's doctrinal approach to this mission was to establish defensive positions and fight from them. Further, the lack of mechanization placed an emphasis on infantry-oriented tactics, with army generals happy to make minor territorial gains along the front.

The army also played a major part in maintaining internal security. It fought its first counterinsurgency in the late 1940s when the Communist Party of India launched an insurrection in the southern state of Andhra Pradesh. Subsequently, in the 1950s the army began a twenty-five-year-long counterinsurgency campaign against the various hill tribes of the northeast. The army used a paramilitary outfit, the Assam Rifles, to deal with the northeastern insurgencies and later, in the 1960s, raised a mountain division (57), which was also to gain counterinsurgency experience. But neither role necessitated a change in doctrine or the need for new types of equipment.

AVAILABILITY OF RESOURCES

Although each armed service had a perceived mission, the force structure required to carry out these missions was not available to the air force or the navy. In the early years after independence the lack of financial resources restricted force development. While India's hard currency reserves stood at $3.17 billion in 1947, by 1949 a sharp rise in imports and a thirty percent devaluation of the Rupee led to these reserves steadily declining. In fact, by 1951-1952 the trade deficit had reached approximately $462 million.[10] In the 1940s and 1950s, the only arms available to India were from the West European countries, and these were paid for in hard currency. In fact, immediately after independence, India had used the favorable sterling balance with Britain to purchase weapons.[11] But India lacked the financial resources to pay for the large-scale induction of weaponry. Thus the navy was unable to get an aircraft carrier until the late 1950s (the carrier was handed over to the Navy in 1961) and what ships it did acquire were surplus vessels from the World War II.

What made it especially difficult for the navy was the lack of a credible threat. India's principal enemy, Pakistan, had a small fleet and its defense planners were placing even less emphasis on the navy than the Indian government was. Further, the principal naval power in the Indian Ocean at that point was Britain, and it was considered a friendly nation. The Indian government, therefore, did not consider naval expansion a priority and the navy continued to receive less than five percent of the defense budget until the late 1960s.[12] Given the cost of surplus naval equipment at that time and that India did not have the hard currency to pay for these weapons, the naval expansion had to be carried out on a piecemeal basis (a light carrier, for example, cost around £6 million or almost half the naval budget in the 1940s).[13]

Similarly, the air force purchased surplus fighters from the West and for its bombing role made do with cannibalizing Liberator aircraft left behind in India after the World War II.[14] Coupled with the lack of hard currency, was the fact that the Indian leadership wanted to build an aeronautical industry in India and for this reason resources were invested in the Marut project. The Army, on the other hand, because its doctrine and mission required the least modern weapons, could afford to arm itself with surplus weaponry. Its principal opponent, Pakistan, was building up its forces with World War II vintage equipment. This situation changed by the late 1950s when, due to the infusion of American arms into Pakistan, the Indian Army faced an enemy equipped with better armor.

India's first military expansion became possible in the late 1950s when the Korean War boom, and the economic growth that followed it, led to a favorable hard currency situation—its reserves stood at $483 million.[15] This allowed it to purchase, at commercial prices, an aircraft carrier for the navy as well as new aircraft for the air force. The air force procured 110 French Mystere interceptors, 160 British Hawker Hunters, and 78 British Canberra bombers.[16] In fact, by the time the Sino-Indian war broke out in 1962, India had one of the largest air forces in Asia.

THE DEFENSE INDUSTRY

The third set of bureaucratic pressures came from the defense industry. In 1947, the Indian arms industry consisted of sixteen ordnance factories and Hindustan Aircraft Limited—the aircraft overhaul facility. Apart from ammunition, the ordnance factories produced largely nonlethal equipment— uniforms and tents. Further, the government wanted to scale down defense production and a number of the plants that had surplus capacity were used in the 1950s to produce consumer products—coffee percolators and sewing machines. The aircraft industry was the exception to the general downswing in defense production for reasons cited earlier. There, a dual path to production was followed with India simultaneously trying to license-produce and indigenously design and develop aircraft. Another problem arose from the fact that India did not have the necessary infrastructure or scientific personnel to undertake the indigenous development of other weapons systems. Consequently, the armed services depended on imported weapons systems to fulfill their requirements. All these problems were reflected in the difficulties faced in the Marut project.

In the 1950s, an Air Staff Requirement was formulated for the development of a Mach 2 speed combat aircraft, later named the HF-24 Marut, and Hindustan Aeronautics Limited (HAL) was given the task of designing and producing it. HAL did not have the necessary experience, however, and Dr. Kurt Tank, the famous German design engineer, was invited to come to India and head the project.[17]

The first flight of a Marut took place in 1961, but the project turned out to be a failure with only 145 of an initial target of 214 aircraft built. The plane could never achieve supersonic speeds; the Bristol Orpheus 12 engine originally intended as an interim one, could not be used because Bristol refused to carry out further development work unless the Indian government paid the cost. India then turned to Egypt and later the Soviet Union for engines, but neither attempt was successful. HAL finally decided to power the aircraft with two unreheated Orpheus 703 engines, but the aircraft still could not attain supersonic speeds. Worse, "Marut relied heavily on imported parts and materials and [it] was more expensive to produce in India than it would have been to import a complete plane. The plane was technically obsolete by the time it was first delivered in 1964."[18]

In the aftermath of independence, therefore, it was the wishes of the political leadership, the situation in the external environment, and the availability of resources, rather than the existence of threats, that shaped the force structure and doctrine of the armed forces. In the years that followed, the relationship between these factors changed and with it so did the armed forces themselves.

THE NUCLEAR PROGRAM

As mentioned above, the initial period after independence was a low-threat period and one in which India did not face a nuclear threat. Instead, Nehru's commitment to disarmament and world peace saw India make several proposals in the 1950s to halt the spread of the nuclear arms race between the two superpowers. In the period after independence, therefore, the development of India's nuclear program was shaped by four factors: the role played by influential scientists; political sponsorship of the atomic energy program by Jawaharlal Nehru; the ability of the nuclear bureaucracy to obtain autonomy; and the successful use of external suppliers.

Indian scientists had started theoretical work in the nuclear field in the 1930s and two of the scientists who became institution builders in independent India had international reputations in the preindependence era. Meghnad Saha was known for his work in astrophysics and Homi Bhabha was known in the 1930s for his work in cosmic ray and elementary particle theory.[19]

It was Homi Bhabha who was primarily responsible for the direction India's nuclear program took after independence because it was his organizational and political skills that gave the necessary impetus to an atomic program in what was a newly independent country of the South. Bhabha, who was a student of Lord Rutherford, was unable to return to Cambridge after the outbreak of World War II and instead sought to develop fundamental research in India. Bhabha was the nephew of a wealthy industrialist, J.R.D. Tata, and was able to get funds from the Sir Dorab Tata Trust to set up the Tata Institute for Fundamental Research in 1944 to conduct research in the then relatively new field of high-energy physics.

Bhabha argued that such a research institution was necessary for India because, ". . . such a school forms the spearhead of research, not only in the less advanced branches of physics but also in the problem of immediate practical application to industry. . . . Moreover, when nuclear energy has been successfully applied for power production, in say a couple of decades from now, India will not have to look abroad for its experts but will find them ready at home."[20] Bhabha was, therefore, both aware of the potential of nuclear energy in national development as well as the need to create a body of trained personnel in the country to remove dependence on external powers. Bhabha's record in achieving these goals is remarkable. By the time of his untimely death in 1965, the Department of Atomic Energy (DAE) had established ten major research units and projects:

1. Atomic Energy Establishment, Trombay
2. Tarapore Atomic Power Project
3. Rajasthan Atomic Power Project
4. Madras Atomic Power Project
5. Jadguda Mines Project
6. Thumba Equatorial Rocket Launching Station
7. Space Science and Technology Center
8. Experimental Satellite Communication Earth Station
9. Atomic Mineral Division.
10. Trombay Township Project.[21]

Thus Bhabha had laid the foundations for three nuclear power plants, for the mining and extraction of uranium, for the development of an indigenous space program, and for the training of an indigenous group of nuclear scientists. Bhabha was also able to claim by 1965 that India was eighteen months away from having a nuclear blast.[22]

Bhabha's success was attributable in part to his ability to successfully cultivate political links—to the extent that he had direct access to Nehru—and being able to use his bureaucratic skills to preserve the autonomy of the Indian nuclear establishment from political and bureaucratic interference. Leading Indian scientists had recognized the need to develop political linkages even before independence. Meghnad Saha had invited Nehru to preside over the Indian

National Science Congress, making Nehru the first nonscientist to do so. Saha also successfully urged the then president of the Indian National Congress, Netaji Subhas Chandra Bose, to establish a National Planning Committee on Science and Culture. Once the committee was established, Saha was instrumental in ensuring that Nehru chaired it. His logic was that unless an important member of the Congress chaired the committee it would be merely regarded as an academic set-up by the leadership of the Congress Party. Once Nehru was the chair, Saha used this forum to influence Nehru's thinking on science and industrialization. Saha was able to get Nehru to agree that he did not believe in the Gandhian approach to industrialization, that of setting up cottage industries but rather favored large-scale industrialization. Saha favored the Soviet approach to industrialization.[23]

Bhabha was equally astute in his cultivation of Nehru. Through family connections and their mutual interest in science he developed a friendship with Nehru. "These men shared the same patrician background with proximity to wealth and political influence; both had been to Cambridge, lived like bachelors, considered themselves connoisseurs of art, music, food, etc. Their mutual attraction enabled them to speak the same language."[24] The friendship was so strong that Bhabha and Nehru were having tea or dinner every two weeks and Bhabha called Nehru "bhai" [brother].[25] On the strength of this friendship Bhabha was able to secure the autonomy he required, as well as the governmental funds he wanted, to further his nuclear agenda.

In 1948, Bhabha set up the Indian Atomic Energy Commission (AEC) with the underlying assumption that India would use atomic energy for peaceful purposes. The AEC, therefore, would promote Indian national interests in the future development of nuclear energy, conduct surveys for natural resources, and promote research in the nuclear field in both its own laboratories as well as in those of Indian universities. The three members of the commission were under the guidance of the prime minister in the fulfillment of these objectives.[26]

The success of the AEC led Bhabha to suggest in 1954 that the Indian government establish a Department of Atomic Energy for research and development in nuclear technology. The chairman of the AEC was the ex-officio secretary of the DAE and reported directly to the prime minister. In order to achieve greater autonomy, Bhabha, in consultation with Nehru, was by 1958 to reorganize the AEC with "full authority to plan and implement the various measures on sound technical and economic principles and free from all non-essential restrictions and needlessly inelastic rules." Further, it was the chairman who appointed the full-time and part-time member of the AEC board. The chairman himself was also responsible to the prime minister and all recommendations of the AEC had to be passed through him to reach the prime minister. The chairman could overrule the other members of the commission except the Member for Finance and Administration who in a financial matter could ask to be referred to the prime minister.[27] Thus by 1958 Bhabha had complete control over nuclear affairs in the country, bypassing both the bureaucracy and the Indian cabinet. In a national security system where the military reported to civilian authorities and the defense industries had to function within the organizational pressures generated by the bureaucracy, the armed forces, and the politicians, Bhabha had secured remarkable freedom for himself and his agenda.

The last reason that Bhabha was so successful was his ability to use his international scientific links as well as the willingness of external suppliers to provide the kind of technology India wanted to initiate a nuclear program. In 1945 Bhabha tried to purchase a betatron from General Electric but was turned down. He then successfully approached the Canadians in 1947 to supply a ton of crude uranium oxide for his experiments. After getting permission from the United States and Britain, Canada made the shipment. The Western nations hoped this would ensure future access to India's thorium supplies.[28] With a little foreign assistance—the enriched uranium fuel elements were purchased from Britain—Bhabha led a team of Indian scientists who went on to build a 1 MW experimental reactor, Apsara, and to carry out a chain reaction in 1956. This was the first experimental reactor in Asia outside the Soviet Union.[29]

Nehru also gave Bhabha a free hand to negotiate with the Canadians for the purchase of a research reactor. The Canadian government offered the NR-X research reactor (which India subsequently acquired and named CIRUS). The notable aspect of Bhabha's diplomatic skills in this case was his ability to get the reactor without adequate safeguards. "India pledged that products resulting from the reactor would be employed for peaceful purposes only. Bhabha insisted that India's word was a sufficient safeguard between members of the Commonwealth and expressions of Canadian doubt only served to call into question Indian credibility, a subject which diplomats found easy to avoid."[30]

Two other key transfers of technology were the CANDU and Tarapore deals. At the 1954 Atomic Energy Conference Bhabha laid out his three-stage plan for the development of India's nuclear program. The first stage consisted of establishing a nuclear power generation capacity of 2700 MW by setting up pressurized heavy water reactors (PHWR) using uranium oxide and heavy water. In the second stage, fast breeder reactors of 1000 MW capacity would use the plutonium produced as a by-product in the PHWR to breed more plutonium and uranium-233. The third stage would consist of converting India's abundant thorium reserves into fissile material in the breeder reactors.[31] To set the first stage rolling Bhabha was attracted to the Canadian CANDU-type reactors. There were several reasons for this. By the early 1960s, Indo-Canadian nuclear cooperation had worked quite effectively and as Dhirendra Sharma describes it, "could be termed as a model of cooperation between the technologically advanced and the less advanced nations."[32] The Canadians agreed to bilateral cooperation on equal terms. They offered to give the blueprints for the Rajasthan Atomic Power Plant and promised access to subsequent R&D in CANDU technology. The Canadians were eager to sell the reactor because it was a prototype. Further, the cost for all this was to be borne by the Colombo plan.[33] Thus, in financial and technology transfer terms, the CANDU deal was considered a good one.

Given Bhabha's plans for self-reliance, the decision to negotiate the Tarapore deal seemed a strange decision. Tarapore was a turnkey project provided by the United States, with G.E. as the principal contractor, and it used a reactor that ran on an enriched uranium fuel cycle. Further, the fuel was to be provided for the life of the reactor by the United States. Thus the deal did not fit into Bhabha's plans for self-reliance. Sharma's explanation is that it was signed because it gave India access to enriched uranium and took the country closer to plutonium technology.[34] By the early 1960s, India's civilian nuclear power program had advanced considerably due to critical inputs from friendly foreign states. Anderson argues that such technology was sold to further Western interests in India, for profit, and because of Bhabha's worldwide network of contacts in the scientific community. These contacts allowed him to overcome Western governmental opposition to technology transfers.[35]

By the early 1960s, Bhabha was able to lay down the framework for a nuclear program with the potential for dual purpose uses. Bhabha was also keen to take the next step and have a nuclear blast, although the reasons for this seemed to change over the years. In private conversations in the mid-1950s, Bhabha spoke of the desire to have Plowshare-type blasts in India for construction purposes.[36] But as a result of the growing confrontation with China, there was some discussion about the need to have a nuclear deterrent. From 1958 onward India began to pursue a "forward policy" in the Himalaya to lay claim on uninhabited territories that were considered to be a part of India. It was at this time that Nehru reportedly wrote a memo to Bhabha on the nuclear program which said that apart from generating electricity, "there is always a built in advantage of defense use should the need arise."[37] But despite such declarations little was done in the pre-1962 period to further the nuclear option. The reason for this lay in Nehru's nuclear and security policies.

NEHRU'S NUCLEAR AND SECURITY POLICIES

Nehru's security worldview was based on mitigating the adverse effects of bipolarity on the international system. He believed that India should keep itself out of the two armed camps that seemed to be forming around the superpowers and instead follow a policy of nonalignment. Nonalignment as Nehru saw it was not simple neutralism but rather the use of an independent position on international affairs to try to influence the structure of the international system. One aspect of nonalignment, therefore, was for India to press for global disarmament measures. Contrary to popular belief, this desire for disarmament did not come out of any idealistic Gandhian notions of universal peace. Instead, it came out of the recognition that the continued escalation of the Cold War would swallow up the newly independent nations of the South and make them lose their recently gained freedom. There was also the recognition that if the arms race could be curtailed, some of the money wasted by the superpowers on armament could be transferred to develop the nations of the

South. Only with global development, Nehru believed, could true peace be achieved in the international system.[38]

The second aspect of nonalignment germane to Indian nuclear policy in that era was the belief that India was an important nation. Implicit in this belief was the idea that the country's importance would ensure its security, for none of the great powers would allow it to be conquered by another. As one observer described it, ". . . every non-alignmentist, without exception, has been taking it for granted, consciously or unconsciously, that the forces of some other Powers will come to India's aid if and when she is threatened by conventional forces far in excess of her own defensive capacity, or by nuclear blackmail or attack."[39]

As a consequence of such thinking, India's nuclear policy in the 1950s was essentially one of pursuing disarmament in the global arena. Thus, in 1954 it proposed a moratorium on testing, a Comprehensive Test Ban Treaty (CTBT), and a subsequent attempt to eliminate nuclear weapons. In 1955 it called for the establishment of an international body to study the atmospheric effects of testing and in 1956 called for a conference for controlling plants that made nuclear explosive materials.[40]

At the same time, the Indian government was not willing to allow for the establishment of nuclear safeguards, which were seen as "unequal obligations." Thus, in 1956, India for the first time protested the discriminatory system of safeguards proposed by the great powers—a decade before it raised objections to the NPT.[41] India's objections came out of a desire to retain technological autonomy and avail itself of the advantages of nuclear energy for developmental purposes (Plowshare-type projects).

What we see, therefore, is that India's national and international nuclear policy in this period was marked by developmental, technological, and bureaucratic factors rather that threats. The success of the domestic program came out of the bureaucratic skills of Homi Bhabha as well as the willingness of external suppliers to provide critical technologies—particularly the CIRUS reactor. Internationally, Nehru pursued a nuclear policy that was not aimed at a particular nation but instead sought global disarmament for pragmatic developmental and security reasons. The focus of the Indian nuclear debate was to change in the 1960s due to the Sino-Indian war and the subsequent nuclearization of China.

1962–1971: REARMAMENT

The 1962 Sino-Indian war brought about a sea change in Indian defense planning. India was humiliated in the war, as the Chinese first overran India's hastily prepared fixed defensive positions in the Himalayas, and then unilaterally declared a cease-fire. Nehru's attempts at using diplomacy to offset the nation's military weakness had failed, and he was forced to undertake a major military buildup. It was believed that India now faced a two-front threat that could only be met by raising force levels. Yet the defense buildup that followed was only partially related to the events in the war. It is important to remember that the war had been a land battle with the Indian Air Force providing only transport support and assistance with search and rescue missions. As for the Indian Navy, it played no role in the conflict given the long distance from the Chinese coastline.

In 1964 a defense perspective plan was drafted that recommended expanding all three services. The army was to be enlarged by raising ten mountain divisions (basically infantry divisions with more vehicles and lighter weaponry), six additional infantry divisions, and a second armored division, thereby allowing it to increase its pre-1962 strength of nine divisions to twenty-five by the time the Indo-Pak war of 1971 broke out. It was to also receive more modern weapons and for this purpose six new ordnance factories were set up to produce small arms and ammunition.[42] Prior to the war plans had also been laid to produce Japanese and German trucks in the country and, more importantly, to license produce a Vickers tank.

The air force, similarly, was to be raised to forty-five squadrons and a phased withdrawal of the subsonic Hunters, Mysteres, Ouragons, and Canberras was to be carried out. Instead, the air force was to be built around two types of supersonic aircraft (the MiG-21 and the HF-24) backed up by the transonic Gnat.[43] Vertical lift capacity was to be increased with the licensed production of the French Allouette III helicopter.

Plans for naval expansion were also laid after the war but they clearly were not in response to the new threat. One of the initial concerns of the Navy was to acquire submarines, although the precise role these vessels would play was never made clear. One vague explanation given was that the Chinese Navy had the capability to operate in the Bay of Bengal and the Indian Ocean. Raju Thomas argues that the reason may not have been a threat as much as the opportunity provided by the availability of subsidized weaponry on easy terms from Britain and the United States.[44] Ultimately, the submarine deal could not be cut with the British because India could not meet the costs of the program, but New Delhi was able to sign an agreement with Britain for the licensed production of the Leander class frigates.

Instead, the bulk of naval expansion in the 1960s was undertaken due to the opening up of the military relationship with the Soviet Union. The Soviets transferred four surplus Foxtrot class submarines to the navy along with five Petya class frigates and an undisclosed number of Osa class missile boats. The navy, while still a junior service, was beginning to acquire the capability to fight a major maritime offensive, especially against a weak maritime state like Pakistan. The crucial factor that shaped the military expansion program of the 1960s, however, was the availability of resources.

The 1960s were a decade of turmoil for India. The Indian National Congress, the umbrella organization which had ruled the country since independence, was beginning to come apart due to factional infighting. Militarily, the nation had suffered a humiliating defeat at the hands of the Chinese.

The country was also in the worst economic crisis since attaining independence. In the mid-1960s two successive years of sparse rainfall led to a famine in parts of Northern India and plunged the nation's economy into a downward spiral. As a consequence India could not afford to invest in an unlimited expansion of its armed forces. The gravity of the economic crisis was felt in both procurement and in the shaping of perceived missions and doctrines.

Procurement was hampered by the lack of hard currency. India, in fact, could not go in for the outright purchase of any weapons system from the West in the 1960s. Instead, the deals cut with Western armament companies—like the Allouette helicopter and Leander frigate deals—were for licensed production. Further, the various ordnance factories were established because the Western nations were providing military aid on concessional terms as a result of the Sino-Indian war. Such aid, however, dried up after the 1965 India-Pakistan war, when the Western nations imposed an arms embargo on both combatants. What facilitated the Indian buildup after that war was the opening up of the Soviet military connection.

THE SOVIET CONNECTION

In 1962 the then Indian Defense Minister, Krishna Menon, overrode the objections of the air force and opted for the MiG-21 as India's first supersonic fighter. Menon argued that while the aircraft might be inferior to the aircraft the air force wanted—the Lockheed F-104 Starfighter—the Soviets were willing to transfer the technology to India. This would serve, he argued, as the foundation for an Indian aircraft industry that would be as technologically advanced as those of the Western nations.[45] Such an attempt may seem overly ambitious given the cost, lack of technological expertise, and the fact that the Marut project was already facing problems. But as Wainwright argues, the rationale may have been the prestige value such a project had in the international community.[46]

The major advantage of the arms link with the Soviets was that it had a cushioning effect on Indian weapons procurement. At a time when India faced a severe shortage of hard currency, the Soviet link allowed the country to import significant numbers of aircraft, tanks, and ships and to modernize the inventories of Indian armed forces. The reason for this was the terms on which the Soviets sold arms: the weapons were to be paid for in Indian Rupees rather than scarce hard currency; there was a seven-year grace period before payments began and total repayment period of seventeen years; and the Soviets charged a low interest rate of 2.5 percent.[47]

The cushioning effect of the Soviet arms connection can be seen in the procurement patterns of the 1960s. The only outright purchase of a fixed wing combat aircraft in the 1960s, for example, was the Rupee purchase of the Su-7 ground attack aircraft form the Soviet Union.[48] India also undertook licensed production of the MiG and by the 1971 war had about 140 MiGs in its inventory. Thus, by 1971, close to 40 percent of the air force's inventory consisted of Soviet aircraft. The Ouragons had been phased out, but other obsolescent aircraft like the Hunter and the Canberra continued to soldier on as the IAF was unable to reach its target of forty-five squadrons.

DOMESTIC ARMS INDUSTRY

In the general buildup after the 1962 conflict, defense research and production received a major boost. Apart from the earlier mentioned expansion of the ordnance factories there was also an expansion of the Defense Public Sector Undertakings (DPSUs)—state owned companies. Two new undertakings—Bharat Earth Movers to build tractors and bulldozers for the military and Bharat Dynamics to build missiles—were established. Older DPSUs were charged with building electronic equipment and precision machine tools for the armed forces. Along with the increase in defense production units came the expansion of the laboratories engaged in defense research.

The Defense Research and Development Organization (DRDO) was set up in 1958 but was to expand rapidly after the Sino-Indian war. The reason for this was twofold: it lay partly in the traditional interest of the Indian leadership in attaining technological self-sufficiency; it also became necessary because of the Western arms embargo. The decision was taken, therefore, to expand India's defense laboratories to cover research in Aeronautics, Electronics, Naval Technology, Materials, Life Sciences, and Engineering Equipment.[49]

Coupled with the increase in defense science laboratories was the growing civilian scientific establishment, whose research had dual-purpose uses. India established an atomic energy commission in 1948 and by the mid-1960s had both a nuclear power reactor and a research reactor in operation (the power reactor was sold by the US to India under the Atoms for Peace program while the research reactor came from Canada). Further, the early 1960s were marked by a debate in Indian intellectual, scientific, and political circles about the need to go nuclear. Nuclear weapons were seen as consolidating India's nonaligned status as well as providing it with the currency to join the club of major powers.[50]

The other major civilian program with military implications was the space program. The space program started with the launching of sounding rockets in the 1950s. By the 1960s plans were laid for building launch vehicles and satellites. By the mid 1970s the first rocket had been successfully launched and the first satellite put into orbit with Soviet assistance.

To sum up, in the aftermath of the Sino-Indian war the defense industry was expanded to develop or license-produce systems across the board to satisfy the needs of the armed forces. License-production programs for aircraft, ships, and tanks were established, as were programs for the manufacture of electronic components, explosives, small arms, and missiles. Scientific programs on the civilian side, particularly the atomic and space ones, were also to have a major impact on the future development of India's defense strategy.

THE AGENDA OF THE ARMED FORCES

The nature of the post-1962 buildup, the existence of a two front threat, and the 1965 India-Pakistan war had differing impacts on the doctrines of the armed services. In the 1965 India-Pakistan war each of the services essentially fought its own war. The army, to weaken the Pakistani effort in Kashmir where the terrain placed Indian forces at a disadvantage, broadened the conflict by trying to penetrate the plains of Pakistani Punjab. The defensive buildup in the region by the Pakistanis limited the room for armored maneuver and few territorial gains were made by India during that war. Indian armor was, in fact, used defensively to support the infantry to repel Pakistani attacks, and the conflict ended in a stalemate.

The air force decided that instead of providing close support to the army it would fight a virtually independent air war. Its principal goals, derived from its doctrinal philosophy, were to go after Pakistani air bases and carry out interdiction efforts. These tactics met with limited success because Pakistan based its aircraft deep inside its territory and the Indian Air Force suffered unnecessary and considerable losses trying to attack these targets.[51] Worse, India had virtually no forward bases along the south-western border and this allowed the Pakistani ground forces to penetrate the region without aerial interference. Finally, there was little coordination with either the army or the navy to provide air defense and close support to their forces.

The air force followed a World War II organizational procedure to give support to the army in which, "self-contained Tactical Air Forces operated closely alongside Army formations. Lacking such forces and organization and without a highly developed communications system, the text-book procedures were next to useless; if anything, they created chaos and confusion and left the troops on the ground bewildered and frustrated."[52] Nor was a plan drawn up to defend naval bases along the western border and the Pakistan Navy, therefore, was allowed to attack the Dwarka naval base in Gujarat.

But undoubtedly the worst performance in the war was by the navy. As one cynical observer points out the lack of coordination between the services led to the situation in which the navy was totally unprepared for the forthcoming war.[53] At the outbreak of hostilities it had just completed a set of exercises and consequently put its aircraft carrier, *Vikrant*, in dry dock. The navy, therefore, played a marginal role in the conflict and after the attack on Dwarka both navies withdrew from the conflict.

The 1965 war had a mixed impact on the doctrines of the three armed forces. The army persisted with its defensive tactics along the western border with Pakistan. It built up a series of Ditch cum Bunds (DCBs)—basically a series of antitank ditches—parallel to the border in Indian Punjab to prevent the Pakistanis from using armor to achieve rapid breakthroughs.[54] Thus the strategy was set for the western sector. India would seek to hold territory in the region rather than try and break through the Pakistani defenses—the Pakistanis having built their own antitank ditches in that sector. In the 1971 war the effort was to conduct holding operations in the west, while seven divisions were used to invade and subsequently liberate East Pakistan. Again the emphasis was on using the infantry to lead the attack with the armor in support.

By 1971 the air force had learned its lessons from the 1965 war and under a new commander, Air Chief Marshall Pratap Chand Lal, decided in 1969 to reshape the priorities for air operations. The doctrine of strategic bombing that had dominated the 1965 war was viewed as a carry-over from the World War II and not considered a priority in the South Asian context. Instead, the air force leadership decided that the service's role in the forthcoming conflict, in a descending order of importance, would be (1) to defend the air space of the country, (2) to provide support to the army and the air force, (3) to undertake strategic bombing, and (4) to carry out operations like paratrooping and transport.[55] An effort was also made to improve communications between the services. Lal recounts that during the 1965 war it took the army one or two days to get a request for air support from the front to air headquarters. By assigning squadrons to specific corps or areas, the air force was able to get the response time down to one to one and one-half hours by 1971. Thus in the 1971 war the air force was to fly over 5,000 sorties in support of the army, thereby providing effective support in the ground battle in both the western and eastern sectors.

In the late 1960s, the navy, despite its lack of presence in the 1965 war, sought once again to obtain a fleet to carry out blue water operations. When the British announced that they would be withdrawing from the east of Suez in 1968 the then naval chief of staff, Admiral Chatterji, called for India to take over policing the Indian Ocean from the British. For carrying out this task Chatterji wanted a fleet with four aircraft carriers in it. The government, however, struck down the proposal because it was seen as having imperialist connotations. The navy was successful, however, in persuading the government to expand the fleet in other directions by claiming that a larger navy was an integral part of an overall maritime policy.

At the operational level, in the 1971 war the navy decided to pursue three principal roles: to protect Indian shipping and keep the sea lanes open; to deny the use of the seas to Pakistan for naval and trade purposes by blockading both wings; and to undertake offensive forays on the coast of both parts of Pakistan for the maximum destruction of its naval strength and harbor facilities.[56] During the war the Navy divided its vessels into two commands: the aircraft carrier and its support vessels were to carry out offensive operations against the weakly defended East Pakistan coast; and the rest of the surface fleet, along with the missile boats, was placed in the western sector. The eastern fleet was able to freely carry out air strikes against targets in East Pakistan because it enjoyed both maritime and air superiority. The western command was to carry out a daring raid against Karachi harbor itself. It towed the Osa class missile boats to the vicinity of the harbor and then used the Osa's Styx antiship missiles to blow up the oil storage tanks in the harbor. A second raid later in the campaign wiped out Pakistani tankers anchored in Karachi harbor and Pakistan lost approximately half of its oil reserves.

The 1971 war showed that given sufficient time, the Indian armed forces had the capacity to launch a concerted and effective attack against an opponent. Planning for the war, which broke out in late November, began in May of that year and the different services had months to practice their tactics. Further, the existence of commanders willing to coordinate their activities helped surmount what could otherwise have been an acrimonious relationship between the services.

THE NUCLEAR DEBATE

Following India's defeat in the Sino-Indian war and the subsequent nuclearization of China, there was a debate in India about the implications of developing a nuclear weapons capability. The debate occurred at two levels: one focused on the specific threat posed by China; and the other looked at the more general implications of nuclearization on India's role in the international system.

After the 1962 war official Indian policy toward China rested on several planks. India would continue to remain nonaligned rather than enter an alliance. It would seek guarantees from the nuclear powers that they would come to the aid of nonnuclear states threatened by nuclear blackmail or attack. While capable of making a nuclear device, the country would refrain from doing so. Instead, it would actively seek arms control and global disarmament.[57] India would also refrain from the nuclear option, the government reasoned, due to economic considerations and because it led to the risk of heightening tensions in the region.

The argument made by one antinuclear analyst was that China's nuclear capability was too limited to provide it with a defense capability against the superpowers and therefore it was governed by prestige reasons.[58] He argued that given the lack of a defensive capability China would not launch a nuclear attack on India because this would provoke an attack by a stronger power. Thus the old argument of India's importance acting as a deterrent was still being echoed.

The economic argument against nuclearization was equally important because the Indian government had a commitment to the development and building up a full-scale nuclear capability was beyond the economic capacity of the nation. Minoo Masani, then an Indian parliamentarian, said that because Indian cities were within a 300-mile range from Chinese military bases in Tibet, while major Chinese cities were 2,500 miles away from India, the economic costs of a credible nuclear deterrent would be too high for India to bear. To develop such a capability would require three-quarters of the entire outlay of India's fourth Five Year Plan.[59] Similarly, Raj Krishna argued that a truly independent deterrent capability required the acquisition of IRBMS and ICBMs, a strong navy, a long-range air force, and a second-strike capability. The economic cost of establishing such a force, he believed, would be too much for the Indian economy to bear.[60]

Some analysts believed that although India could not bear the economic and political costs of nuclearization, it still required a nuclear guarantee. Masani and former Defense Secretary H. M. Patel suggested that India abandon non-alignment and seek alliance with the West.[61] Another argument in this vein was to seek a joint assurance from the two superpowers that they would intervene if India was subjected to nuclear blackmail or attack.

The alternative was to go nuclear. The pronuclear lobby felt that this was the best alternative given the incredibility of security guarantees. Dismissing potential alliances with the West, or the idea of a joint guarantee, Raj Krishna pointed out that the United States would be reluctant to attack China because "it involves, inter alia, commitment of masses of Western infantry against the flood of Asian infantry—a prospect which evokes infinite horror in the Western mind." He concluded, therefore that "It is difficult to visualize Europeans and Americans bombing China just for the sake of a few thousand South Asian lives or a few thousand miles of South Asian territory."[62]

The type of nuclear force the pro-bomb lobby wanted, however, was a modest one. It was to be based on what Krishna called "the division of labor in deterrence." It was assumed that China would remain a revolutionary state and continue its rivalry with the United States and the Soviet Union. The West and the Soviet Union would, therefore, provide long-range deterrence in the form of their nuclear missiles, while India would provide short-range deterrence. India would acquire the capability to wage tactical and short-range deterrence in the land in the air. Thus India should have a regionalized atomic capability.[63] The logic behind such a modest force (they were calling, among other things, for the development of nuclear artillery shells), was that it did not leave India vulnerable to the decisions of the great powers and at the same time did not place a staggering economic burden on the nation. It was estimated that a modest force could be acquired with an annual outlay of Rs 200 crores ($418 million). Such a force structure could work, Sisir Gupta argued, because it meant that the Chinese would have to factor in the Indian nuclear capability along with the overwhelming superiority of the US and the USSR in their security calculations—thus raising the risks for China of initiating a nuclear war.[64]

At the systemic level, a modest nuclear force was also seen as preserving India's influence in international affairs. Anti-nuclear analysts suggested that it was immoral for the land of Gandhi and Nehru to have bombs. They further argued that Indians lacked the psychological makeup to use nuclear weapons, that nuclearization would heighten international tensions, and that it would lead to worsening relations with the West, which was pushing a nonproliferation agenda.[65] The proponents of nuclear weapons countered all of these arguments. Discussing the role of nuclear weapons in international politics, Sisir Gupta stated that nuclear weapons were central to a nation's quest for power in the international system of the 1960s. In fact nations were willing to compromise on economic problems in order to continue acquiring the bases of such power. Thus he believed that India had two options: "It can either enter the [nuclear] club by defying the world and making a bomb or see to it that the bomb as a status symbol loses its significance because of effective progress towards disarmament."[66]

As to heightening international tensions and worsening relations with the West, the argument was made that what mattered was not India's nuclear status but what it did when it became a nuclear power. If India was to be a responsible status quo state, unlike China, it would assuage Western fears. And if it did not use its nuclear weapons but instead used the influence gained by possessing them to push for disarmament, then its role would continue to be one which was both moral and moderating in the international system. Further, as Sisir Gupta argued, true global security did not just involve checking the proliferation of nuclear weapons. It was also one of "taking steps to advance the world to a higher level of international order and collective security."[67]

So by the mid-1960s there was a body of opinion in India that believed that nuclear weapons were needed both to counter the Chinese threat and to maintain India's role and influence in international affairs. The Indian government did not move rapidly in this direction. In declaratory policy there was still the quest for guarantees and disarmament. In action policy there was a move toward exploring the nuclear option. With Nehru's death in 1964 Bhabha had to deal with a new prime minister, Lal Bahadur Shastri. Bhabha was able to convince Shastri of the need for a Subterranean Nuclear Explosion Project (SNEP), and in 1965 cabinet approval was granted to explore the feasibility of the project.

The SNEP did not come about in the 1960s for a variety of reasons. Bhabha died in an air crash leaving a large scientific and organizational hole which was difficult to fill. His successor, Vikram Sarabhai, was supposedly against nuclear option and instead wanted to pursue the peaceful applications of atomic energy. Shastri also died and his death signaled the beginning of infighting in the ruling Indian National Congress. It took Indira Gandhi, Shastri's successor, nearly five years to gain full control over the party. The economic burden of the Bihar famines also worked against entering into an expensive nuclear program. Finally, the Sino-Soviet split of 1969 lessened the need to overtly go nuclear since Beijing had a far more serious security threat to worry about.

By the end of the 1960s, therefore, the Indian government had backed away from exercising the nuclear option because of domestic constraints and the emergence of a more favorable international system. The 1971 war and the Indo-Soviet treaty that preceded it further negated the need to exercise the nuclear option. At the same time, the Indian government continued to resist attempts to constrain India's nuclear option. It refused to sign the NPT, labeling it discriminatory for its safeguard provisions, and for the fact that it did little to spur disarmament.

1972–1979: LOW THREAT PERIOD

This was a period in which the threat level declined to its lowest point since independence. Pakistan had been dismembered and India was the predominant military power in South Asia. Relations with China improved as the two countries resumed diplomatic relations and India was able to lower the level of forces it maintained along the Sino-Indian border. Finally, the superpowers, which had played a crucial role in arming the region in the 1960s, shifted their focus of attention to other crisis areas. But while it was a low-threat period it was marked by other factors which shaped Indian defense planning.

First, the economic situation once again took a turn for the worse and with it India faced yet another shortage of hard currency. This had an adverse impact on weapons procurement. The Indian Air Force had test flown the British Aerospace Jaguar as early as 1968 but by 1973 the negotiations had to be put on hold because of hard currency restrictions. The Navy similarly carried out the first shipboard tests of the Sea Harrier in 1972 but was unable to consummate the deal because of a lack of hard currency. Thus India was not in a position to replace its obsolescent weaponry with purchases from the West.[68]

Second, problems were also emerging in the Soviet connection. Moscow wanted India to provide it with a naval base and to endorse its plans for an Asian Collective Security scheme. India refused to provide the base because it would violate the country's nonaligned status and was unwilling to endorse the latter proposal because it was viewed, among other things, as being anti-Chinese in its orientation. The Soviet response was to constrict the supply of spares to India and to refuse to sell some new weapons systems to it.[69]

Third, the Indian arms industry failed to provide indigenous systems for the use of the services. By the early 1970s the Marut project had turned out to be a complete failure. The plane never attained supersonic speeds because a powerful enough engine could not be obtained and even the subsonic version proved ineffective resulting in only a small number of aircraft entering service. The workable weapons that the armed forces got from the arms industry were essentially those that were license-produced such as the MiGs, the Leander frigates, and the Allouettes. But the problem with most of these systems was that they were beginning to become obsolete. The worst hit by this crisis was the air force, whose inventory continued to consist of mainly obsolescent aircraft like the Hunter, the Canberra and the Su-7.

Fourth, the combination of low financial reserves and the failure of the arms industry to provide modern weapons systems impacted on doctrinal development. The navy, unable to procure a new carrier or new aircraft to complement the old one, shelved its plans for a blue water navy in the early 1970s and instead decided to use the *Vikrant* as an antisubmarine warfare helicopter carrier until the end of its service life.[70] No new carriers were to follow. The air force also shelved its plans for a deep penetration strike aircraft, the Jaguar, which would have been used to take out strategic targets deep in Pakistan. Yet while the lack of resources dictated the unfulfillment of doctrine it did not stop the development of military thought on the subject.

After the dismemberment of Pakistan, military planners began to think in terms of what the next war would look like. The main emphasis was placed on what to do in a future conflict with Pakistan. In both the 1965 and 1971 wars the emphasis had been on repulsing Pakistani attacks, but by the early 1970s there was a shift in military thinking. The emphasis in military writings shifted to how to deal a crushing and final blow to Pakistan in a future war. The means to do this, it was believed, was to shift the emphasis in military strategy from infantry-oriented defensive tactics to armor oriented offensive ones. Armored thrusts were to be carried out deep into Pakistani territory so as to destroy that country's war making potential.[71] But the lack of financial resources prevented the necessary buildup of the army necessary to fulfill such a strategy. Instead the Army opted for a more modest growth plan which reflected the financial and external environment of the 1970s.

In 1975 the Indian government appointed an expert committee consisting of generals K. V. Krishna Rao, M. L. Chibber and K. Sundarji to develop a twenty-year perspective plan for the army.[72] The recommendations of this committee, with a few modifications, were carried out into the 1980s by the army brass. The committee stated that the primary goal of the army was the prevention of war at as small a financial investment as possible. Its second major recommendation was that India's research and development capability be used to minimize the army's dependency on imports.[73]

The expert committee viewed Pakistan and China as the main threats to Indian security and recommended that a force structure be evolved that would deter the other side. The idea was to create a force structure which would convey to the other side that if it started a war it would be unlikely to achieve its objectives. In operational terms this meant that the Indian army should have a force advantage of two corps (six divisions) over the Pakistani Army (the existing balance of forces with China was considered sufficient to deter a Chinese threat).[74] Further, the tank regiments in the army were to be doubled from 27 to 58 and the committee also recommended that two mechanized infantry divisions be added to the existing force structure.

The committee's recommendation to reduce the dependence on imports was couched in terms of providing the country with greater autonomy of action and the need to lessen the defense burden. But this decision was primarily taken because of the hard currency crisis in the early part of the decade. In fact the decision had already been taken in the early 1970s to draw up a follow-on tank to the Vijayanta—the Chetak. Along with the Chetak, the army was also to benefit from the planned development of an Advanced Light Helicopter (ALH). Neither the Chetak project nor the ALH came to fruition in the 1970s and both programs were carried into the 1980s (with the Chetak's name being changed to Arjun). There were several reasons why indigenous arms production did not bear fruit by the 1970s.

First, as K. Subrahmanyam points out, the importation of sophisticated materials continued, despite licensed production, because there was no aggregation of civil industrial and defense demand for most of these materials. He argued that no country had tried to develop a combat aircraft industry without developing an adequate civil aeronautical industry. If these two went together there would be aggregated and economical demands for aircraft, alloys, instruments, various accessories, and hydraulic systems.[75] An aircraft industry based solely on military requirements, such as India's, did not provide an adequately broad base to develop R&D for various subsystems and materials, with the result that the defense aircraft industry had to depend on a certain amount of imported components. To indigenously produce those components was deemed uneconomical.

Second, delays in forcing indigenous equipment developments through to the production stage also affected the industry's ability to satisfy the needs of the armed forces. The delay in producing HAL's Kiran II jet trainer in the mid-1970s led to the import of the Polish Iskra. Delays in development could not, however, be laid solely at the doorstep of the Indian defense industry. The armed forces were largely responsible for the protracted delays in the development of a weapons system. The tendency was for the armed forces to continue adding requirements well past the project definition stage and into the actual developmental stage. This had the effect not only of prolonging the project but of making design development work extremely difficult.

The development of the Ajeet Mark II demonstrated how changing requirements could have a detrimental effect on the most feasible of weapons programs. The idea behind the Ajeet was to improve the Gnat Mk I's ground attack role by increasing its armament carrying capacity and its radius of action. This was a manageable task for HAL and it was what was agreed upon in Air Staff Requirement 22 of 1972 (the project definition report). But the Public Accounts Committee of the Indian Parliament noted that "progressive addition of tasks till as late as 1978–1979 has had a significant impact on the development expenditure schedule as well as ultimate target set for the delivery of production aircraft." The report continued: "The Air Force authorities had no precise idea of the real nature of the development effort required, particularly in the context of the new role the aircraft was intended for. Decisions were taken in an ad hoc manner from time to time resulting in escalation in cost as well as in heavy time overrun."[76] Such additional requirements were permitted because of the position of the arms industries in the defense hierarchy. The Indian national security system was structured in such a way as to lessen the influence of the production units. Until recently, HAL's chairman was a serving officer in the Air Force. Similarly, the head of the Avadi tank production factory was an officer of the Indian Army. This quite obviously led to a weakening of the bargaining power of the production units. But while the domestic production of conventional weapons was running into trouble, significant steps were being taken in the nuclear sector.

THE NUCLEAR PROGRAM

The 1970s were marked by major achievements in the Atomic Energy and Space programs. In 1974 India exploded its first nuclear device at Pokhran, in Rajasthan, and established itself as a potential nuclear power. By the end of the decade India was able to launch its first indigenously developed rocket and satellite. Thus India had not only become a de facto nuclear state but had also taken the first step to build a guaranteed delivery system. Indian nuclear policy in the 1970s evolved into one that retained the nuclear option without having an overt nuclear weapons program. At the same time, India continued to seek what Sisir Gupta had argued for—the creation of effective order in the international system—through global disarmament measures. The reason behind pursuing such a policy of restraint lay in the fact that India did not face a serious threat to it security in the 1970s. In fact the decision making on the nuclear explosion was driven by factors other than just the threat of a nuclear China.

The decision to go nuclear arose from a complex set of circumstances. In 1971, Mrs. Gandhi informed the Parliamentary Consultative Committee of the DAE that the government would experiment with nuclear explosions for scientific purposes. This intent was reiterated in 1972 in parliament by Mrs. Gandhi when she stated that the AEC was studying conditions under which Peaceful Nuclear Explosions (PNEs) could be carried out underground to prevent environmental hazards.[77] The security environment in South Asia in 1971 probably led to Mrs. Gandhi's decision, but by 1972 the security rationale had died down due to India's success in the 1971 war. P. R. Chari believes that a combination of security concerns, bureaucratic momentum, and internal political reasons led to the 1974 test. India's nuclear scientists urged that the test be carried out. By 1974, the country was going through a severe economic crisis and Mrs. Gandhi faced increasing domestic challenges to her authority. In such a situation the Pokhran test was seen as increasing her domestic prestige (not, as many observers believe, the country's external prestige).[78]

The immediate fallout of the Pokhran test was its impact on India's civilian nuclear program. Canada first suspended and then canceled the supply of design data and nuclear equipment for the Rajasthan and Madras atomic power plants, thereby creating delays in the plants becoming operational.[79] Indian production of heavy water, which was the moderator for the CANDU-type reactors, had yet to commence, so India asked the Soviet Union to be an alternative supplier of fuel. The Soviets provided the heavy water but insisted on safeguards on the project.[80] The Madras plants were also delayed due to construction problems and the first plant did not become operational until 1985—a twelve year delay. Fuel supply problems as well the problem of what to do with the spent fuel at the Tarapore plant became contentious issues in U.S.-Indian relations.

From 1975 onward the United States put pressure on India by "delaying, restricting and denying consignments of fuel for TAPS."[81] It also postponed the "joint determination," under the 1963 agreement, of how to dispose of the spent fuel from the reactor. As Mansingh points out, the economic costs of these delays for India were high because the Tarapore plant ran well below capacity and an indigenously built reprocessing plant also lay idle (Tarapore provides electricity to India's major industrial belt along the West coast).[82]

In 1984, the Estimates Committee of the Indian Parliament examined the success of the Indian atomic energy program at generating electricity and its report showed the impact Western sanctions had on the civilian nuclear program. The Atomic Energy Commission, for example, had stated in 1968 that by 1980 atomic energy would generate 2,700 MW of electricity in the country. But, as the Estimates Committee noted, by that date only 860 MW of power was being generated—a shortfall of 68 percent from the planed estimate.[83] The AEC's explanation for this shortfall lay in two constraints "limited industrial infrastructure capable of supporting the nuclear programme and the restrictive practices in international trade in nuclear materials."[84] The impact of U.S. fuel restrictions for Tarapore was also described, "we have had to reduce the maximum operating power level at Tarapore to 160 MW from 210 MW in order to conserve the available fuel."[85]

International concern against proliferation led to the formation of the London Club of Western suppliers, who now began to demand full-scope safeguards on the export of nuclear materials and technology. It also led to the U.S. Congress passing the Nuclear Non-Proliferation Act (NNPA), which became law in 1978. The establishment of such national and international laws obviously hurt India's nuclear power program. An imposition of full-scope safeguards could hurt India's efforts to retain the nuclear option. But more particularly the NNPA was going to hurt the future of Tarapore. The provisions of the act that most concerned the Indian government were that any nation receiving U.S. nuclear exports would have to place all its installations under IAEA safeguards and that within eighteen months of the act's going into effect agree to the more comprehensive fullscope safeguards.[86]

The Indian response under both Prime Ministers Morarji Desai and Indira Gandhi was to try to prove to the Carter administration that India had no intention of going nuclear and, for its part, would abide by the terms of the 1963 Tarapore agreement. It would not use outside fuel in the reactor and it would not divert spent fuel from it. India, after several delays, got the fuel it wanted but the net result was to seriously hurt Tarapore's capacity to function.

While external pressure slowed down India's nuclear program it needs to be explained why India desisted from further tests after the Pokhran explosion. The internal political situation was one reason. By 1975, faced by rising dissent in the country, Mrs. Gandhi imposed a national emergency on the country. In effect this meant the abrogation of the constitution and the imposition of authoritarian rule on the country. The emergency focused Mrs. Gandhi's attentions on maintaining political control. External economic pressure also probably prevented a second test. Japan, for example, terminated economic aid after the Pokhran test and future testing would most likely have hurt foreign aid from other countries as well as multilateral sources. Wasting scare national resources on building an expensive nuclear force did not make sense given the low-threat environment.

In 1977, Mrs. Gandhi lost the national elections and was replaced by the octogenarian Morarji Desai. Desai was a committed Gandhian and had a deep personal repugnance for nuclear weapons. While Desai could not scrap the nuclear program—the internal constituency to preserve the option was too strong—he did make policy statements that effectively constrained the program. Desai stated that, first, India would use atomic energy for peaceful purposes and not, under any circumstances, manufacture nuclear weapons. Second, India would not sign the NPT unless the major nuclear powers renounced their nuclear weapons. Third, PNEs would not be conducted (although earlier he had said that PNEs could be carried out openly and after consultations with other nations).[87] Further, Desai continued to push the disarmament agenda. He called for a CTBT and for universal disarmament. What makes Desai's self-imposed constraints on Indian policy all the more interesting is that they came at a time when evidence was beginning to come in that Pakistan had initiated its own nuclear weapons program. Desai's term ended all too quickly when his party split in 1979 and, after a six-month caretaker government, Mrs. Gandhi returned to power in 1980.

Thus, in the 1970s, it was political will—or the lack of it—along with continued domestic political and economic constraints, and restrictions placed by external suppliers that shaped the nature of the Indian nuclear program.

1980-1987: THE INDIAN MILITARY BUILDUP

The period from 1980 to 1987 was marked by a major Indian military buildup. The army acquired T-72 tanks, Bofors 155 mm Howitzers and BMP-2 ICVs. The air force emerged from the decade with one of the most modern fleets in the world. It acquired Mirage 2000s, MiG-23s, 27s and 29s, and the Jaguar ground attack aircraft. It also built up a strategic transport component with the acquisition of the IL-76 Candid. The most spectacular growth, however, was that of the navy. It acquired twelve submarines (8 Soviet Kilo class and 4 German Type 1500s) a second aircraft carrier, squadrons of Sea Harrier aircraft to equip both carriers, Tu-142 long range maritime patrol aircraft, and a leased Charlie I nuclear attack submarine.

India was able to go in for this buildup for a number of reasons. First, the hard currency situation improved in the late 1970s and early 1980s to the extent that India was able to procure weapons from Britain, France, Germany, and Sweden. Lesser deals were cut with the United States, Holland and Italy. Second, the Soviet Union viewed these purchases from the West with concern, fearing a reduction in influence (the Soviets were also keen to secure India's support for their Afghan policy). Thus by 1979 the Soviets had made some tempting offers in the effort to retain the Indian market. This led to the signing in 1980 of a $1.6 billion deal for the supply of Soviet weaponry.[88] Thus through the early and mid-1980s the Soviets offered India virtually every conventional weapons system available, often before supplying them to Warsaw Pact countries.

Third, a new India political leadership emerged that sought to use India's military strength to pursue its foreign policy goals. When Mrs. Gandhi returned to power in 1980 she faced a changed threat environment in South Asia. The

Soviets were in Afghanistan and the United States was rearming Pakistan because it was considered a frontline state in the struggle against communism. Mrs. Gandhi viewed this development with concern because Pakistan had previously used American-supplied weaponry not to fight communism, but to fight India. This conflicted with India's desire for a South Asia that was free from superpower influences, thereby allowing it to be the predominant power in the region. To achieve this goal, therefore, Mrs. Gandhi espoused the Indira, or South Asian Doctrine, in 1983. According to this doctrine Indian concerns were predominant in South Asia, especially over those of external powers who must not be allowed to exploit the internal crises of other South Asian states to enhance their own positions in the region. By implication, any attempt by another South Asian nation to invite such outside intervention would be considered hostile to India and grounds for Indian retaliation. Instead, states in such a situation were to first seek the assistance of India.[89] This political doctrine required a buildup of the Indian forces particularly to give them an improved regional reach. This doctrine was operationalized when India sent peacekeeping troops to Sri Lanka (1987–1990) and to crush the Maldives coup in 1988.

THE ROLE OF THE DEFENSE INDUSTRY

Another aspect of the buildup was the resuscitation of the domestic arms industry. By the late 1970s the Indian arms industry was in a slump as its indigenous arms production projects were not getting off the ground. The Arjun program was behind schedule and it was proving difficult to build an engine with sufficient power for the tank. The ALH project had fared no better due to major disagreements between the air force and HAL over the shape of the aircraft. Further, work at India's missile production unit had ground to a halt and there was talk of disbanding the project.[90]

What changed the state of affairs was the availability of financial resources and key changes in the decision making structure. In the late 1970s Dr. Raja Ramanna was appointed Scientific Adviser to the government. He had headed the team that constructed the 1974 nuclear device and therefore wielded considerable influence in political circles. Ramanna recognized that if the arms industry was to survive, it had to develop systems that could meet the challenges of the modern-day battlefront. This meant producing high-technology weapons systems. It was decided, therefore, to both revive old projects and initiate new one in order to satisfy the needs of the armed forces in the 1990s. With this is mind the arms industry pushed for the revival of the ALH and Arjun projects and for the initiation of a light combat aircraft (LCA) project.

Ramanna's successor was Dr. V. Arunachalam, who in 1983 was able to convince the political leadership and the armed forces of the need for an entire range of missiles, including ballistic ones (another crucial figure was the army chief in the mid-1980s K. Sundarji who pushed for both the computerization of the army and for upgrading its communications and electronic warfare technology).[91] This project was expanded by the then defense minister, R. Venkatraman, into an Integrated Guided Missile Development Program (IGMDP) in 1983 (according to Dr. Arunachalam the armed forces gave their complete backing to the project).[92] It was from this program that India's short-range missile Prithvi, (in 1988), and intermediate range missile, Agni (in 1989), were developed. It was also recognized that for such programs to succeed the critical electronic and subcomponents had to come from external sources. Thus the Agni's onboard computer, inertial guidance system, and gyroscopes were procured from external suppliers.[93]

Along with the major projects, there was an attempt to improve the communications, surveillance, electronic warfare and electronic countermeasures capabilities of the armed forces. The arms industry developed the Indra low-level radar for the army as well as naval radars for the detection and tracking of sea-skimming missiles. The army also obtained an Army Radio Engineered Network (AREN), which provides "ground forces with a secure computerized area grid communications system connecting all parts of the country."[94]

THE LCA, ALH, AND MBT

A discussion of India's three major conventional arms production projects indicates that the problems faced with arms production in earlier periods continue to plague the defense industry. The ALH project was first proposed by the C. Subramaniam committee on aeronautics in 1969, and in 1971 India entered into a ten-year agreement with Aerospatiale of France for the design of a single-engine ALH, the first prototype of which was to fly in 1982. In 1977 the IAF asked the government to change the ALH into a twin-engine aircraft, and its recommendation was accepted in 1979 despite the fact that HAL had nearly completed a single-engine design. This led in 1981 to a termination of the contract with Aerospatiale, and the government had to pay $4 million in cancellation fees. In 1984 a new seven-year collaboration contract with MBB of West Germany was signed and work began from scratch.

This collaboration, however, led to disputes between the MBB and HAL designers over technical specifications of the aircraft. The MBB-proposed design lowered the crashworthiness of the aircraft from 95 percent to 50 percent and in addition reduced its load-carrying capacity. The ALH designers also got approval for the removal of indigenous avionics equipment (altimeters and sonars), replacing it with lighter imported equipment so as to bring down the empty weight of the aircraft.[95] Since the engine and the fiber composite rotors were also imported this led to both a reduction in the indigenous content of the aircraft and an increase in its price. The Indian government also acquired several Mi-25s from the Soviet Union to make up for the protracted delay in the ALH project. The ALH did eventually come through as project. Flight testing of the aircraft took place in 1993 and HAL hopes to get orders in both the civilian and military markets. But even with a successful program there are doubts that the ALH will be commercially viable within the country, and it is likely that the army will want more advanced attack helicopters rather than the cheap hybrid the ALH provides—the helicopter is to be used for both naval and close-support purposes.

Like the ALH program, the Main Battle Tank (MBT) project also went through developmental snags. Started in 1974, the MBT was supposed to be in service by the mid-1980s. The tank was to be powered by an indigenous 1,300 to 1,500 hp. diesel engine, but the power plant was able to produce only 500 horsepower without a turbocharger, and even after being turbocharged it fell short of its planned output. This led the Combat Vehicle Research and Development Establishment to fit an imported MTU engine with ZF transmission into the vehicle as an "interim measure." Production with an imported engine was supposed to commence in 1991 and from 1995 onwards the indigenous engine was to be used. But the decision was taken to manufacture the German engine under license—the problems with the domestic engine having perhaps proved insurmountable. The tank ended up being overweight and was too heavy to traverse bridges in India's main combat sector—the Punjab. It was also too wide to be carried in standard Indian railway bogies. It is asserted that these problems have been solved and the Indian Army has agreed to purchase the Arjun, but doubts remain about how many of these tanks will be inducted into the army, particularly since it would like to buy Russian T-80s.[96] One must also wonder just how successful Indian scientists have been in rectifying the Arjun's weight problems.

The project that best exemplifies the state of India's indigenous arms production efforts in the 1980s is the LCA. Preparatory work on the LCA began in 1980, when it was conceived as a 200-kilometer-radius fighter optimized for battlefield air superiority in a tropical climate but capable of undertaking secondary ground attack roles. HAL undertook a feasibility study that confirmed the country's capability to build the plane, but it was stated that certain technologies such as the radar, the fly-by-wire technology, and the fiber composite materials would have to be imported. The design team then drew up a proposal for an aircraft that would be powered by an RB-199 engine and with MBB as the design consultant. Project approval was given by the government in 1985.

But soon after, the Indian government terminated the agreement with MBB and signed Dassault to be the design consultant. It also decided to buy the GE F-404 as the power plant instead of the RB-199. The air force also did its bit by asking, for example, for a beyond-visual-range capability, which pushed the weight of the aircraft up from 8–10 tons to 12.5 tons.[97] Finally, the U.S. aerospace industry was supposed to play a major role in the development of the aircraft. In 1987 the U.S. government published a Blue Book on releasable technologies to enable U.S. industry to interact with the program. An LOA (letter of understanding and acceptance) "was also signed for utilization of U.S. government facilities and expertise and to provide for interactions in specific fields between concerned aeronautics laboratories of the two countries."[98] Under the agreement four U.S. firms were allowed to participate in the LCA program—Bendix, Northrop, Lear, and Moog.

Despite such a multinational effort the LCA is unlikely to succeed. A low production run of 400 aircraft may make the plane uneconomical, especially since India will probably be license-producing the MiG-29. It also is expected to enter squadron service in 2005 (the original date having being 1994). The question of technological obsolescence must then come into play given that most technologies on the airplane are of the late 1970s to early 1980s vintage.

These three projects exemplify the sort of problems Indian arms production has to face: changing requirements in mid-program; the constant threat of external purchase; and the long delays in research, development and production. In such circumstances utilizing scarce domestic resources to build systems that may not work well or face technological obsolescence is financially extravagant. That such programs have been sanctioned and continue despite delays testifies to the ability of the arms industry to influence decision makers. In contrast, the relative success of the IGMDP shows what could be achieved if the structural pressures which constrained domestic production efforts were removed or lessened.

The IGMDP was established in 1983 to develop an entire range of missiles—surface-to-surface, surface-to-air, air-to-air, and antiship missiles. The program led to the development of the Prithvi and Agni missiles. Unlike other indigenous programs, the IGMDP has been successful for a number of reasons. First, India could not obtain the technology for these systems from any other country, leaving the Indian military with no other option but to back fully the efforts of Indian scientists. Such support was vital in carrying the project through the ups and downs associated with the development of any weapons system.

One senior scientist, Dr. M. Krishnamurthy, has written about how different the attitude of the armed forces was to regular defense projects and the IGMDP.

In the case of the MBT, the indigenous development of the engine on which the fate of the MBT seemed to have hinged at one time has taken a back seat. This is because the Germans have now offered an engine which they were unwilling to give earlier. The engine development team is no longer getting the same attention or support as it used to get in the early eighties when no foreign source was forthcoming. In the case of the Light Combat Aircraft also, wherever possible foreign collaboration is being sought. The indigenous programs do not get the all out support the IGMDP receives. The present writer was involved in trying to get sanctions for some very important projects in the early eighties for DRDO, but in many cases a foreign source was preferred to indigenous development. In each case the services questioned the competence of Indian scientists to achieve their targets within the time frames specified. This at a time when the same people were willing to entrust the same Indian scientists with such an ambitious and technologically advanced effort as the IGMDP.[99]

Second, the missile program was an integrated one, using as far as possible common subsystems and technologies. By integrating development and tackling issues simultaneously, time was saved and duplication avoided. Third, the missile program was a technologically manageable one. Ballistic missiles, being an older technology, were easier to develop than supersonic combat aircraft—a project at which India had already failed once.

THE IMPACT ON THE ARMY

The import of arms facilitated the Indian Army's movement toward a new Indian military doctrine. Until the 1980s Indian military doctrine had emphasized using the infantry and fighting from positional defenses. In the 1980s doctrine was rewritten, largely through the efforts of General Sundarji, to use India's growing mechanized strength to carry out deep thrusts into enemy territory. Having broken through enemy lines, Indian forces were expected to seize significant amounts of territory and fight the enemy on grounds of their choice. As one Indian writer put it, "The primary operational objectives should be deep enough and important enough for their capture or destruction to exert a strategic effect. These could be the enemy's nerve centers such as Corps Headquarters, operational reserves, military airfields and, to a lesser degree, towns of politico-economic importance."[100] This doctrine was to be followed in conflicts with China and Pakistan, although in the Chinese case the breakthrough was to carried with helicopters.

The evolution of a new doctrine came gradually. When General Sundarji was the head of India's Western Command he had drawn up the operational plans for Exercise Dig Vijay, the Indian Army's triennial military exercise, which was held in 1983. In this exercise the first attempts were made to carry out a new doctrine of using armor to thrust deep into enemy territory. But the real shift in doctrine, and its impact on proposed force structure, was seen after General Sundarji became Chief of Staff and in 1986 oversaw the army headquarters' plan Exercise Brasstacks.

From a doctrinal standpoint the goal of Exercise Brasstacks, the largest military exercise in Indian history, was to try and give the army experience in using multicorps formations.[101] It also saw the use, for the first time, of Reorganized Army Plains Infantry Division (RAPIDS). These were essentially infantry divisions with one mechanized brigade which would give the division greater mobility and allow it to be quickly used for either defensive of offensive purposes. Sundarji also planned on setting up Reorganized Army Mountains Infantry Divisions (RAMIDS) and an Air Assault Division. The RAMIDS were mountain divisions equipped with more modern artillery and were to have greater mobility and firepower due to the use of four types of helicopters—light, utility, heavy, and attack. The mountain divisions were to also receive more recoilless guns and precision guided missiles.[102]

The Air Assault Division was Sundarji's most ambitious venture. In Brasstacks he labeled the 54th Infantry division from Hyderabad an air assault division, but that force did not have the necessary aerial capability to be called one. The eventual goal, however, was to establish a division that would be fully air mobile by moving it to the scene of battle with helicopters. If the Air Assault Division had been put in place it would have allowed Indian forces to be transported scores of miles in a single day, thereby allowing them to strike deep in the heart of enemy territory.

Table 2.1
India's External Debt, 1980–90 (U.S. $ millions)

	1980	1983	1984	1985	1986
Total Debt	20610	32035	34048	41210	48538
International Reserves	11924	9126	8804	9730	10814
Current Account Balance	-2268	-2640	-2945	-5536	5588

	1987	1988	1989	1990
Total Debt	55856	58524	64374	70115
International Reserves	11449	9246	11610	5637
Current Account Balance	-5987	-8509	-7940	-9281

Source: World Debt Tables 1991-1992: External Debt of Developing Countries (Washington D.C.: The World Bank, 1991).

The development of this new force structure was put down in Sundarji's 1987 perspective plan for the army called Army 2000. According to this plan the army, by the year 2000, was to build up to a force level of forty-five divisions (from its then strength of thirty-four divisions), which included four tank divisions, eight mechanized infantry divisions, seven RAPIDS divisions, and two Air Assault divisions. The development of this force structure would have given the Indian Army the capability to move quickly into any area in the region and to impose its will effectively there. Had Sundarji's plan gone into operation it would have also removed one of the major problems associated with the Indian Army's fighting ability: the limited mobility of infantry divisions due to the lack of motor transport. In the mid-1980s the Army had about 1,360 MICVs but this was considered a small complement for taking a force of thirty-four divisions into battle.[103]

Even without such an expansion, the Indian army was a formidable force by the mid-1980s, and it was used to try and enforce India's foreign policy goals. Thus in the winter of 1986, in Exercise Brasstacks, the army was amassed along the border in an attempt at coercive diplomacy against Pakistan. The idea was to show Pakistan the possible consequences of continuing to support Sikh terrorists in Punjab. Later in the year Sundarji was to amass the army along the border with China because of suspected Chinese encroachments on Indian territory. Next, in July 1987, the Indian Army was dispatched to Sri Lanka to serve as a peacekeeping force. Finally, in 1988 Indian paratroopers were flown over 2,000 kilometers to crush the coup in the Maldives.

Sundarji's proposed expansion, however, could not be completed because of a worsening economic situation. By the late 1980s India's external debt, fueled by unrestricted imports in the early 1980s, had soared to a record of $48 billion. By 1991 the figure had risen to around $70 billion (Table 2.1). Hard currency holdings also fell to their lowest level in a decade. Faced with this adverse economic situation the government curtailed spending and one of the major casualties was the expansion of the armed forces. The army shelved plans for the RAPIDS and RAMIDS and dropped the idea of creating two Air Assault divisions because it would have involved raising a costly helicopter force.[104] The raising of four armored, and eight mechanized infantry divisions was also slowed by the financial crisis.

THE IMPACT ON THE NAVY

The Indian Navy, while seeking a blue water role, was forced by circumstance, since independence, to assume a more modest mission. Lacking sufficient funding, faced with an indifferent political leadership, and consisting of a fleet of antiquated vessels, the navy was forced to play a limited role in the defense of the nation. The navy's role was to protect India's maritime assets—its commercial and fishing vessels—guard harbor installations, and arrest smugglers and poachers.[105] The navy was also to deter a Pakistani attack by the sheer existence of a large, though admittedly antiquated, force. This existential deterrence, as Tellis calls it, was to end with the 1965 war when the Pakistani Navy attacked the naval base at Dwarka.

The Indian Navy in the 1971 war, therefore, planned a campaign of Sea Denial by wrecking havoc in Karachi Harbor in the west and bottling up Pakistani surface shipping in the east.[106] But the event of the 1971 war that had the most long-term effect on Indian naval planning was the U.S. decision to send the USS *Enterprise* into the Bay of Bengal. This provided Indian security planners with graphic evidence of the effect of coercive superpower naval diplomacy and set the rationale for further naval expansion. A few vessels were added to the Indian fleet, therefore, because of the impact of the 1971 war. But it was regional events in the mid and late 1970s that gave the navy the threat rationale it required to make a case for modernization. The growing superpower presence in the Indian Ocean, the militarization efforts of the Shah of Iran, and the Soviet occupation of Afghanistan were all seen as leading to a deteriorating regional environment. Hence the modernization of the Indian Navy in the 1980s, with purchases from both the West and the former Soviet Union.

Given such a perceived growth in external threats, the role of the Indian Navy became one of fulfilling two contradictory roles. One was to "maintain command of the sea in the event of a conflict with smaller regional adversaries [sea control], while concurrently deploying a modest but effective deterrent against extra-regional powers operating within the environs of the Indian subcontinental barrack [sea denial]."[107] In operational terms this meant that the Indian Navy was applying a British conception of defense—concentric circles— to the maritime environment. The British in their defense of India built two concentric circles of defense. The inner circle consisted of the north-eastern and north-western borderlands and the small Himalayan states. The outer ring consisted of the Persian Gulf states, Afghanistan, Tibet, and Thailand. Total control was to be maintained over the inner ring while the outer one was to be neutralized into a buffer zone through the use of both diplomacy and occasional force.

The new naval strategy of the 1980s consisted of developing an inner ring of Sea Control in the peninsular region that extended from Pakistan in the west to as far as Burma and Indonesia in the east. This entailed the complete denial of access routes available to its regional competitors and the maintenance of absolute control over their contiguous sea zones, through which overwhelming naval power could be brought to bear on them either in a coercive or a supportive mode.

The outer ring had at times been described as stretching to the channel between South Africa and Madagascar on the southern end, to the Red Sea Suez Canal area on the western side, and to the Straits of Malacca on the eastern border. In this outer ring India was to pursue a policy of "Sea Denial": in which, despite lacking the capability to destroy extraregional fleets, it could inflict a level of damage disproportionate to the political gains sought by an alien power. It would utilize these perceptions to deter extraregional application of naval power in the first place. While it was never clear which extraregional powers had been targeted, some senior spokesmen had identified South Africa, Iran, Malaysia, Australia, and China, besides the two superpowers, as potential threats.[108]

The Indian Navy was and remains fully capable of securing its objectives within the peninsular region because it enjoys maritime superiority in that area. None of the peninsular states could take on the Indian Navy in a localized conflict since it is the most balanced naval force in the Indian Ocean littoral. With a large submarine fleet, an integral air arm, long-range maritime reconnaissance, and a surface fleet of which over 50 percent is armed with missiles, the navy is unmatched in the region. Despite financial fluctuations, the naval buildup is likely to continue. The naval dockyards are building a new generation of destroyers for the navy, and an indigenously produced aircraft carrier is to be designed with French assistance. Indian defense factories now manufacture a range of naval weaponry and the navy is to get an antiship missile—the Trishul—from the IGMDP.

Concern about Indian activities in the outer circle. however, have forced the Indian government to reassure the nations in the Indian Ocean littoral about its intentions. The impressive naval expansion of the 1980s made the southeast Asian countries and Australia concerned about India's intentions in the Indian Ocean region. This led to the Indian government calling for joint naval exercises with these countries in an effort to alleviate their concerns.

THE IMPACT ON THE AIR FORCE

The induction of aircraft like the Jaguar, the MiG 29, and the Mirage 2000 have made the Indian Air Force one of the most modern air arms in the world today. With this change in capabilities has also come a return to earlier ideas of conducting air warfare.

The former chief of air staff, Air Chief Marshall S. K. Mehra spelled out in an interview what the air force's role would be in a future conflict. In case the enemy struck first, the air force would absorb the attack while trying to cause maximum damage to the enemy's offensive air capability. The air force would then retaliate "against the aggressor's airfields, road/railway network, military, industrial, and command and control centers." Secondly, should the initiative rest with us the air power effort in the first instance would attempt to put the enemy air force out of action to the extent possible.[109]   The emphasis, therefore, seems to be returning to the strategic bombing and interdiction missions of the 1965 war.

As for close air support to the army, the Air Chief Marshall commented that the army and the air force were engaged in ongoing negotiations on how to reduce the reaction time for such operations. The air chief pointed out that the organizations and procedures that existed today had been around since World War II and were tried and tested so no major organizational changes were required. The problems at the operational level lay in how far bases were from the Forward Edge of the Battle Area. Further, given the type of battle visualized—swift flowing mechanized operations and tank to tank battles—target recognition would be a major problem (both Pakistan and India operate versions of the original T-54 tank).[110]

In the 1980s the air force also began discussing the need for a Strategic Air/Aerospace Command. With the Jaguars and the Mirages being nuclear capable and with the development of Prithvi and Agni, there was a demand for a Strategic Air Command to better employ these resources. Air Marshall Mehra seemed to expand the function of such a command when he stated that it would include both strategic transport and reconnaissance missions.[111] He also stressed that such a Command would copy the United States and the former Soviet Union in that it would not bring all strategic systems under one head. It should be stressed that such a command would require the prerequisite of India going nuclear and the implications of such a move are discussed in the next section.

As for the air force itself, its own role has not changed as dramatically as that of the Navy. Its primary mission is intraregional, countering the Pakistani and Chinese Air Forces, and it does not envisage playing an extraregional role. The fact is that it does not have the necessary systems to do this: tankers for refueling and—at least operationally—airborne warning and control systems to serve as force multipliers. Without these the air force would neither be able to reach far flung targets nor defend itself in the hostile environment that would prevail there.

Further, the adverse economic situation is likely to have a major impact on future force modernizations in that service. The air force has been trying to obtain a new subsonic trainer since 1986 but the financial crisis of the early 1990s has kept the deal from being concluded (and in the mid-1990s the decision has yet to be taken).

A more serious problem will arise when the need to replace India's 400-odd MiG-21s occurs. The Indian solution to this problem has been stop-gap one. It recently awarded Russia's Mikoyan bureau a contract for refurbishing some of the later-generation MiG-21s.[112] This would allow the LCA to be fully developed for squadron service, or even a later purchase of Western aircraft. The escalating costs of Western produced fighter aircraft, however, make anything more than a token purchase unlikely.

Nor is the LCA a sure bet. The LCA project has been marred by delays, escalating developmental costs, the existence of a small domestic market, and the fact that the aircraft may be technologically obsolete by the time it enters squadron service.[113] The project was started in the mid-1980s, but the full production of the aircraft is expected to begin only in 2005. So far the Indian government has spent approximately $468 million on the aircraft's development, and current estimates are that an additional $834 million would be required to successfully complete the project. Faced with such mounting costs the Indian government is seeking international collaboration to both lower the developmental cost and to enter the arms market.[114]

THE NUCLEAR FACTOR

In the 1980s India continued to pursue its policy of ambivalence in the nuclear sphere. The policy of ambivalence, which was borrowed from the Israelis in the 1970s and aimed at deflecting Western pressure, required that India build up all of the requirements for producing and delivering a nuclear weapon without openly going nuclear.[115] Following this policy the nation developed and tested delivery systems—the Prithvi and Agni ballistic missiles. It also acquired nuclear-capable field howitzers and aircraft—the Bofors 155mm Howitzer and the Jaguar and Mirage 2000. Research was also carried out to develop a nuclear propelled attack submarine that would fire cruise missiles.

While India was seeking to develop such systems, Pakistan also sought to build its own bomb in the basement. By the late 1980s Pakistan had acquired a nuclear capability but India still held an asymmetric advantage over it.

Pakistan's missile program produced a missile with a range of only 250 kilometers. Further, India was estimated to have greater holdings of fissile material than Pakistan and had acquired the capacity to produce more if necessary.

Indian concerns about Pakistan's nuclear program began to emerge in the late 1970s when evidence began to gather that Islamabad was seeking to deter India's nuclear superiority. The Indian reaction to the Pakistani weapons program see-sawed from an aggressive reaction to attempts to stabilize the situation in South Asia. In 1984 Mrs. Gandhi, concerned with the impending Pakistani threat, sought to carry out an Osirak-type action—where Israeli F-16s in 1981 had destroyed the Iraqi reactor. Indian Jaguars were to be used to take out the uranium enrichment plant at Kahuta.[116] But the Indian government backed away from such an attack. There are two possible reasons for Mrs. Gandhi's decision to back off. One could be the Pakistani government's message to India that if attacked they would respond with air strikes on all of India's nuclear facilities. The other could be that Mrs. Gandhi was not confident that international public opinion would be favorable to such an attack.[117]

Once India backed away from the preemptive strike the policy of dealing with Pakistan was based on several strategies. First there an was attempt to make Pakistan keep its bomb in the basement. In the mid-1980s Indian writings began to change as they started suggesting that while both India and Pakistan were developing nuclear weapons it would be in their mutual interest to keep them in the basement, thereby preventing an open, destabilizing, and costly arms race.[118] Second, Indian government and nuclear officials made statements indicating that India was ahead of Pakistan in the nuclear field. These included the 1985 start-up of the Dhruva research reactor at Trombay, which gave India the ability to produce plutonium from domestic technology and fuel—the fuel coming from the unsafeguarded MAPP plants. Later, in 1986, when American press reports claimed that Pakistan had weapons-grade uranium, Raja Ramanna responded that India could enrich uranium to any level (though subsequent reports suggested that India had only reached the more modest 2% level). Later there were also reports that India was conducting research into developing thermonuclear weapons.[119]

Third, there were attempts to set up confidence-building measures between the two countries. Rajiv Gandhi and Zia ul-Haq reached an agreement to not attack one other's nuclear facilities (a deal that was subsequently signed by Benazir Bhutto and Rajiv Gandhi). Yet while reaching such an agreement India was unwilling to sign on to any regional disarmament measures, preferring instead to have broader universal disarmament treaties. Thus Pakistan's call for a nuclear weapons free zone in South Asia was rejected by India because it did not include China. Similarly, India was to reject the 1987 call of the Junejo government for a nuclear test ban in South Asia. Fourth, by the late 1980s leading Indian strategists like K. Subrahmanyam started suggesting that both countries openly go nuclear since this would bring about a state of mutual deterrence between them.

While India pursued such a multilayered policy toward Pakistan some writing began to emerge on the what type of possible force structure and doctrine an Indian nuclear force should have. General Sundarji in his M. Phil. thesis discussed the nuclear challenges India now faced.[120] His contention was that the possession of nuclear weapons by both India and Pakistan has stabilized the situation between the two countries by making it impossible for either nation to achieve a conventional victory. Sundarji argues that even though an asymmetry exists in the India-Pakistan nuclear relationship it is not large enough to allow India the freedom to launch a major conventional onslaught against Pakistan. In fact, if Pakistan were to drop even a few bombs on India the effects would be calamitous since it would cause "considerable damage which no government can ignore."[121]

Sundarji continues:

If India had a conventional edge, Pakistan would be fully deterred from taking a conventional initiative, while India in theory could have an option of exploiting it in low intensity actions which are unlikely to trigger a nuclear riposte by Pakistan. However, in practice this is most unlikely because of the danger of upsetting the nuclear quasi-stability which would cause considerable damage to both sides. The same would apply with even greater force if Pakistan had a conventional edge. Therefore, one may conclude that even in this scenario, even if one of the two powers had a conventional edge, it would be unlikely to exploit it in practice.[122]

China, Sundarji feels, poses a different problem. There the asymmetry between Indian and Chinese nuclear forces is so great that Beijing would not be deterred from launching a conventional attack against India. Sundarji, therefore, recommends that India build up a secure second strike capability against China. He writes, " In this scenario it is assumed that India has sufficient operational SSBNs and a mix of land based ICBMs and IRBMs to give her an assured destruction capability against China in the second strike mode. It should be emphasized that for a strategic nuclear balance, India does not need to have matching numbers of various categories with China. . . . What is necessary, however, is the ability to inflict assured destruction against China in a second strike mode, thus having an essential equivalence leading to essential nuclear balance. In such a situation nuclear stability with China would prevail."[123] A more recent study put the number of nuclear weapons required to have a deterrent against both Pakistan and China at 132. The study suggested a countervalue strategy against China which involved destroying five or six major cities and two ports—with submarine launched ballistic missiles doing the damage. Against Pakistan it advocated both a countervalue and counterforce strategy with IRBMS and attack aircraft.[124]

Sundarji's call for a second-strike capability against China has been echoed by others but the cost of attaining such a capability, the prevailing state of India-China relations, and the international environment do not warrant such a move. Estimates on building up a nuclear force for India are hard to come by, but one study written in the early 1980s claimed that it would cost up to $70 billion over a period of 15 years for India to build even a modest triad—a figure that was well beyond the country's reach.[125] Further, Sino-Indian relations have improved dramatically since 1989 when Rajiv Gandhi made the first trip by an Indian prime minister in thirty years to Beijing. In 1993 the two countries reached an agreement to reduce their troop levels along the border and to freeze the border issue. As things stand, therefore, India's principal nuclear opponent remains Pakistan.

While the nuclear threat in South Asia grew larger in the 1980s it did not lead to the weaponization of the Indian program. Instead the political leadership continued the policy of retaining the option as well as seeking broader disarmament goals. Retaining the nuclear option was a policy measure that had broad support in India, and in fact the right-wing Bharatiya Janata Party wanted to go further and have a public nuclear force. But the ruling Congress party, and from 1989-1991 the Janata Dal coalitions, did not pursue this path because of the international repercussions of such a move. Rajiv Gandhi had begun a policy of economic liberalization and technological advancement of India that required large-scale foreign investment. These goals would have been endangered if India had a public nuclear force and was subjected to international sanctions. Western reaction to the Agni and Prithvi tests was an indication of these trends.

Following the test of the Agni IRBM India faced problems in acquiring further technology in the missile field. The United States refused to provide India with a device to test the ability of reentry vehicles to withstand the heat and stress of flight. U.S. pressure was also put on the Russian space agency Glavkosmos to prevent the sale to India of a cryogenic engine required to put large satellites into orbit. The need for cryogenic-engine technology came from the continued problems with the Indian launchers.[126] Recognizing such pressures and the potential threat Agni posed in the region, the Indian government almost immediately sought to play down the strategic significance of the missile, calling it a technology demonstrator.[127] Thus sensitivity to international concerns continued to dominate Indian thinking on the creation of a public nuclear force.

The pursuit of global disarmament also continued as the Indian government, in 1986, along with six other nations, tabled an initiative on disarmament. But the more comprehensive plan on disarmament was offered by Rajiv Gandhi to the third United Nations Special Session on Disarmament. The Rajiv Gandhi plan called for a phased cutback in nuclear weapons and their total abolition by 2010. It also called for a moratorium on the testing and deployment of SDI, for a treaty to eliminate chemical weapons, and a CTBT.[128] In a post-Cold War international system most of these objectives have been achieved. START II goes a step further than the Rajiv Gandhi plan in cutting strategic forces. A chemical weapons convention has been signed, as has the CTBT. Such shifts took place due to systemic transformation, and what these changes have created is a new environment in which the utility of Indian nuclear weapons has to be discussed.

THE PRESENT, THE FUTURE

In the 1990s India initially faced both a financial crisis and a supply side problem with the breakup of the former Soviet Union. The high debt incurred through import liberalization in the 1980s led to a reduction in defense spending. The devaluation of the rupee also reduced the buying power of the armed services. Subsequent growth in the economy however allowed the 1994–95 defense budget to be raised to Rs 230 billion ($7.4 billion) the first real increase in defense spending in the 1990s. Moreover, "Given India's burgeoning foreign exchange reserves, it is believed special provisions may even be made to buy much need systems to replace obsolete equipment crippled by spares shortages."[129] This may be a short-term situation because, as past indicators have shown, hard currency reserves tend to fluctuate.

More worrisome for Indian defense planners is the demise of the Soviet Union. Approximately 70 percent of India's defense equipment is of Soviet origin and replacing it—in fact even maintaining it—is a difficult and costly process. The soft currency purchase of weapons is a thing of the past as Russia and other successor states now demand hard currency for the sale of weaponry. A more critical problem was the shortage of spares as the breakup of the Soviet Union left India dealing with the various republics and the individual weapons factories within them. Attempts to manufacture spare parts indigenously were slow and the readiness of the armed forces was affected.

In 1995 India was able to revive this military link when it signed a $1 billion deal for MiG-29 combat aircraft, Tunguska surface-to-air missiles, and spare parts for Russian systems in the Indian arsenal.[130] In 1996 the Indian government successfully negotiated $1.66 billion deal to purchase forty Su-30 combat aircraft from Russia. It also entered into an agreement to have the Russian arms industry refurbish its fleet of 150 MiG-21 bis combat aircraft.[131]

The availability of external suppliers is crucial because the Indian arms industry is unlikely to meet most of the armed forces' requirements. India's armor and aircraft, two critical components of its conventional arsenal, will have to be imported because its indigenous tank and aircraft programs have run into trouble. The Arjun MBT has yet to enter full service with the army, and its cost and weight make it an unattractive weapons system for the armed forces—the tank is too heavy to cross the bridges in Punjab. India's chief of army staff, General Shankar Roy Chowdhury, stated that: "challenges still remained with regard to enhancement in the performance capabilities of the Arjun MBT, in the fine tuning of systems, and producing the tanks within a desired time-frame.[132]

The LCA project has been marred by delays, escalating developmental costs, a limited domestic market, and the fact that the aircraft may be technologically obsolete by the time it enters squadron service. The project was started in the mid-1980s but full production of the aircraft is expected to begin only in 2005 (the aircraft was supposed to begin flight tests in 1996 but is now expected to fly by the end of 1997).[133] Until 1993 the Indian government had spent approximately $468 million on the aircraft's development and current estimates are that an additional $834 million would be required to successfully complete the project. Faced with such costs the Indian government is seeking international collaboration to lower the developmental cost as well as to make the plane more attractive in the global arms market.[134] More recently the Indian government has entered into negotiations to license-produce 200 Sukhoi-30 fighters in India, and this creates further pressure to terminate the LCA project.[135]

The arms industry will also remain technologically dependent on the West and the former Soviet Union in the years to come. The systems that are coming through heavily depend on imported components, and according to Anand Parthasarthy of the IGMDP the supply of such components was progressively constricted through the 1980s due to Western controls on the export of technology.[136] While this will not effect the current generation of weapons since India insists on license-producing these technologies, it will prevent the arms industry from building a next-generation of tanks, aircraft, and missiles.   India could continue to build older systems since these would still be assets in a South Asian battleground, but it would seriously affect any attempts at extra-regional power projection where the armed forces could   face technologically superior opponents.

The industry is also unlikely to achieve success in the export market, thereby removing one of the means to subsidize military expenditure. My impression after talking to officials in various defense production units was that no clear thinking had gone into developing an export capability for major weapons systems: markets had not been identified; marketing strategies had not been developed; and strict restrictions exist on what can be exported.[137] Dr. Arunchalam pointed out that India had turned down $150 million worth of military-related business with Iraq in the 1980s and also rejected Libya's attempts to invest in Indian weapons programs.[138]

The doctrine of the armed forces may also be affected by internal events. In the 1980s internal security missions increasingly tied down Indian armed forces—particularly the army. The military's internal security role consists of two functions: fighting counterinsurgency campaigns and maintaining law and order. The army has been increasingly dragged into the latter role due to the failure of the police and the paramilitary to check communal violence in Indian cities. Both the police and elements of the paramilitary are heavily politicized and are not trusted by the Muslim minority. In such situations the army alone can maintain law and order because it is still seen as an honest broker by all Indian religious groups. The army, however, would prefer not to carry out this role for a number of reasons: it distracts it from its main mission; reduces its war fighting ability; and it breaks down discipline in the ranks and encourages corruption. It is also seen as a suicidal career move by Army officers to have crowd control on their resume.

A more serious challenge emerges from the growing number of insurgency movements in the nation. As the fruits of development are unevenly spread in the country discontented groups are beginning separatist movements and resorting to violence to settle their grievances. The extent to which such operations tie down the army can be seen from its experience in Punjab. During Exercise Bluestar, the 1984 operation to clear the Sikh Golden Temple in Amritsar of terrorists, seven divisions had to be deployed to tie down the states of Haryana and Punjab. In 1990, during the war scare with Pakistan, four divisions were used to maintain internal security in Punjab. In a future war with Pakistan the existence of such insurgencies would prove to be a serious handicap for the Indian Army.

THE NUCLEAR OPTION

The end of the Cold War created a complex strategic environment for India's nuclear program. Indian analysts argue that within the South Asian region India faces a threat from a politically unstable Pakistan—still seeking revenge for the dismemberment of the country in 1971—and to a lesser extent from China. Extraregionally, the Saudi possession of the CSS-2 IRBM and the existence of nuclear armed Muslim majority states in central Asia are seen as being threats to the country.[139] The response to these threats has been to continue developing the means for exercising the nuclear option. The Indian space program has improved India's communications facilities and, it is hoped, will also provide it with improved satellite imagery to monitor troop movements and facilities in Pakistan. The improved satellite capability is also expected to help in the targeting of cruise and ballistic missiles.[140] Work also continues on the indigenous nuclear submarine project. India reportedly received the plans for a Soviet vessel on which it will base its own designs for a nuclear submarine. India has also tested a nuclear reactor to power the vessel.[141]

While India continues to acquire the means to deliver nuclear weapons it has also refrained from carrying out any further tests and continues to press for global disarmament in international fora. It also continues to oppose treaties that are seen to impose unequal obligations on the signatories. The reason for continuing this policy of pursuing restraint yet retaining the option lies in the complex set of economic and political pressures India faces as a result of the end of the Cold War and transformation of the international system.

First, the death of the Soviet Union took away India's superpower ally and forced it to seek a stronger relationship with the United States. The need for such a relationship also arose from India's ambitious plans for economic liberalization which required American investment both in terms of technology and capital. But creating such a relationship has meant addressing the thorny issue of India's nuclear option. Second, as Shekhar Gupta points out, the end of the Cold War has actually heightened the nuclear stakes in South Asia: "India fears being a peripheral power in a unipolar world. Pakistan fears being left without superpower protection in a future conflict with India."[142] How to deal with a nuclear Pakistan in the context of a changed international system remains a central concern for Indian policy-makers. Third, there is a serious move towards disarmament and arms control in the international system that India cannot ignore. Fourth, the changing conditions in the international system also have to be taken into account, specifically the utility of nuclear weapons in a changed international environment. All of these issues impact the shape the Indian nuclear option can take.

India's relationship with the United States on the nuclear issue is complicated by the pursuit of contradictory objectives by the two nations. The United States in its pursuit of global nonproliferation policies has sought to control India's nuclear option through both international regimes and regional measures, hence the pressure on India to join the NPT and to adhere to the MTCR. India's continues to oppose both international regimes because of their discriminatory structures. It condemned indefinite extension of the NPT in May 1995 saying it was an unfair treaty that legitimized the arsenals of nuclear weapons states. Instead the Indian government, which did not attend the UN conference on the NPT, said that its own 1988 plan, that called for the elimination of all nuclear weapons, was the type of measure that had to be followed to achieve genuine nonproliferation.

It has refused in the past to sign the MTCR because it did not prevent vertical missile proliferation, provided no mutuality of obligations between missile and nonmissile states, would have kept critical space and missile technologies in the hands of a few states, and discriminated against Third World civilian space programs.[143] The United States countered by asking India to join the MTCR as an observer state in return for greater cooperation in space technology. But the Indian government held out for full membership, presumably to be in a position to shape the future direction the treaty takes.

At the regional level U.S. policy moved to one of getting India and Pakistan to cap their nuclear and missile capabilities. The State Department stated in a 1993 report to Congress that its goal in South Asia was ". . . first to cap, then over time reduce, and finally eliminate the possession of weapons of mass destruction and their means of delivery."[144] The Clinton administration also proposed a regional summit on nuclear issues in which the five nuclear powers and India, Pakistan, Japan, and Germany would participate. India's objection to the summit lay in the fact that "Chinese participation in the summit was premised on the exclusion of its nuclear arsenal from consideration."[145] For despite the thawing of relations with China, India still takes, at least publicly, the Chinese nuclear force into consideration when discussing regional disarmament measures. India's response, in fact, was to broaden the notion of region and include Russia and the Asiatic republics of the former Soviet Union in the summit.

The problem lay, and as some Indians believe continues to lie, in how the United States perceives India. Raja Ramanna, the father of the Indian bomb, has written that the United States views India as a "revisionist power bent on restructuring the international system at the expense of America's global interests."[146] This view goes against the image of responsible behavior that India has tried to promote in the international system: one of refraining from a public nuclear force and pushing for global disarmament. Further, it does not appreciate the legitimate security concerns for which India has to retain the nuclear option.[147] It is this belief that has led to continued multipartisan support for India's retention of the nuclear option and an actual increase in the funding for the missile program.

This approach, however, has begun to change as India has had some success in convincing the United States of its intentions in the international system. There is some recognition that it would be politically difficult for any government in New Delhi to sign the NPT, for it would be seen as bowing to American pressure. The reason for this being that both the left- and the right-wing opposition parties have put pressure on the government to resist American demands on nonproliferation, terminating the missile program, and on the liberalization of the Indian economy.

In fact, Indian commentators have approvingly pointed to the fact that the United States has adopted a low-key approach to deal with the issue without dropping its concerns about proliferation. Thus, during the 1994 visit of Prime Minister Narasimha Rao to Washington, President Clinton did not raise the proliferation issue with the Indian prime minister—it was raised instead in Congress by Representative Lee Hamilton. Another indicator Indian observers point to is that the State Department classified the fourth report on progress in nuclear proliferation in South Asia because it felt it would be counterproductive to make it public.[148] More recently in 1996, when India refused to sign the CTBT it did not lead to a breakdown in relations between the two countries. The Clinton administration accepted that there was a divergence of views on the nuclear issue and, instead, engaged in talks on regional security issues and the Kashmir problem with the Deve Gowda government.[149]

Being a responsible power in the new international system, however, requires taking more positive steps in the direction of global disarmament. But there is an inherent contradiction between such steps and current Indian security perceptions, as well as the continued Indian desire to acquire greater status in the international system. In a nutshell, India's resistance to most multilateral disarmament measures stem from the shortcomings of being a late-nuclearizing state. As a late-nuclearizing state India has had to face international sanctions on its nuclear program and consequently has been unable to secure the advantages to which the pre-NPT nuclear states could avail themselves. It has been unable to openly conduct successive nuclear tests to refine its weapons option, particularly toward a thermonuclear bomb. It has been denied access to technologies which would have enhanced its delivery capability. Its stockpile of fissile material is minuscule compared to that of the pre-NPT nuclear powers. And the current concern about restricting dual-purpose technology hurts India's scientific effort. This is particularly the case in the space program where India has an ambitious agenda to launch a series of satellites for developmental purposes.

The Indian response to multilateral treaties reflects such concerns. After supporting the CTBT for decades there was concern in both political and scientific circles about the implications signing the treaty had for international security and India's nuclear program. The arguments against the CTBT were that it permits hydronuclear testing, which is needed to build "mininukes"—low-yield nuclear weapons that can be used for nuclear war-fighting in the Third World.[150] Additionally, the fact that only Western laboratories can carry out these tests at this juncture is viewed as perpetuating the technological hierarchy in the international system.

As for the Indian nuclear program, there was unhappiness in Indian scientific circles because the CTBT would prevent India from conducting "scientific experiments." But, as Giri Deshingkar points out, the type of experiments and how they would be impeded was not explained.[151] It was suggested that Indian reluctance stemmed from the fact that under the provisions of the CTBT India would not be able to develop a thermonuclear bomb and join the same league as China because a fusion weapon would require multiple tests. The implication of this constraint would be that "those who look for shortcuts to great power status through purely military means are loath to see India's capability confined to the fission level. Hence the bizarre equation of the CTBT, for which India has campaigned since 1953, with evil itself."[152]

India subsequently refused to sign the treaty because citing both security concerns and the inadequacies of the treaty itself. Indian government officials argued that the treaty had no effect on the South Asian security environment and it did not bring about global nuclear disarmament. Indian officials also stated that they could not accept a CTBT with loopholes. The treaty allowed for, "non-explosive techniques like laboratory simulation, hydro-nuclear explosions which yielded invaluable data and simulation using laser techniques."[153]

The problem with such an approach is that it essentially puts India in the passenger seat rather than as a nation shaping the debate on the emerging international system. Also, while complaining about the technological advantages conferred to the West from the CTBT and the NPT, India would find it economically and, given the lackluster performance of the AEC, technologically difficult to carry out the sort of programs that would make not acceding to such regimes worthwhile.

The reshaping of the international system has created obvious territorial changes such as the emergence of the Central Asian states—potentially Islamic—which complicate Indian security planning. The continued belief in the Islamic bomb testifies to this. But a more important problem for India is one of coming to terms with the changing basis of power in the international system. In the international system of the 1960s nuclear weapons were the basis for international power. But in the system of the 1990s nuclear weapons play a more complex role. Their acquisition does not automatically confer major-power status. No nation viewed North Korea's atomic program as the basis of power just as India's own PNE did little to raise its international standing. In certain conditions, which are discussed below, they do provide security from external intervention. But they do not serve as a deterrent to internal dissension nor do they prevent external support to such dissent. Further, without a substantial economic base, the mere possession of nuclear weapons does not enhance a nation's prestige and status. Indeed, it may very well lead to its demise. The former Soviet Union had a First World military but a Fourth World economy, a fact Indian planners are acutely aware of. Hence the effort, especially since 1991, to spur economic liberalization and growth in the country. Being a responsible state is part of achieving that goal. One could in fact argue that the lesson of the Cold War is that a clear victory over Pakistan at the regional level and greater status within the international system are more likely to materialize if the Indian developmental model, now one of a liberalizing economy, is successful. Just as victory in the Cold War was due to the fact that the United States's economic model proved more attractive to other nations around the world.

Assuming the role of a responsible power is also of vital interest in the South Asian context. The economic and political costs of having a public nuclear force, as discussed earlier, are too high for a nation like India which has a major developmental agenda—especially given the move toward liberalizing the economy. This developmental imperative adds to the Indian desire for restraint on the nuclear option. Indian policy in South Asia has therefore sought to keep the nuclear option, maintain a nuclear and delivery edge over Pakistan, without facing the international censure that comes from a public nuclear force, and haltingly move towards confidence-building measures with Islamabad. In the 1990s this task has become easier, as the public excuse of a Chinese threat has diminished with the relaxing of tensions along the Sino-Indian border. Thus India continues its missile program and the civilian space program to give it the edge over Pakistan in delivery vehicles as well as a better reconnaissance C^3 I capability. Given the depth of the Indian scientific base it would be difficult for Pakistan to match it through indigenous efforts.

While retaining the nuclear edge, India is also trying to stabilize the strategic environment with Pakistan through a series of confidence-building measures. Despite the rhetoric of mutual suspicion and the continuing tensions between the two nations over Kashmir, there is progress in this area. Since the late 1980s, the two countries have established "hot lines" between military commanders, have signed a no-attack on nuclear facilities agreement, and have given each other prior notification of military exercises.[154] In February 1994 Indian diplomats submitted six "nonpapers" to their Pakistani counterparts on building a regime of new confidence-building measures. These measures included a commitment by each country to not wage nuclear war on the other; a mutual withdrawal of forces from the Siachen Glacier without either side giving up its territorial claims; better and more secure communications between the military commanders of both sides, and a proposal to resolve the territorial dispute over Sir Creek in the Arabian Sea.[155] These papers, in part, served as the basis for official talks between the two governments in March-April 1997.[156] While these initial discussions were inconclusive, further rounds of negotiations are scheduled to continue and India's new prime minister, Inder Kumar Gujral, has said that he wants relations normalized in his lifetime.[157]

The reason such confidence-building measures may work is that despite Indian claims about Pakistan's warlike intent in its nuclear program, Islamabad has been pursuing a policy that is a mirror image to India's on the nuclear issue. While the father of the Pakistani bomb, A. Q. Khan, had declared that Pakistan had the capacity to make nuclear weapons in 1987, successive Pakistani governments did not go ahead and build a public nuclear force. In fact, the same pressures that affect India's nuclear option—international censure and economic difficulties—would affect a Pakistani decision to go nuclear. Thus Pakistan has followed a policy somewhat similar to India's: retain the option, make ambiguous statements about capability, and refrain from signing multilateral agreements that could hurt the capability to go nuclear should a significant security threat arise. This inspite of the conventional superiority of the Indian armed forces, the periodic calls in Pakistan to avenge Bangladesh, and that maintaining a public nuclear force would possibly enhance Pakistan own quest for prestige in the Islamic nations of the Middle East and Central Asia.

In terms of actual costs—both political and economic—continuing such a policy would work in favor of both states. Economically, it saves both nations from a costly arms race because both countries would have to build survivable second-strike forces. In the Indian case, an overt nuclear force could also create unease in China as well as the Middle East. One of the problems with declaring other nations a threat is that they begin to take your concerns seriously and start acting on them. An undeclared nuclear force makes it easier for external investors to live with because it both increases stability in the region and lessens fears of nonproliferation sanctions. Politically, the exercise of restraint allows India and Pakistan to keep pushing a disarmament agenda, in the Indian case with greater success, with the major players in the international system. Thus the Cold War model of two rivals engaged in a bitter and escalating arms race need not apply in the South Asian context. Instead, a South Asian version of nuclear deterrence based on the bomb in the basement seems to be operating.

CONCLUSION

The fact that Indian acquisition efforts and doctrinal shifts are largely determined by resource availability and external suppliers rather than by threats and bureaucratic politics puts obvious limits on the development of India's military capability. At the same time, the fact that acquisition demands and doctrinal shifts come from threats and bureaucratic politics—demand factors— leads to the creation of a security dilemma and hurt indigenous procurement efforts. First, because resources and supplier constraints determine weapons procurement, the acquisition programs of the armed forces have an on-again, off-again nature. The Navy's quest for an aircraft carrier and subsequently for one to complement it, is indicative of this trend. Further, it leads to the creation of incomplete force structures—with the armed forces having only bits and pieces of the systems they require for pursuing a particular military doctrine.

Second, the fluctuations in resource availability and supplier reliability work against the development of an indigenous capability. Indigenous weapons programs, in the Indian context, have taken a long time to mature and have been continually threatened by the ability to buy weaponry abroad. Once resources or suppliers become available, domestic programs tend to be sidelined as the armed forces prefer the quality of imported systems. Thus India gets caught in the development of expensive weapons systems that do not satisfy the armed forces needs. The Marut fighter, and probably the LCA and the Arjun tank, are examples of this.

Further, the dynamics of Indian weapons procurement has allowed programs not affected by bureaucratic politics or resource constraints to succeed. Thus, the Indian missile program succeeded because it did not take away resources from the pet projects of the armed services. Moreover, there was no possibility of importing alternative systems to the Agni and Prithvi missiles. Similarly, the Indian shipbuilding program has enjoyed some success because the naval budget could not fully fund the import of vessels for the fleet. The problem here is that these are the very programs that have extraregional implications and therefore are viewed with concern by the other states in the Indian Ocean littoral.

Third, the interaction of these demand and supply factors not only leads to the development of incomplete force structures but also heightens the Indian security dilemma. Other states do not dwell over the on-again, off-again nature of Indian force development. Instead they prepare for the worst by modernizing their own armed forces. This was particularly the case with the Indian naval buildup, which sparked concern in both South-East Asia and Australia. Thus the organizational desire for weapons procurement based on vague threats is dangerous since it can become a self-fulfilling prophecy.

India's attempt to build its military capability reflects the problems that other regional powers face. Its scientific base, while capable of producing weapons systems, is constrained by pressures emanating from the domestic security policymaking process. At the same time, its continuing economic constraints force it to rely on external sources for a successful militarization effort. As long as this state of affairs continues, India's ability to become a major military power will be constrained.

NOTES

1. Ravi Rikhye, The Militarisation of Mother India (New Delhi: Chanakya, 1990), p 38.

2. Ibid.

3. The defense v. development debate in this period is best covered in Raju Thomas, *The Defense of India: A Budgetary Perspective of Strategy and Politics* (New Delhi: MacMillan, 1977).

4. Ibid., 105.

5. For a discussion of the underlying assumptions of Nehru's foreign policy, see, Sisir Gupta, *India and Regional Integration in Asia* (Bombay: Asia, 1964), 1-27.

6. P.M.S. Blackett, *The Scientific Problem of Defense in Relation to the Needs of the Indian Armed Forces, Report to the Honorable Defense Minister of India*, 10 September, 1948.

7. The best discussion of civil-military relations in India is in Stephen P. Cohen, *The Indian Army: Its Contribution to the Development of a Nation* (New Delhi: Oxford University Press, 1990).

8. Blackett, *Scientific Problem of Defense*, 9-15.

9. Sukhwant Singh, *India's Wars since Independence*, 3 (New Delhi: Vikas, 1981), 8.

10. Thomas, *Defense of India*, 104-5.

11. A. Martin Wainwright, *Inheritance of Empire: Britain, India, and the Balance of Power in Asia*, 1938-55 (Westport, Conn.: Praeger, 1994), 87-88.

12. In the first defense budget, the navy received a mere 3.75 percent of the total budget and by 1969-70 it still received only 4.6 percent of the budget. Cited in Thomas, *Defense of India*, 146.

13. Letter to P.M.S. Blackett from the Department of Operational Research, British Admiralty, 2 May 1950.

14. Pratap Chand Lal, *My Years with the IAF* (New Delhi: Lancer, 1986), 73.

15. Thomas, *Defense of India*, 105.

16. Ibid., 177.

17. Pushpindar Chopra, "Spinal Cord of the Indian Air Force," *Air International* (January 1975): 10-11.

18. Thomas W. Graham, "India," in *Arms Production in Developing Countries: An Analysis of Decision Making*, James Everett Katz, ed. (Lexington, Mass.: Lexington Books, 1984), 170.

19. Robert S. Anderson, *Building Scientific Institutions in India: Saha and Bhabha*, Occasional Paper Series, no. 11 (Montreal: McGill University, 1975), 1.

20. Ibid., 33.

21. Dhirendra Sharma, *India's Nuclear Estate* (New Delhi: Lancer, 1983), 14-15.

22. Anderson, *Building Scientific Institutions*, 81.

23. Ibid., 26-29.

24. Ibid., 40.

25. Sharma, India's Nuclear Estate, 33.

26. Ibid., 27-28.

27. Ibid., 31-32.

28. Anderson, *Building Scientific Institutions*, 39.

29. Onkar Marwah, "India's Nuclear and Space Programs: Intent and Policy," *International Security* 2, no. 2 (Fall 1977): 98.

30. Barrie Morrison and Donald Page, "India's Option: The Nuclear Route to Achieve Goal as World Power," *International Perspectives* (July-August 1974): 25.

31. G. S., Bhargava "The Nuclear Power Industry: Need for Reappraisal," *IUMDA Newsletter* 2&3, 1990, 133.

32. Sharma, *India's Nuclear Estate*, 51.

33. Ibid., 51-52.

34. Ibid., 52.

35. Anderson, *Building Scientific Institutions*, 100-102.

36. Ibid., 68.

37. Ashok Kapur, *India's Nuclear Option: Atomic Diplomacy and Decision Making* (New York: Praeger, 1976), 194.

38. Sisir Gupta, *India and Regional Integration in Asia*, 1-27.

39. Raj Krishna, "India and the Bomb," *India Quarterly* 21, no. 2 (April-June 1965): 122.

40. Marwah, "India's Nuclear and Space Programs," 114.

41. Ibid., 114-5.

42. Thomas, *Defense of India*, 159.

43. Ibid., 191.

44. Ibid., 210.

45. Harjinder Singh, *Birth of an Air Force* (New Delhi: Palit and Palit, 1977), 278.

46. Wainwright, *Inheritance of Empire*, 141.

47. Amit Gupta, "The Indian Arms Industry: A Lumbering Giant?," *Asian Survey* 30, no. 9 (September 1990): 850-853.

48. Thomas, *The Defense of India*, 178.

49. Gowri Sundaram and Mike Howarth, "India: Indigenous Programs Flourish Amid Modernization," *International Defense Review* no. 4 (1986): 437.

50. For an excellent overview of the early Indian debate, see Sisir Gupta, "The Indian Dilemma," in *A World of Nuclear Powers*, Alastair Buchan ed. (Englewood Cliffs, N.J.: Prentice Hall, 1966), 55-67.

51. Pratap Chand Lal, *My Years with the IAF*, 164.

52. Ibid.

53. Sukhwant Singh, *India's Wars since Independence*, 2 (New Delhi: Vikas, 1981), 335.

54. Ibid., 3: 31.

55. Pratap Chand Lal, *My Years with the IAF*, 174.

56. Singh, *India's Wars Since Independence*, 2: 343.

57. Krishna, "India and the Bomb," 121.

58. R. K. Nehru, "The Challenge of the Chinese Bomb—I," *India Quarterly* 21, no. 1 (January-March 1965): 8.

59. Minoo Masani, "The Challenge of the Chinese Bomb—II," *India Quarterly* 21, no. 1 (January-March 1965): 21.

60. Krishna, "India and the Bomb," 127.

61. H. M. Patel, "Arrangement with the West," *Seminar* (January 1965): 18-19.

62. Krishna, "India and the Bomb," 125.

63. Ibid., 128.

64. Sisir Gupta, "The Indian Dilemma," 65.

65. Masani, "Challenge of the Chinese Bomb—I," 15-20.

66. Sisir Gupta, "Break With the Past," *Seminar* (January 1965): 31.

67. Sisir Gupta, "The Indian Dilemma," p. 67.

68. Amit Gupta, "India's Military Buildup: To What Purpose?," *Armed Forces Journal International* (October 1989): 58.

69. Ibid.

70. Inder Malhotra, "Hankering after the Harrier," *The Times of India*, (New Delhi) 17 July 1973.

71. See, for example, Ravi Rikhye, "Rethinking Mechanized Infantry Concepts," *USI Journal* (April-June 1972) and "A New Armored Force for India," *USI Journal* (April-June 1973).

72. Interview with Lt. Gen. M. L. Chibber, September 13, 1990, Urbana, Illinois. All three generals were to play a major role in the development of the army in the 1970s and the 1980s. Krishna Rao and Sundarji later became chief of Army Staff and Chibber commanded India's Northern Command and was director of Military Operations.

73. Ibid.

74. Ibid.

75. K. Subrahmanyam, *Indian Security Perspectives* (New Delhi: ABC, 1982), 143.

76. Public Accounts Committee, Seventh Lok Sabha, *Delay in Development and Manufacture of an Aircraft* (New Delhi: Government of India, 1982), 4.

77. P. R. Chari, "India's Nuclear Choices: Some Perspectives," in *Great Power Relations, World Order and the Third World*, M. S. Rajan and Shivaji Ganguly eds. (New Delhi: Vikas, 1981), 360.

78. Ibid., 360-61.

79. Ibid., 361-62.

80 G. S. Bhargava, "India's Nuclear Policy," *India Quarterly* 34, no. 2 (April-June, 1978): 138.

81. Surjit Mansingh, *India's Search for Power—Indira Gandhi's Foreign Policy, 1966-82* (New Delhi, Beverly Hills, London: Sage, 1984), 103.

82. Ibid., 103.

83. Eighty-Second Report Estimates Committee, *Seventh Lok Sabha, (1983-84), Department of Atomic Energy—Generation of Electricity* (New Delhi: Lok Sabha Secretariat, 1984), 3.

84. Ibid., 6.

85. Ibid., 13.

86. Mansingh, *India's Search for Power*, 100.

87. Bhargava, *India's Nuclear Policy*, 139.

88. For a discussion of the reasons behind the buildup, see Gupta, "India's Military Buildup," 58-60.

89. Devin Hagerty, "India's Regional Security Doctrine," *Asian Survey* 31, no. 4 (April 1991): 351-52.

90. Interview with Dr. P. C. Angelo, Staff Officer to the Scientific Advisor Government of India, 10 July, 1991.

91. Interview with Dr. V. Arunachalam, Director, Defense Research and Development Organization, 8 August 1991.

92. Ibid.

93. Interview with Anand Parthasarthy, Senior Scientist IGMDP, Hyderabad, 24 July, 1991.

94. Sundaram and Howarth, "Indigenous Programs Flourish," 442.

95. Srinivas Prasad, "Designed Delays: Advanced Light Helicopter," *India Today*, 31 January, 1986, 138-43.

96. Sandy Gordon, *India's Rise to Power in the Twentieth Century and Beyond* (New York: St. Martin's Press, 1995), 85.

97. Rajendra Prabhu, "Misgivings over LCA Plan Changes," *Hindustan Times*, 24 January, 1987 and Raj Chengappa, "LCA Project: A Testing Time, " *India Today*, August 31, 1988, 85.

98. K. Santhanam, "Indian Defense Technology and Infrastructure and Prospects of Indo-U.S. Cooperation," paper presented at the Indo-U.S. Defense Workshop, National Defense University, Washington, D.C., September 1989, 15.

99. M. Krishnamurthi, "Self-Reliance: Lessons of Agni," *The Hindu* (Gurgaon) 5 July, 1989.

100. Major Gurmeet Kanwal, "Strike Corps Offensive Operations—Imperatives for Success," *Indian Defense Review* (January 1988), 82.

101. Interview with Lt. General Chibber.

102. "Interview with General K. Sundarji," *Indian Defense Review* (January 1988): 38.

103. Anthony Cordesman, "The India-Pakistan Military Balance," Unpublished Paper, 1987.

104. Rikhye, *Militarization of Mother India*, 76.

105. Ashley Tellis, "Securing the Barrack: The Logic, Structure and Objectives of India's Naval Expansion, Part I," *Naval War College Review* (September 1990): 84.

106. Ibid., 84.

107. Ibid., 87.

108. Ashley Tellis, "Securing the Barrack: The Logic, Structure and Objectives of India's Naval Expansion, Part II," *Naval War College Review* (October 1990): 45.

109. "Interview with Air Chief Marshall S. K. Mehra," *Indian Defense Review* (January 1990): 25.

110. Ibid., 26.

111. Ibid., 26.

112. "Indian MiG-21 Upgrade," *Jane's Defense Weekly*, 21 May 1994.

113. For a detailed discussion of the problems with the LCA program, see Gupta, "The Indian Arms Industry," 851-53.

114. Rahul Bedi, "Collaboration Invited for LCA Program," *Jane's Defense Weekly*, January 29, 1994, 4.

115. P. R. Chari, "India's Nuclear Choices," 367-68.

116. The proposed air strike is discussed in Leonard S. Spector with Jacqueline R. Smith, *Nuclear Ambitions: The Spread of Nuclear Weapons 1989-1990* (Boulder, Colo.: Westview, 1990): 66. A more sensational version is provided in William E. Burrows and Robert Windrem, *Critical Mass: The Dangerous Race for Superweapons in a Fragmenting World* (New York: Simon and Schuster, 1994), 349-350.

117. Interview with Giri Deshingkar, Director, Center for the Study of Developing Societies, Delhi, August 5, 1991.

118. Bhabani SenGupta and Amit Gupta, "The Roots of Conflict in South Asia," in *Regional Cooperation and Development in South Asia*, Bhabani SenGupta ed. (New Delhi: South Asian, 1986), 1: 274.

119. Spector with Smith, *Nuclear Ambitions*, 66-72.

120. K. Sundarji, "Strategy in the Age of Nuclear Deterrence and Its Application to Developing Countries," M. Phil. thesis submitted to Madras University, June 11, 1984.

121. Ibid., 33.

122. Ibid.

123. Ibid., 36.

124. Vijay K. Nair, *Nuclear India* (New Delhi: Lancer International, 1992), 171-172, 181.

125. Quoted in Akhtar Ali, *Pakistan's Nuclear Dilemma* (New Delhi: ABC, 1984), 67.

126. Brahma Chellany, "An Indian Critique of US Export Controls," *Orbis* 38, no. 3 (Summer 1994) 446-448.

127. *India Today*, 15 June, 1989, 11.

128. For details, see Sandeep Waslekar, "Abolishing Nuclear Weapons: Rajiv Gandhi Plan Revisited," *Acdis Occasional Paper*, University of Illinois, Urbana, July 1994.

129. Rahul Bedi, "India Stems Fall in Defense Spending," *Jane's Defense Weekly*, 12 March, 1994.

130. *The Hindu* (Madras), 21 February, 1996.

131. *Deccan Herald* (Bangalore), 17 March, 1997.

132. *The Times of India* (New Delhi), 10 January, 1996.

133. *Deccan Herald* (Bangalore), 11 April, 1997.

134. *Jane's Defense Weekly*, 29 January, 1994, 4.

135. *The Hindu* (Madras) 16 February, 1997 and *Deccan Herald* (Bangalore) March 3, 1997.

136. Interview with Anand Parthasarthy.

137. Interviews with officials at the Aeronautical Development Agency, Bangalore, 15 July, 1991, at the Defense Research and Development Organization, Hyderabad, 16 July, 1991, and at the Defense Metallurgical Research Laboratory, 17 July, 1991.

138. Interview with Dr. V. Arunachalam.

139. K. Subrahmanyam, "The Islamic Bomb, U.S. Silence On Saudi Effort," *The Times of India* (New Delhi) 2 August , 1994.

140. Gordon, *India's Rise to Power*, 42-43.

141. Ibid., 90-91 and *The Hindu* (Madras), July 11, 1996.

142. Shekhar Gupta, "India Redefines Its Role," *Adelphi Paper* No. 293 (London: Oxford University Press, 1995), 46.

143. Chellany, *An Indian Critique*, 455.

144. U.S. Department of State, *Report to Congress on the Progress toward Regional Nonproliferation in South Asia* (Washington, D.C.: Department of State, 1993).

145. Deepa Ollapally and Raja Ramanna, "U.S.-India Tensions— Misperceptions on Nuclear Proliferation," *Foreign Affairs* 74, no. 1, (January/February): 14.

146. Ibid., 17.

147. Ibid., 13-14.

148. K. Subrahmanyam, "Strategy of Engagement," *The Times of India* (New Delhi), December 6, 1994.

149. C. Raja Mohan, "Indo-U.S. Relations: A New Maturity?" *The Hindu* (Madras), September 13, 1996, 13.

150. Giri Deshingkar, "CTBT: The State of the Debate in India," *International Security Digest* 1, no. 10 (September 1994): 3.

151. Ibid., 3.

152. Praful Bidwai, "India and the NPT Review," *The Times of India* (New Delhi), 22 September, 1994.

153. *The Times of India* (New Delhi), 21 June, 1996.

154. Poonam Sethi Barua, "India-Pakistan Confidence Building Measures," *International Security Digest* 2, no. 8 (May 1995): 3.

155. Shekhar Gupta, "India Redefines its Role," 54.

156. *Indian Express* (New Delhi), 11 April, 1997.

157. *The Times* (London), 23 April, 1997.

3

Building an Arsenal:
The Israeli Experience

Israel has one of the most impressive arsenals among regional powers: its acquisition of imported weapons has given the country the most technologically advanced military force in the Middle East; its scientific-industrial base has provided the country with nuclear weapons and ballistic missiles, and, as the Israelis claim, a conventional military capability. Thus analysts point to the Israeli Jericho missile, its nuclear program, and at the conventional level to the development of the Kfir fighter-bomber, the Merkava tank, and a series of guided missiles as examples of Israeli capability to indigenously build an arsenal.

Coupled with this productive capability is the mystique about Israeli weapons development and organizational behavior. Israel is portrayed as a state in which the national security system operates as a smoothly oiled machine geared towards maintaining the country's defenses against overwhelming odds. Edward Luttwak argues that," Israel has had a true defense-planning process since the immediate aftermath of the 1948-1949 war of independence. Its weapons requirements have reflected force-structure goals themselves derived from evolving operational concepts of war as well as changing definitions of national strategy."[1] Discussing the role of the Israeli arms industry, Martin Van Creveld says that Israel enjoys a large domestic market for its products and is able to produce weapons effectively. Van Creveld writes that Israel enjoys some unique advantages including the availability of highly skilled but low-paid labor, vast combat experience, and a close interaction between users and producers,

that is without parallel in most other developed countries. As a consequence, Israel is currently the only country of its size and degree of development capable of designing and producing a whole series of modern weapon systems ranging from fighter aircraft and missile boats to communications, electronic warfare, and surveillance gear.[2]

This chapter argues that despite the existence of a high-threat environment and a large scientific base, Israeli weapons acquisition and arms production process suffers from constraints similar to the ones that beset the Indian acquisition and production efforts. The economic constraints of the nation as well as its relations with external powers determine the acquisition and production of weaponry. They also determine the eventual shape of Israel's force structures. The chapter first lays out the framework of analysis and then examines the Israeli case through four discrete historical periods: the first period, which lasts from independence in 1948 to the Suez War in 1956, is labeled the prealliance period; the second period, the French period, is from 1956 to 1967; the American period is from 1967 to 1991, and the last period discusses Israeli efforts in the post-Gulf War period.

THE THREAT

Since its creation in 1948 Israel has existed in a hostile regional environment, facing threats to its territorial integrity. Unlike other states that face claims to parts of their territory, the very notion of an Israeli state is challenged by some Arab groups and states—and initially was by all of them—in the region. Further, from the 1950s to the 1980s, Israel was engaged in a qualitative arms race with the Arab states that were able to get weapons first from the Soviet Union and later also from the West. Lack of territorial depth also poses a threat because it does not provide Israeli forces with the luxury of giving up territory to regroup and wage a counteroffensive.

According to Martin Van Creveld, Israel has traditionally faced the following problems in ensuring its security. First, it is a small state and, therefore, suffers from both manpower and resource shortages as well as a territorial disadvantage. In terms of its population, Israel is a small state and the loss of personnel hurts both militarily and psychologically. Militarily, the Israeli armed forces cannot afford heavy casualties in combat. Psychologically, the smallness of the country ensures that every one knows someone in the armed forces and, therefore, reacts adversely to the news of combat casualties.[3] The sensitivity about casualties has demanded that the Israeli armed forces seize the initiative in a potential conflict (preemption), inflict heavy damages on the enemy early, and ensure a quick end to the war.

The lack of resources has posed a potential problem in that Israel has to try to secure both guns and butter for its citizens. While the threat environment has demanded high levels of militarization, political and ideological considerations have required the creation of a welfare state in Israel. The Israeli economy did not have the capability of generating these resources indigenously, particularly in the early years. The defense budget, for instance, fell from $88 million in 1950 to $60 million in 1953.[4] The search for external resources, therefore, has been critical to ensuring the survival of the state.

A third part of the Israeli security dilemma emerged from Israeli dependence on external suppliers for its military equipment. The Jewish Army (Hagannah) in British Mandate Palestine set up small factories to produce ordnance and this led to the birth of TAAS— Israel Military Industry. But the new nation lacked a sizable military industrial base to wage a war against the Arab states. Thus, Israel required an external supplier of weaponry and this requirement has essentially continued since the early days of independence. The problem with this requirement has been twofold. First, there was the difficulty of finding suppliers willing to provide arms to a country which, for the bulk of the Cold War, was viewed as a pariah state. Further, the Cold War rivalry drove the superpowers to try to both accommodate Arab interests in the region and balance the two rivals. Second, Israel was also vulnerable to the termination of foreign military assistance, as was the case when the Czechs cut off the supply of weaponry after the 1956 Suez War and, later, the French government terminated military programs after the Six Day War of 1967. In more recent times Israel has been concerned about the suspension of American military aid, or, as in the case of the 1991 Gulf War, the constraints it puts on Israeli security policy.

THE NATIONAL SECURITY SYSTEM

As in the Indian case, the three main groups in the Israeli national security system are also the political leadership, the military, and the defense industry. Unlike India, however, the Israeli system is portrayed as a highly cohesive one with high levels of cooperation between the three groups. Thus, the development of military doctrine and the acquisition of weapons systems, as mentioned earlier, are seen as being shaped by the constructive interaction of these three groups. This would seem to suggest that the high-threat environment that Israel faces marginalizes bureaucratic pressures and leads to the development of coherent internal programs for building force structures.

In fact the existence of these three groups leads, at times, to significantly differing views on security issues and, consequently, on the development of force structures. The Israeli political leadership, for instance, has recognized since the early days of the state that a degree of self-reliance was required in defense matters. David Ben-Gurion, speaking before the national assembly in 1949, laid down self-reliance in defense production as one of the goals that Israel had to achieve. In pursuit of this goal the Israeli political leadership has encouraged the creation and development of an indigenous defense capability and, on occasion, sought to give it weapons production programs that are only partially determined by threat considerations.

The Israeli armed forces, on the other hand, have played a role which is at times inimical to the interests of the Israeli arms industry. As the principal guarantor of the nation's security, the armed forces have tended to prefer importing weapons systems to having them manufactured indigenously. Imported weapons have a proven quality, while the indigenous development of weapons is both a lengthy and uncertain process. Consequently, indigenous weapons programs have suffered from a lack of financial and bureaucratic support.

The Israeli arms industry has become a major player in the national security system, but not entirely for its ability to provide weaponry to the nation's armed forces. As mentioned earlier, the arms industry was established during the British Mandate of Palestine, and from its inception research was conducted in a variety of areas ranging from the production of munitions to research into rocketry. Since then weapons production has taken place both in the private and public sectors and the arms industry has become a valuable earner of hard currency. The industry until the early 1990s was also a major employer within the Israeli economy. All of these factors worked to give the industry leverage in its attempts to secure new projects.

Israel has been heavily dependent on the availability of resources and external suppliers for its militarization efforts. As mentioned earlier, the initial dilemma for the Israeli state was how to provide both guns and butter for the citizens. The need for both security and development could not be satisfied through internal efforts. In the late 1940s and early 1950s the new state had to resettle a wave of immigrants and try and upgrade its arsenal.[5] Israel's economic base was inadequate to meet this challenge and it was only able to meet these competing demands with the inflow of external assistance in the form of private donations from international Jewry, reparations from the West German government, and the supply of foreign aid. Coupled with the supply of monetary resources was the existence of a guaranteed supplier weapons—first Czechoslovakia, then France, and later the United States. Concern about the decline of incoming financial resources and the existence of an external supplier is a continuing problem for Israeli security planners.

1948–1956: THE PREALLIANCE PERIOD

After the armistice of 1949 the Israeli government had to shape a security policy and the force structure to implement it. The policy and the force structure were shaped by systemic circumstances, regional considerations, and domestic constraints. Israeli security policy in the early period was influenced by the transformation of the international system. The international system had shifted from a multipolar to a bipolar one, and the major powers in the Middle East, Britain, and France were retreating powers. The problem for Israel was that it did not fit into the strategic calculations of either of the two superpowers, nor the two retreating powers. The United States, while one of the first to recognize Israel, did not want to become a major weapons supplier or an ally of the new state. The Soviet Union, through Czechoslovakia, was initially willing to provide arms but by the time of Stalin's death had started shifting toward the Arab states because such a relationship provided a better fit with the Soviet

Union's strategic interests. As Shlomo Avineri points out, the Soviet move to establish closer ties with Egypt "was not primarily aimed against Israel. It was based on two common interests of the Soviets and radical Arabs in curtailing Western influence in the region: first, to put and end to the vestiges of British and French influence (as in the case of control over the Suez Canal, as well as French rule in Algeria) and, second, to counter growing American influence which was greatly enhanced by the discovery and production of oil."[6]

Both Britain and France still had economic and political interests in the Arab world, and in France's case major colonial possessions. Further, the armies of both Egypt and Jordan remained under British military commanders. Given such considerations it was believed that Israel could not secure a dependable external supplier of weapons in that period. This concern was in part alleviated with the Tripartite Declaration of 1950, whereby the United States, Britain, and France guaranteed to not allow the military balance in the region to shift in favor of either side.[7] While this declaration controlled the sale of weapons to the Arab states and allowed Israel to purchase weaponry from the West, it is argued that it also hampered Israel's efforts to build up a credible military deterrent. Another aspect of the great-power calculations that influenced Israeli security planning was their position on territorial gains. It became apparent that the Israelis would not be allowed to keep any territorial gains they made during the course of conflict with the Arab states. Ben-Gurion, in fact, was forced to return territory captured in the Sinai during the 1948 war.

At the regional level Israel faced the Arab states, which had the advantage of population, strategic depth, weapons acquisition, and staying power. While the Arab advantage in population does not need to be elaborated, the problems associated with weapons acquisition, strategic depth, and staying power do. The standard Israeli argument is that in the initial years after state formation, they had to struggle to find weapons while the Arabs were busily arming themselves. In actual fact the Arabs were just as poorly armed because of the British and French decisions to leave these nations with small and not particularly effective armed forces. The Tripartite Declaration also restricted the amount of arms flowing in from Western sources. Further, the Arabs lacked the resources to purchase weapons on the Western market (the Soviets having not yet worked out the advantages of arms transfers).

Israel's problem with weapons acquisition in the prealliance period was not, therefore, one of facing a quantitative or qualitative arms race because the Arab states, until the Czech-Egyptian arms deal of 1955, did not have the capability to alter the military balance. Nor was it a supply-side issue even though the usual argument is that no nation was willing to provide Israel with the arms it needed. In fact, by the early 1950s, Israel was buying weapons from both the British and the French. Instead, Israel faced the same problem other newly independent countries of the South faced—a resource crunch.[8] In the late 1940s and early 1950s, weapons transfers had yet to become a tool for foreign aid, and, instead, were carried out on a strictly commercial basis—a similar resource crunch affected India's efforts to modernize its armed forces.

The staying power argument was a more serious one. Israel's small population base required that the armed forces depend heavily on reservists because economic considerations did not permit the existence of a large standing army.[9] Further, once its reservist army had been mobilized, economic conditions dictated that it could not remain so indefinitely. This constraint required that the army, once mobilized, had to be used quickly and that it had to achieve a rapid victory. Unlike the Arab states, the Israelis could not afford a long drawn out war of attrition.[10]

The lack of strategic depth and the policy of not conceding an inch of ground created problems as well. The fact that Israel was a small nation meant that it could not trade land for time in a conflict. Further, the political decision to not cede an inch of ground for nationalistic reasons also shaped the creation of early Israeli security policy and doctrine. During the last decade of the British Mandate of Palestine, the new Jewish agricultural settlements had been created with a hidden paramilitary purpose—to try and hold off an Arab attack. Thus these settlements were fortified, ringed with trenches, fences, and minefields and during the 1948 war were able to exact a high price from the invading Arab armies.[11] The success of these settlements helped shape postwar doctrine.

The lack of strategic depth also created the determination to carry the war to the enemy's territory. Ben-Gurion articulated this policy shortly after the creation of the Israeli state when he said: " If we are attacked and war is again forced on us, we shall not adopt a defensive strategy, rather we will move to an attack on the enemy—and as far as possible into enemy territory. . . . If they attack us, as they did this time, we shall transfer the war to the gates of their country. . . . If they attack us again, in the future, we want the war to be waged not in our country but in the enemy's country, and [we want] not to be on the defensive but to attack."[12]

The constraints posed by the threat environment shaped Israeli policy in a number of ways. First, the military lessons of the 1948 war and the constraints imposed by Israel's lack of strategic depth led to the adoption of a twofold and in some ways contradictory defense policy. The new Israeli government decided to combine a policy of spatial defense with an offensive military capability designed to quickly carry the conflict onto enemy territory. The spatial defense policy created a string of agricultural settlements along the border that would serve as the first line of defense in the event of a future war with the Arab states. The system, called Nahal, was Ben-Gurion's idea, and at his insistence young people who would otherwise have been prime candidates for recruitment by the Israeli Defense Forces (IDF) were sent to these settlements.[13] The IDF saw the spatial defense policy as taking away resources—both in terms of personnel and finances—from the creation of an effective and professional military force.

Second, Israel continued to seek an external ally among the major powers, the logic being that such an alliance would prove to be a deterrent to the Arab states. The decline of the imperial European powers and the rise of the two superpowers, however, created circumstances that worked to shut out Israel as a possible security partner for these countries.

Third, Israel's military doctrine had to be essentially defensive in nature. Israeli leaders argued that Israel could not be the first to initiate a conflict since this could possibly antagonize the major powers with whom it sought an alliance. Thus, it was argued that the combination of spatial defense and an external ally would have to serve as a deterrent. If this deterrent failed and the Arab states attacked, "Israel would quickly mobilize and seek to shift the fighting to the adversary's territory as soon as possible. In the event of such a war, Israel would not limit itself to the repulsion of the invader. It would retaliate massively, seeking to inflict on the adversary the most severe punishment in its power."[14]

BUREAUCRATIC AGENDA

Israel's military doctrine, therefore, was based on the twin pillars of spatial defense and the creation of a rapidly mobilizable army which, if the country was attacked, would carry the war onto Arab territory. These two pillars, however, did not complement each other. The creation of the Nahal system meant drawing away talented personnel from the IDF. It also meant taking away the funds required for buying the modern weaponry the IDF required to carry out its offensive mission (funds being siphoned off for the establishment of the Nahal system and the setting up of defenses in these settlements).

Another problem arose within the sphere of arms procurement: Should weapons be produced indigenously or should they be imported? The armed forces wanted to buy new weapons systems from the West rather than rely on indigenously produced weapons systems. This reluctance of the armed forces was understandable given the proven quality of Western weapons systems, and that Israel had yet to develop the necessary scientific-industrial base to successfully produce these weapons. Further, the creation of an arms industry was opposed by both military and civilian experts on the basis of economic and social considerations. Experts argued that the arms industry had too small a domestic market and the export market was too limited to absorb the production surplus.[15] The social constraints came from the need to accommodate the new migrant population that had flooded into the state. Lastly, it was recognized by the military that resources would have to be diverted from its modernization budget to establish the arms industry.

Despite such opposition, Ben-Gurion decided to establish an indigenous weapons production capability both for reasons of self-reliance and due to technological considerations. Recognizing that Israel could not completely depend on an external power for its survival, Ben-Gurion felt that an arms industry would enhance the nation's quest for security. Speaking before Israel's Knesset in 1949, Ben-Gurion laid out his four principles for Israel's national security: self-sufficiency in agriculture, the development of an arms industry to prevent dependence on others, the development of shipping and the establishment of maritime links, and the development of an air service.[16] He also saw an arms industry facilitating the development of a broader technological base in the country.

ARMS INDUSTRY—EARLY DEVELOPMENT

To develop the arms industry, Ben-Gurion had to break down the bureaucratic bottlenecks that restricted indigenous weapons production. The organization that could develop defense science in the country—the Science Corps—was located within the IDF and therefore could not function with the autonomy necessary to develop weapons systems. Munya Mardor (who would later head Emet, the R&D branch of the arms industry) argued that its location within the IDF would relegate it to the solution of short-range problems caused by the 1948 war rather than the long-range development of sophisticated weapons systems. Not only was the Science Corps made autonomous, but the Defense Ministry, again under the urging of advisors like Shimon Peres and Mardor, was given functions separate from the IDF. Peres argued that the IDF should deal exclusively with military matters—organization and command of forces, training and organization—while the Defense Ministry should have jurisdiction over all remaining functions—finances, and the acquisition, production and development of arms and equipment.[17]

The Israeli government first sought to expand TAAS in 1950, but the scarcity of resources and personnel caused the plans to remain at the blueprint stage. Despite these constraints, TAAS had started development of the UZI submachine gun and begun overhauling and modifying tanks. [18] It was only after Emet was established as a part of the Defense Ministry in 1952 and Ben-Gurion took the step of setting up an aircraft industry in 1953 with the establishment of an aircraft maintenance plant (called the Institute for the Reconditioning of Planes but better known by its Hebrew acronym Bedek) that the arms industry began to take shape. Emet's early work was in the area of missilery with development of sabotage boats, air-to-surface missiles (the Luz series), and later the G-25 antishipping missile.[19]

The origins of the Israeli aircraft industry, which was to become the nation's largest employer, lay in both a shift in strategic thinking as well as in organizational politics. The air force had not played a major role in the 1948 war, and in the late 1940s and early 1950s it was given low priority in the defense planning process. Israel's military doctrine of that period emphasized the role of the infantry and consequently it was in that direction that defense expenditure was targeted. The poor funding of the air force, in fact, led two air chiefs of staff to resign in protest.

What boosted the fortunes of the air force, and with it those of the aircraft industry, was the shift in Israeli military thinking toward an offensive doctrine. As mentioned earlier, the lack of strategic depth and the quantitative advantage of the Arab states demanded that Israel quickly carry the war over onto Arab territory. That an offensive doctrine over open territory required air superiority soon became obvious, and by the early 1950s the Israeli Air Force formulated the following set of missions in a descending order of priority: (1) gaining air superiority by attacking the enemy airfields; (2) interception of hostile aircraft over the skies of Israel; and (3) providing air cover and support for the ground forces and navy.[20]

Ben-Gurion agreed with the new preemptive mission of the air force and was willing to support its expansion. This in turn led to his support of the development of Bedek. Yet, in creating Bedek, Ben-Gurion had to overcome resistance from economists, military advisors, cabinet ministers, and industrial experts who opposed the establishment of the plant. Their argument was that the domestic market was too small to justify the indigenous production of aircraft. Further, it was unlikely that Israel would find an export market for these aircraft because other countries would be skeptical about the quality of aircraft produced in Israel.[21] But the thinking of the Israeli political leadership was that national development and national security took precedence over economic arguments, and Bedek was created.

What finally laid the foundation for the Israeli defense industry, however, was the Israeli cabinet's approval in 1953 of a three-year long, eighteen-point plan for Israel's defense policy (drafted by Ben-Gurion who was by then the defense minister). The plan called for "maximum utilization of the civilian economy, for military supply, transport, construction, production of other military services."[22] While the politicians had laid down the foundations for a defense industry, its actual development was facilitated by the availability of resources and the link with an external supplier. These factors were also to play a role in the implementation of an offensive military doctrine.

RESOURCES AND SUPPLIERS

The availability of financial resources and external suppliers plays a key role in the development of regional power military arsenals. In the Indian case it became apparent that whenever resources and suppliers were available, the modernization of force structures and shifts in doctrine were possible. In the Israeli case, conventional wisdom is that the Israelis have indigenously developed a war machine that can ensure the survival of the state. In actual fact, Israeli weapons acquisition and arms production has been heavily dependent on the availability of financial resources and a guaranteed supplier of weaponry.

By the early 1950s, the doctrinal thinking for the Israeli armed forces was beginning to emerge. So too was the need for an arms industry. But for both the doctrine to succeed and the arms industry to be established, a heavy infusion of capital was needed. Yet up until 1952, Israel had a scarcity of capital and funded its defense planning efforts through deficit spending. Further, the new nation's industrial base was small and its capacity to export limited. Until 1952, Israel had depended on donations and grants from world Jewry, the sale of bonds, and on foreign aid. These amounts were limited and U.S. governmental aid had begun to decline. What changed the situation in Israel's favor was the Reparations and Restitutions Agreement with the West German government in

1952. German reparations started at $40 million in 1953. The amount grew every year and by 1961 had reached $199 million. Coupled with these reparations was growth in personal donations and American foreign assistance. The latter figure was to reach approximately $200 million during the 1950s.[23] This infusion of capital allowed for both the purchase of weaponry and for the Israeli government to invest in the development of defense related industries like steel.

The infusion of capital also led to the procurement of new weaponry. Arms imports gradually began to increase after 1952, going from approximately $24 million in 1952 to $38.1 million in 1955. [24] Between 1950 and 1955 the IDF began to raise force levels and acquire more modern systems. It bought surplus equipment from the United States and Canada and more modern systems from Europe. Israel was also able to buy its first jet fighters from Britain and France in 1953, and to purchase AMX tanks from France.[25] These purchases, while for small quantities and in cash, allowed Israel to maintain the military balance in the region, since the Arab states were also hampered by the lack of resources and suppliers. What changed the situation for both the Arabs and the Israelis was the infusion of weapons into the region by external powers in the mid-1950s.

The post-Stalin leadership of the Soviet Union moved to secure better ties with Third World countries as part of the Cold War struggle against the United States. This led to the signing of the Czech-Egyptian arms agreement in 1955, through which the Egyptians received jet fighters, bombers, artillery, tanks, destroyers, mine sweepers, and submarines.[26] The Egyptian acquisition of such weapons was seen as altering the military balance in favor of the Arab states. In contrast, the Israeli government had been unsuccessful in finding an external ally to provide it with both political support and a steady supply of weapons. By 1949 the supply of Soviet arms had begun to dwindle as the Soviet Union started demanding that Israel identify itself with the Eastern bloc—something Israel refused to do.

Israeli attempts to seek allies in the Western camp were also unsuccessful. The United States, Britain, and France all sought to maintain ties with the Arab states for Cold War reasons or due to past imperial ties and were unwilling to provide the sort of assistance and guarantees Israel sought. Moreover, some of the compromises that the Western powers expected Israel to make with the Arab states were not acceptable to the Israeli government—to stop reprisals and to agree to the armistice lines being final ones.[27]

What changed the circumstances in Israel's favor was the Egyptian-Czech arms because it led to an alliance with France. In 1954, the Algerian uprising began and Nasser, as the champion of the Arab cause, soon became its strongest supporter, providing safe heaven to the FLN guerrillas. A marriage of convenience emerged between Israel and France and from 1954 till the 1967 war France supplied a range of weaponry to Israel. Thus in 1954 France agreed to sell the first batch of Ouragan fighters to Israel.[28] The 1955 Egyptian-Czech arms deal created the fear in Paris that Egypt would intensify its support to the

Algerian rebels, and this led France to forge an alliance with Israel. The military relationship with the French was beneficial both in terms of arms imports and in the development of the arms industry. In 1956 France agreed to transfer a large amount of weaponry to Israel and also agreed to the coproduction of defense systems—particularly aeronautics and missilery—and later to the transfer of nuclear technology.

Israel was also to use its alliance with France to resolve its immediate security problems. The Arab blockade of Israeli shipping in the Gulf of Aqaba and the continued incursions into Israeli territory led the Israeli government to join forces with the Anglo-French expeditionary force (which sought to reverse Nasser's nationalization of the Suez Canal) and attack Egypt in 1956. While militarily successful, the expeditionary force was forced to withdraw due to superpower pressure, and this setback led to nuclear cooperation between Israel and France.

THE EARLY NUCLEAR PERIOD

Israel's nuclear program is shrouded in secrecy and there is little public debate in the country on the issue. Even when something as important as the Vanunu affair took place " it did not lead to a national debate in Israel on issues such as the role of nuclear weapons in Israel's conception of national security, the question of democratic control over nuclear development, and moral concerns about possible nuclear use."[29] Instead there was both governmental and self-censorship of the issue. The Israeli academic community and media see nuclear weapons as a topic of high-level security and refrain from discussing it in public. Consequently, any discussion of Israel's nuclear program is based on certain conjecture about the path it took and where it stands today. What is apparent about the Israeli program is that like the Indian program it has several discernible trends. Israel's quest for nuclear weapons came out of a perceived threat posed by Israel's numerical inferiority to the Arab states. The lack of a credible ally also made the Ben-Gurion government seek the nuclear option. As in the Indian case, there was also a developmental agenda of using nuclear power to hasten the development of the country.

Israeli research in the nuclear field had begun in the late 1940s, and by 1950 the Weizmann Institute had established a section for nuclear research and development. The institute also employed Professor Ernst Bergmann, the father of the Israeli bomb.[30] Like the Indian case, the Israeli program was marked by a high degree of secrecy and the centralization of powers. The deal with France to purchase the Dimona reactor was only disclosed to the Israeli Knesset in 1960, three years after the deal was consummated. Further, when the Israel Atomic Energy Commission (IAEC) was set up in 1952 within the framework of the Defense Ministry, it was assigned an advisory and supervisory role and not officially given decision-making powers in the field of nuclear energy. But at the same time there was no attempt to define its range of action in a codified manner. Fuad Jabber argues that this was done to limit decision-making on nuclear issues to the highest levels of political and military authority. It should be pointed out that Ben-Gurion was both the prime minister and defense minister from 1948 to 1953. It also allowed these authorities to assign new tasks and prerogatives to the IAEC without having to go through the legislature, and to avoid unwanted publicity and public debate.[31]

Such secrecy was necessary because members of the ruling Mapai Party opposed the plan to go nuclear, viewing it as "suicidal, too expensive, and too reminiscent of the horrors that had been inflicted on the Jews in World War II."[32] In fact the real push toward nuclearization came only in Ben-Gurion's second term as prime minister and with the Suez War of 1956 providing the security rationale.

The role of France as a willing external supplier also paved the way for the establishment of Israel's nuclear program. The basis for Israeli-French nuclear cooperation lay in Israel's ability to provide needed inputs to the French nuclear program, as well as in Israel's desire to collaborate in the nuclear area with a country that was at a comparable technological level.[33] The fact that the three leaders in the nuclear field in the early 1950s, United States, the Soviet Union, and Britain, would not permit such collaboration also restricted Israel's choice.

Israeli scientists were able to develop two procedures that were useful for the French nuclear program. One was a process enabling the separation of uranium from other ores and the other was a process to make heavy water. The French nuclear establishment was also interested in obtaining computer skills from Israel.[34] Consequently, in 1953, France agreed to purchase the uranium separation and heavy water manufacturing processes from Israel. In return Israeli scientists were given access to the French nuclear program.[35] Seymour Hersh argues that the large number of French scientists who were Jewish, as well as members of the former resistance in the French nuclear program, provided Israel with a receptive group within the French scientific community. These were people with intense feelings about the Holocaust and who therefore felt that Israel needed a nuclear capability.[36]

Thus, by the mid-1950s, Israel had laid the groundwork for a nuclear program, and following the Suez War was able to get a reactor from France, giving it a nuclear weapons capability. Like the Indian case, the Israeli government was to centralize decision making in the nuclear realm and keep the program out of legislative overview.

1955–1967: THE FRENCH PERIOD

The Sinai campaign of 1956 imparted important political and military lessons to the IDF and the Israeli political leadership. Militarily, Israeli troops performed extremely well, having rapidly overrun the Egyptian armed forces and reached the Suez Canal. The success of the IDF vindicated the doctrinal shift to a strategy of quickly transferring the conflict to the enemy's territory. It also brought out just how successful a strategy of preemption could be.

Consequently, there was another shift in Israeli strategic thinking to accommodate the lessons of the war. Israeli military strategy was reshaped to put an emphasis on the use of armor and air power to achieve rapid breakthroughs, and Israel also sought to carry out a policy of deterrence through preemption.

At the political level, there were equally important lessons from the war. First, the intervention of the United States and the Soviet Union in the war once again brought home that the great powers would not permit Israel to hold on to its territorial conquests. It also became clear that the major powers would not allow the complete destruction of the Arab military capability. In fact, Nasser was able to replace all of the weaponry he had lost in the war with more advanced systems from the Soviet Union.

Second, the United States, despite encouraging the sale of weapons to Israel in the postwar period and from 1962 onwards itself openly selling weapons to Israel, continued to seek Arab support in its containment policy against the Soviet Union. This led the United States to provide arms to Iraq and later Jordan. In the Jordanian case, the United States made Israeli acquisition of arms conditional to the Israeli government's consent to the deal with Amman.

THE THREAT

The 1956 war had a major impact on the weapons procurement patterns of both Israel and the Arab states. Israel and most of the Arab states moved away from infantry-oriented armies to those structured around tanks and armor. Further, Egypt, now Israel's principal enemy, was able to replace its war losses with more advanced weaponry from the Soviet Union. The willingness of the Soviet Union to provide weapons at subsidized rates gave the Egyptian government what it had lacked before the 1956 war—a guaranteed and cheap supplier of weapons. Thus, in the post 1956 period, Egypt replaced Israel as the pace setter in the induction of new weapons systems. This heightened Israeli apprehensions about the potential threat posed by Egypt.

The consequences of the Soviet military link with Egypt were also felt in the pro-Western Arab world—states like Jordan, Iraq, and Saudi Arabia. Alarmed by the growth of Egypt's military capability, these nations also began to modernize their armed forces. From the Israeli perspective the modernization efforts of the pro-Western Arab states was a further erosion of their security. Not only did the IDF have to worry about a better-armed Egypt, but also about better-armed pro-Western states that still had hostile relations with Israel.

The interaction of these factors led to the Middle East becoming one of the most heavily armed regions in the world, as the various nations sought to counterbalance each other. Thus, Egypt's procurement of heavy tanks led both Israel and the pro-Western Arabs to purchase medium tanks. The infantry of all the major Middle Eastern nations became motorized. Israel, Egypt, Syria, and Iraq added supersonic aircraft to their inventories. Egypt also decided to augment its sea power, and Israel sought to match it. By 1960, Egypt had eight submarines and four destroyers while Israel had fallen behind and purchased two destroyers and two submarines.[37] Lastly, Egypt decided to follow Israel's lead and embarked on an indigenous weapons production program.

Egypt started to establish its arms industry in the early 1950s in response to the Western-imposed arms embargoes and restrictions to arms transfers of the late 1940s and early 1950s.[38] By the mid-1950s the Egyptian government had acquired the production rights to two types of jet aircraft, and from 1960 it launched a serious program to produce a surface-to-surface missile.[39] Egypt failed in these efforts, largely due to its sole reliance on foreign technicians (who were subsequently pulled out due to Israeli pressure on their governments, especially that of West Germany) and due to the lack of funding to bring these projects to fruition. But the very fact that Egypt was headed in this direction heightened Israeli security apprehensions and require the need to take countermeasures.

Further, Ben-Gurion initiated and Levi Eshkol, the next prime minister, carried on a policy of seeking both regional and extraregional allies to break Israel's international isolation. Ben-Gurion pointed out that the threat to Israel came from Sunni Arab states. But the Middle East, as Ben-Gurion put it, was not just composed of Sunni Arabs. It included Christians, Turks, Kurds, and Persians, all of whom had reasons to fear the growing strength of the Sunni Arabs. Thus, the Israeli strategy became one of trying to forge alliances with the non-Sunni people region, thereby fueling other conflicts within the Arab world and diverting their attention from Israel. By the early 1960s the Israelis were working with the Shah of Iran to support the Kurdish rebels in Iraq. Israel also began to get involved in the politics of Lebanon. Military and developmental assistance was provided to Ethiopia, both for the political reasons mentioned earlier and also for a specific strategic reason. Good relations with Ethiopia prevented the Red Sea, the only access to the Israeli port of Eilat, from being turned into an Arab-dominated waterway.[40] The move to provide military and developmental assistance to nations in black Africa and parts of Asia was also part of the strategy of ending isolation.

ORGANIZATIONAL POLITICS

While the threat environment had heightened after the 1956 war despite the Israeli victory, it was not clear which path to pursue to meet the threat. Should indigenous production take precedence over the import of weapons? Or should indigenous efforts be shelved and the funds saved be used to import proven weapons systems? An organizational struggle ensued between the IDF, which wanted to import systems, and the arms industry, which wanted new projects to develop. The IDF had shifted its strategy to one of preemption and wanted weapons suitable for a first strike deep into enemy territory. Recognizing that a new war would be short and subject to a foreign intervention, the emphasis was placed on building up the air force—which had the best capability to conduct deep strikes. The IAF became the first priority for funding as a new air force was to be built around fighter-bombers. The decision was also taken to create tank battalions thereby moving away from the old tactics of using armor to support artillery. The Navy, at least initially, remained unaffected by the 1956 conflict. The principal maritime threat remained a blockade of Israel's ports and shipping routes, but Israeli planners believed it would be broken by a victory on land and subsequent great-power intervention.[41]

This plan was altered when the Egyptian Navy acquired the Komar class attack boats from the Soviet Union in 1962 and later the Osa class missile boats in 1966. The Israeli Navy's response was to opt for fast and cheap patrol boats armed with missiles. The construction of these vessels was delegated to a West German firm, which carried out the order in France, while the design and development of the missiles was to be undertaken by Rafael (the new name for Emet) and by Israel Aircraft Industries (IAI). But the cost of these vessels and the low priority given to the navy in the Israeli scheme of affairs meant that no real change took place in the navy's capabilities until after the 1967 war. Thus, within the armed forces the new doctrine had provided greater influence to the air force in its modernization efforts. These efforts, as will be seen later, were greatly enhanced by the military relationship with France.

While the different branches of the armed forces were pressing for weapons imports, the civilian leadership and members of Israel's fledging defense industries were calling for increased indigenous production. The military leadership was skeptical about the arms industry's ability to deliver the type and quality of weapons that the IDF required. Moshe Dayan, the chief of staff, was openly skeptical of the long-range plans of the arms industry to produce state-of-the-art weapons.[42] Instead, he and the rest of the armed forces wanted the arms industry to focus on short-range goals (repair, overhaul, and providing modifications) while precious funds were used to buy the best available systems abroad. The indigenous production of weapons was justified, however, on the grounds that it would increase self-reliance and help, at least in the case of IAI, establish a modern aircraft industry.[43] The decision was, therefore, taken to license-produce the French Fouga Magister jet trainer in 1957.

Once the go-ahead had been given for indigenous production, the arms industries were able to make a case for follow-on projects. As the Magister project was winding down in the early 1960s, the then head of IAI, Al Schwimmer, argued that his company needed more projects to keep open production lines and to prevent a brain drain. He was supported by the Ministry of Defense, which argued that a high price had to be paid for independence and that the technological spin-offs would benefit other parts of the economy. It was these arguments that convinced Eshkol to grant permission for the development of a short take-off and landing transport aircraft, the Arava, despite an unfavorable report on the potential marketability of the aircraft.[44] Even the IAF stated that it would not buy the Arava, and by 1982 the production line was closed due to high costs.

Competition also developed within the arms industry for projects and labor. By the mid-1950s there was a critical shortage of personnel for these technology-oriented industries. The new pool of migrants were not coming from the West but, instead, were unskilled workers from the Middle East (Oriental Jews). Thus Rafael created beneficial policies to retain its skilled work force while IAI set up its own technical training program. But in the final analysis the successful retention of personnel lay in securing projects for the industry. This led to fierce competition within the arms industry. The Gabriel antishipping missile, for instance, was originally a Rafael project but Schwimmer argued that he needed the project to retain his personnel. Shimon Peres suggested a division of labor between Rafael and IAI—Rafael would develop the propellant while IAI did the electronics. Eventually Schwimmer's argument prevailed and the project went to IAI.[45] While political and technological imperatives were creating a constituency for the arms industry, its ultimate fate was being decided by the availability of resources and suppliers.

SUPPLIERS: THE FRENCH CONNECTION

Edward Kolodziej writes that the alliance between Tel Aviv and Paris was founded "on different but complementary security interests threatened by the Arab states bordering the Mediterranean basin—Israel's very life as a state and nation and France's empire identified by the Fourth Republic as a perquisite of national survival and grandeur."[46] Whatever hurt Arab efforts to overthrow French colonialism or the Israeli state was seen as being mutually beneficial. Thus, between 1954 and 1962 France transferred significant amounts of weapons to Israel permitting the buildup of the arsenal required for carrying out the new doctrine. As Kolodziej puts it, "The Israeli Air Force was essentially made in France. Its ground forces were largely equipped with French armor or with American made surplus items transferred (not always with permission from Washington) to Israel."[47] Between 1954 and 1962, France supplied Israel with sixty Mystere, sixty Ouragan, twenty-four Vautour, twenty-four Super Mystere, and seventy-two Mirage III fighter-ground attack aircraft. The air force also received 100 Fouga Magister trainers. Israel's armored capability was boosted with the supply of 150 AMX-13 tanks and the transfer of 300 U.S.-supplied M-2 and M-3 tanks and 100 Sherman tanks. Israel also received 200 SS-10, 150 Entac, 150 SS-11, and 300 AS-30 missiles from France. The navy was to commission the development of nine torpedo boats in France.[48]

The French-Israeli military link was mutually beneficial in the field of arms production. French arms sales to Israel helped build up the French aerospace industry. Israeli scientists were able to gain valuable experience in the development of weapons systems through their collaboration with French arms companies. This was particularly the case with the collaboration between IAI and the French aeronautical manufacturer Dassault.

But the French-Israeli relationship changed significantly after the Algerian War of Independence ended in 1962. While previously it had been a mutually beneficial alliance, it became a patron-client one to promote, at least in French eyes, its goals as a great power in the Middle East. Thus, while continuing to provide arms to Israel, France began to also accommodate Arab interests so as to prevent the eruption of another conflict and the subsequent entry of the superpowers into the Middle East—a step that would diminish French influence.[49] The shift in French policy perhaps made inevitable the decision to impose an arms embargo on Israel after the outbreak of the 1967 war. Thus, for the second time, Israel was to lose its principal weapons supplier to global considerations.

But even though Israel had a tacit alliance (or what Kolodziej calls a marriage of convenience) with France, it did not stop the attempt to diversify weapons suppliers. Israel used German reparations to buy surplus NATO weapons from Germany, and when that became politically difficult for the Bonn government to do—because the Arab states threatened to grant diplomatic recognition to East Germany—it used the reparations amounts to purchase weapons from France and Italy. The West German government recognized that this was the best way to honor the remaining portion of the deal.[50]

More importantly, the Israeli government was able to start openly purchasing weapons from the United States. In 1962, the U.S. government reversed its earlier decision and started to sell arms openly to Israel. Washington's rationale in overturning its past policy lay in its attempt to slow down Israel's nuclear weapons program—particularly since members of the Eshkol government were opposed to the acquisition of nuclear weapons.[51] Eshkol, Golda Meir, and Yitzhak Rabin, the new Israeli chief of staff, did not like the idea of nuclearization and, instead, preferred closer ties with the United States, which was seen as a supplier of the best conventional weaponry. Shlomo Aronson claims, therefore, that in return for slowing down the nuclear program and turning over development of the nuclear-capable Jericho missile to France's Dassault, Israel was provided with advanced weaponry by the United States.[52]

Israel's experience with supplier constraints in this period were to continue into the future. Like France, the United States was to give precedence to its political goals over the sale of weapons to Israel. Thus the Israeli fear of embargoes was to continue. Additionally, the availability of weapons from abroad also shaped the internal weapons production process. The armed forces were reluctant to buy at home and, instead, sought the best the West had to offer. Moshe Dayan, while chief of staff felt that Israel's scarce resources should be used to buy weapons needed to fulfill immediate requirements, while Yitzhak Rabin wanted closer ties with the United States as a source of conventional weapons. The arms industry, however, was able to get projects—like the Arava and later the Westwind aircraft—to keep up employment levels. But financial and political constraints made the development of the industry difficult. Political considerations moved the Jericho program to France and financial constraints placed an emphasis on procuring weapons from abroad. Thus, in the French period Israel's arms imports escalated from about $31.2 million in 1955 to $283 million by 1967.[53]

While Israel was the recipient of arms from a various countries in this period and received substantial financial assistance from external sources, the costs of militarization on the economy were becoming apparent. Defense spending had remained around 6–7 percent of the GNP in the period 1949–1956. In the period 1957–1967 it went up to around 10–12 percent of the GNP. While incurring such a heavy defense expenditure, the Israeli government also sought to continue raising the standard of living. Consequently, it had to resort to external borrowings, deficit spending, and, when all else failed, a planned recession (1965–1967) to meet the twin costs of defense and development.[54]

The recession was the result of an Israeli government policy to curb inflation and reduce the country's capital imports. The consequence was that the GNP stagnated, unemployment figures rose significantly, and emigration figures rose to match the growing unemployment levels. Worse, the groups emigrating were the highly skilled and members of the scientific community.[55]

Thus the costs of militarization were becoming apparent by the late 1960s even as Israel was forced to procure more advanced systems to match the arms acquisition efforts of its enemies. Further, the arms industry was not able to significantly lighten the defense burden. By the late 1960s Israel had entered into arms sales relationships with some of the nations of Africa and Asia as well as with West Germany. But the value of these sales was small. Aaron Klieman quotes estimates that put arms sales at $12–15 million in 1966, and it was estimated that the figure would go up to $30 million in 1967.[56]

DIMONA AND THE NUCLEAR PROGRAM

Israel's quest for nuclear weapons began during the Suez War. Although a military success, the war was seen as a political disaster for Israel: the United States condemned the use of force, the UN brought about a cease-fire; and, at the height of the crisis, the Soviet Union issued a nuclear warning to Israel. In response to this threat Shimon Peres and Golda Meir flew to Paris to request a security guarantee from their French allies. When it became clear that France could not offer any immediate guarantee, Peres suggested that once Israel withdrew from the Sinai, France might provide a security guarantee in the form of nuclear assistance.[57] In 1957 France agreed to sell Israel a nuclear reactor, to be set up at Dimona, as well as a reprocessing plant to separate plutonium.[58] No safeguards were attached to the sale of the reactor. In total secrecy the French provided the components to complete the reactor between 1957 and 1964. It has also been claimed that France provided Israel with the data from its first nuclear test in 1960.[59] Seymour Hersh claims that Israel in fact had access to data from several French tests.[60] Coupled with the assistance in the nuclear sphere was the help provided in constructing delivery systems. The Israeli arms industry was originally to design and develop the Jericho missile—Israel's nuclear capable intermediate range missile—but under the Eshkol government the project was passed on to France where it successfully came to fruition.

In 1958, under the U.S. Atoms for Peace program, Israel also obtained a research reactor, which it set up at Nahal Soreq.[61] The Nahal Soreq reactor could not be used for Israel's weapons program because it was safeguarded. The Dimona reactor was to provide the fissile material for Israel but the path to nuclearization was not a smooth one. It had to face, like India, pressure from other countries to disband its program and also, like India, there was a debate within official circles about the wisdom of exercising the nuclear option.

The Dimona agreement was kept secret by the Ben-Gurion government for nearly three years and only revealed to the Israeli Knesset in 1960 after the United States formally asked the Israeli government to explain the purpose of the reactor. The reason for internal secrecy seemed to lie in the divisions within the political, scientific, and military leadership of the country regarding the need for a nuclear program. After the signing of the Dimona deal, seven of the eight members of the IAEC resigned, with only Dr. Bergmann, an avowed supporter of nuclear weapons, staying on. While no public explanation for these resignations was given, it is assumed that the military nature of the program led to the protest.[62] Two of these former members, in fact, went on to form a committee to bring about nuclear disarmament in the Middle East.

The political leadership was also divided on the issue of nuclear weapons and, it was these divisions which shaped Israel's nuclear policy. The supporters of nuclear weapons were Moshe Dayan and Shimon Peres who argued that it would enhance deterrence and insulate Israel's defense preparedness from possible future cuts in the defense budget.[63] The opponents of nuclear weapons included Yigal Allon and Yisrael Gallili, leaders of Achdut Ha'avodah, Mapai leaders Golda Meir and Pinhas Sapir and from Ben-Gurion's own party, Levi Eshkol. The latter believed that nuclear weapons were immoral, and in the years that he was finance minister had opposed the diversion of funds to the program. Further, Eshkol wanted to use the money to build up the nation's conventional military capability. Pinhas Lavon, Moshe Sharrett's defense minister, believed that the nuclear program was taking away much-needed money from the resettlement of European Jews in the country. The feeling in Israeli government circles was that "the project was an act of political adventurism which would unite the world against us."[64]

Gallili argued that Israel did not need nuclear weapons because its conventional superiority was not diminishing. Nuclearization would weaken the military by reallocating resources and hurting its self-image as the center of national security. More importantly, if Israel developed nuclear weapons the Arab countries would follow suit and this would take away whatever temporary advantage Israel had obtained by going nuclear. Nuclear weapons would also raise the incentive for a first strike because each side would fear that the other was preparing to do so.[65] Gallili also argued that the superpowers' ability to achieve nuclear deterrence could not be automatically transferred to the Middle East. The superpowers had a range of political interests that allowed them greater maneuverability in military conflict situations. The countries of the

Middle East lacked such flexibility and the nuclear trip wire would be triggered fairly quickly.[66]

Ben-Gurion accepted this argument and during his tenure as Prime Minister Israel strengthened its conventional forces and did not cross the nuclear threshold. While Israel's military strategy was not based on nuclear weapons, this was not an end to nuclear effort for, as Yair Evron writes, research and development continued in the field. While budgetary allocations for the program were reduced, the pro-nuclear camp was able to secure alternative funding from other sources and the construction of Dimona continued.[67]

External pressure on the program also arose with the change of governments in France. In 1958 Charles de Gaulle returned to power and in May 1960 his foreign minister informed the Israeli government that France had reconsidered the agreement. De Gaulle wanted Israel to lift the secrecy around the plant, open it to inspections, and declare the peaceful nature of the Israeli program. In November of that year a compromise was reached: The French government would end its direct involvement in the project, but French companies would be allowed to complete existing projects, including the reprocessing plant. In return, Ben-Gurion had to secretly pledge that Israel would not build nuclear weapons.[68] Further, de Gaulle's doubts did not stop French-Israeli collaboration in another crucial area—missile technology. As mentioned earlier, Israel contracted Dassault to build the Jericho missile, thereby pumping capital into the French aerospace industry.[69]

The French pressure on Israel was followed by the United States questioning the Ben-Gurion government about the purpose of Dimona. The Israeli reaction was to assert that the reactor was to be used for peaceful purposes, particularly the development of the Negev. The matter was taken up by the Kennedy administration, who wanted on-site inspections of the plant. Washington was concerned about proliferation in the region and wanted assurances from the Israeli government about the peaceful nature of the Israeli program. The Ben-Gurion government, in turn, could not afford an open fight with the Kennedy administration because it would severely jeopardize the relationship with the United States and it might wipe out the "tenuous support for the nuclear program within the party."[70] To help solve the problem the Israeli government allowed two American scientists to visit Dimona and they reported that no suspicious activities were taking place. Subsequently, in a meeting between Kennedy and Ben-Gurion, the American president stressed the United States's commitment to nonproliferation. He also suggested that the report of the two scientists be made public to the Arab states so as to reassure them about Israeli intentions.[71]

As Avner Cohen points out, the general tone of the meeting was vague. Kennedy did not ask about why Israel needed two research reactors or a plutonium separation plant. He did not seek an answer as to why the Dimona deal had been kept secret. Nor did he get a pledge from Ben-Gurion to not make nuclear weapons. Cohen believes the reason Kennedy did not put pressure on Israel was because he knew his political limits and the scientists' report had been favorable.[72]   Further inspections of the site continued under the Eshkol government, which agreed to an annual visit by U.S. scientists. In 1969, the visiting group complained that given the restrictions placed by the Israeli government the team could not guarantee that a weapons program was not being carried out. After 1969 no more visits were permitted.[73]

Thus, domestic and international pressures made Israel maintain a covert nuclear program. The official posture of the Israeli government during Eshkol's times on nuclear weapons became that "Israel would not be the first country to introduce nuclear weapons into the Middle East."[74] Since both the United States and Soviet Mediterranean fleets had nuclear weapons, this statement meant little except a reassurance to friends like the United States. But Cohen argues that the Eshkol government had a genuine commitment to not cross the nuclear threshold and while believing that Israel should prepare for the nuclear option took steps to reduce the program . Eshkol, thus canceled or postponed ambitious projects in the nuclear field proposed by Dr. Bergmann.[75] In actual fact however Israel's quest for nuclear weapons had paid off by 1966-1967, when it reportedly had enough plutonium for its first weapon.[76]

The subsequent decision to build a covert nuclear force resulted from the sense of isolation before the 1967 war, by a change in defense leadership, and by a change in the post-war strategic environment.[77] In the pre-war crisis Israel felt internationally isolated as the United States did not respond quickly to the Egyptian blockade of the Straits of Tiran. The French arms embargo once again brought home the need to be self-reliant. Further, in the post-war setting there was a change in defense leadership with Moshe Dayan getting a more influential role and this allowed him to incrementally move Israel's program from an option to a bomb in the basement.[78] The post-war strategic environment was seen as being a hostile one because there was no peace with the Arabs, and the Soviet Union had now entered the region.[79] Thus in the post-1967 period Israel built up its nuclear forces but refrained from a creating a public force and did not articulate a military strategy based on the use of nuclear weapons. Instead, not being the first to introduce weapons in the region remains the cornerstone of Israeli declaratory policy. The roots of this policy are similar to that of India, with international pressure making it too costly to go publicly nuclear.

1967–1991: THE AMERICAN PERIOD

The Six Day War of 1967 not only achieved a decisive military victory for Israel but also left it the occupier of a large chunk of Arab territory—the Sinai, the Golan Heights, and the West Bank. The acquisition of such territory was advantageous because it provided Israel with strategic depth, the advantage of physical barriers (the Suez Canal was an effective antitank ditch), a lead time for alerts, and several bargaining chips.[80] At the same time, the war also created new security problems for Israel. As part of the West Bank, Israel acquired a large and hostile Palestinian population that was to become the source of both security threats and political embarrassment. The Soviet Union increased its military and political commitment to the Arab states and the Arabs were unwilling to enter into political negotiations with the Israeli government.

Second, the success of the Israeli armed forces bred a sense of complacency in the strategy and force structure of the IDF. The IAF had decimated the Arab air forces on the ground and achieved complete air superiority by the end of the first day of the war. Israeli armor had made the deep thrusts into enemy territory in the Sinai and the Golan Heights. It was expected that the same formula for success would work in the next war. Consequently, the Israeli general staff was to ignore developments in the Egyptian and Syrian armed forces, particularly the acquisition of precision guided munitions.

Third, the threat Israel had to deter expanded significantly and was complicated by systemic factors. In the past, the threat had consisted of encroachments on Israeli territory, naval blockades, and outright warfare. After 1967, the lower end of the threat scenario included guerrilla warfare in the occupied territories and international terrorism. Middle-range threats included continued attrition warfare with the Arab states, while the upper end of the spectrum included the possibility of the Arab states developing their own nuclear capability or being covered by a Soviet military canopy. Coupled with the increase in threats was the détente process between the two superpowers. This created a situation in which the superpowers at times had a commonalty of interests in the Middle East. Such a mutuality of interests could work against Israeli strategy in the region.

Fourth, Israel continued to face a spiraling arms race in the region as both the Egyptian and Syrian armed forces were reequipped with more advanced Soviet weaponry. The race to maintain a qualitative edge over the Arab states is seen in the changing composition of the Israeli force structure between 1967 and 1973. In 1967, the IAF had an aging fleet of 460 French combat aircraft— Fouga-Magister, Ouragan, Mystere, Vautour, and the Mirage III. By 1973 the IAF was reequipped with 432 American F-4 Phantoms and A-4 Skyhawk fighter-bombers. The army in 1967 had close to 1,000 tanks, 250 cannons, and 50 antiaircraft batteries. By 1973 its force level had increased to 1,700 tanks, 1,000 armored personnel carriers, 352 artillery pieces and 48 antiaircraft batteries. The navy was to reequip with new submarines, missile boats and a destroyer.[81]

The 1967 war had brought home the threat posed by supplier embargoes as the French terminated military assistance to Israel. This, in combination with other factors, led to the growth of the Israeli arms industry. The post-1967 growth of the Israeli arms industry is impressive. Naftali Blumenthal cites figures to show that investments in the industrial sector were 2.5 times greater in 1968 than in 1967, and by 1972 they were greater by a multiple of 3.5.[82] The impact of this growth was visible as the arms industry quadrupled its output between 1967 and 1970, and the number of people employed by the arms industry rose by 20,000.[83] Further, the French embargo forced the Israeli government to ask the arms industry to produce major weapons systems for the armed forces. IAI was to produce the Nesher, a reverse engineered copy of the Mirage V, and later to put a new engine and electronics in the aircraft and call it the Kfir. Based on the combat experience of the Israeli armed forces, the arms industry also began to develop a new tank—the Merkava.[84] Arms exports also increased substantially. While weapons sales had constituted 14 percent of the country's exports in 1967, they made up 31 percent of exports by 1975.[85]

There were several reasons behind the rapid growth of the arms industry. The French embargo created the renewed desire for arms independence. The economic recession of 1965-1967 had created large-scale unemployment and emigration. To overcome these trends the government decided to jump start the economy by investing in industrial growth—most notably the defense industry. This policy was facilitated by the territorial acquisitions in the 1967 war because Israel now had a large supply of Arab labor. This allowed the release of skilled Jewish labor to enter the arms industry. The strengthening of relations with the United States provided both the financial and technological input needed to build up the arms industry.[86] Also, the production of arms and their subsequent export were viewed as reducing the nation's trade deficit and providing economies of scale for domestic procurement efforts.[87]

In this period the armed forces, which had traditionally supported the import of weaponry, also called for the indigenous development of weapons. The shift in the attitude of the armed forces took place for security, personal incentive, and financial reasons. The French embargo, Britain's reneging on the supply of next-generation Chieftain tanks, and the United States's reluctance in the period 1967-1969 to provide the type and quantities of weapons Israel required on favorable terms and conditions, made the IDF amenable to domestic production efforts. This was particularly the case with the decision to develop the Merkava tank, which resulted from the cancellation of the Chieftain deal and the United States's reluctance to sell the more advanced version of the M-60 tank. Personal incentive, as Gerald Steinberg writes, came from the growing number of military officers who retired from the armed forces and then took up positions in the burgeoning arms industry.[88] The availability of financial resources also helped shift financial attitudes. After U.S. economic and military aid started flowing to Israel, the armed forces could, as Reiser puts it, have their cake and eat it too. U.S. aid allowed for the delivery of advanced weapons within short time frames. This created, Reiser believes, a willingness within the IDF to allow the development of long-range domestic weapons programs.[89]

Finally, it needs to be pointed out that while Israel's defense expenditure was escalating, it was also trying to maintain personal consumption levels. Thus the strategy of guns and butter was not abandoned despite the need for higher spending on national security.

The growth in the arms industry and the subsequent spectacular record of arms exports paint the picture of an Israeli national security system that was able to indigenously cater to its defense needs and to develop the means for power projection. In actual fact, despite the growth of Israel's military industry, the post-1967 period saw Israel bear a far greater economic burden for the costs of militarization and develop a higher level of military dependence on its external supplier, the United States.

SUPPLIERS AND RESOURCES: THE UNITED STATES

After the 1967 war the United States became the principal supplier of economic and military assistance to Israel, and this influenced the course its force structure and arms industry took. First, as Israel's new armorer, the United States provided the weaponry to modernize and subsequently retain a qualitative edge over the Arab armed forces. Thus, as mentioned earlier, by the 1973 war, Israel had modernized its air force, one of the crucial arms of its preemptive deep strike strategy, with American Phantom and Skyhawk aircraft. The impact of U.S. military assistance can be seen by the fact that of the $4.03 billion worth of arms Israel imported between 1966-1975, $3.85 billion was imported from the United States.[90] Second, the United States facilitated the development of the arms industry through technological collaboration. In 1971, the United States and Israel signed an agreement for technological collaboration in defense production. Third, the inflow of American arms allowed for the export of older weapons in the Israeli stockpile. Israel was, for example, able to sell seventy-eight fighter and six trainer aircraft of French origin in Latin America between 1970 and 1980.[91] But the new military relationship with the United States also had its down side. Israel developed a dependence on the United States for critical technologies like engines—for the Merkava and the Kfir—radars, and electronics. This dependence was later to hurt Israeli arms export efforts as it gave the United States a veto over potential arms sales.

Thus, by the time the 1973 war took place Israel's military industry had expanded and become a major part of the industrial sector of the nation. By 1973 the United States had also become Israel's principal provider of foreign aid and the armorer of its armed forces. But while the inflow of weapons and assistance from the United States provided Israel with a guaranteed supplier of weaponry and the ability to create a domestic arms industry, it was unable to halt the escalation of military expenditure. Instead, through the 1970s and the early 1980s military expenditure was to keep growing, and this posed a major economic burden on Israel.

THE BURDENS OF MILITARIZATION

The 1973 war began badly for Israel, as Egypt and Syria were able to launch surprise attacks and breach Israel's static defenses. The use of Soviet surface-to-air missiles (SAMs) and precision guided munitions exacted a heavy toll on the IAF as well as on the armored forces. Israeli scholars also point out that the military relationship with the United States made Israel politically vulnerable. Alex Mintz and Gerald Steinberg argue that American political pressure prevented Israel from carrying out a preemptive strike despite evidence of a major buildup of Egyptian and Syrian armed forces and the vulnerability of Israeli forward positions—especially the Bar-Lev line.[92] The United States in the early part of the war was also slow to provide replacement weaponry and spare parts to the IDF. It did so only after it was able to extract an Israeli willingness to enter into a ceasefire. By the end of the war, however, the Israeli armed forces had regrouped, captured the western bank of Suez, and encircled the Egyptian Third Army.

The postwar threat environment was a complex one. On the one hand the military threat from Egypt diminished. Anwar Sadat had dismissed his Soviet military advisors in 1972 and terminated the military link with Moscow after the war. Egypt thus held a large inventory of Soviet weaponry but lacked the spares to maintain and operate these weapons (this led to efforts to seek spares first from India and to later have European firms reverse-engineer parts). The impact of the break with the Soviets can be seen by the dip in Egypt's weapons procurement levels. The Stockholm International Peace Research Institute (SIPRI) estimates show that in the period 1971-1975, Egypt was the second-largest importer of weapons in the developing world with purchases of $10.5 billion. For the period 1976-1980, however, arms imports shrank to $2.9 billion.[93]

At the domestic level, Egypt's economy was in a crisis and governmental efforts to remove subsidies and create a more realistic price structure resulted in the famous bread riots of 1976. Recognizing that Egypt's future economic health and military security lay in peace with Israel and a linkage with the United States, Sadat initiated peace talks with Israel. The subsequent signing of the Camp David accords, which were brought about mainly through the diplomatic skills of the Carter administration, locked Egypt into a military and economic assistance deal with the United States and removed Cairo from Israel's threat perceptions.

Although Egypt was neutralized, the Syrian military was able to rebuild after the 1973 war as the Soviet Union rearmed the country and upgraded its weaponry. Syrian arms imports declined in the mid-1970s because war losses had been amply replaced with more modern equipment. But Soviet arms transfers to Syria increased once again in the late 1970s and peaked in 1982 when equipment losses from the Lebanon war were quickly replaced.[94]

Also, by the late 1970s and early 1980s, potential threats emerged from nations that had hitherto been in the background of the Arab-Israel conflict. The hike in oil prices allowed the Gulf states to rapidly militarize as the West sought to recycle petrodollars. The most ambitious effort in the mid-1970s was made by the Shah of Iran, who sought overnight to create modern air, ground, and naval forces for his country: "The procurement program of the Iranian armed forces comprised new fighter aircraft, a large helicopter fleet, a blue water navy, air defense systems, tanks and artillery. In addition there was an extensive program to build up a modern arms industry."[95] During the Shah's reign, Iran continued its political and military relationship with Israel, but after the Islamic revolution Israel faced a new enemy in the region. The Islamic regime, however, immediately canceled most of the arms import programs, and after the U.S. embassy was attacked the United States and its allies stopped arms sales to Iran.[96]

The availability of oil money also funded the modernization efforts of Saudi Arabia and Iraq. Iraq was the largest importer of weapons in the period 1971-1985 in the Middle East, and it had over thirty countries as suppliers.[97] It also started its own missile and nuclear weapons programs.

Saudi Arabia's oil money allowed it to build up one of the most advanced armed forces in the Third World. Until 1970 Saudi Arabia had had a modest and ill-equipped military force. By the mid-1970s, in response to Iran's military modernization efforts, Saudi Arabia began its own weapons procurement program. It acquired F-15 fighters, AWACS, and the Shahine Air Defense System from the United States, and the U.S. Army corp of engineers constructed an extensive defense infrastructure in the country. The difficulty in getting weapons sales approved through the U.S. Congress as well as Saudi fears of becoming overly dependent on American weapons also prompted diversification efforts by Riyadh. By the mid-1980s, over 25 percent of Saudi Arabia's weaponry was of French origin and, when refused more F-15s by Congress, which determined its veto at least partly due to Israeli protests and lobbying efforts, purchased Tornado interceptor and ground-attack aircraft from Britain.[98] Israel's effort to block the F-15 sale backfired because the Tornado was a more capable aircraft for the purpose of carrying out long range strikes against Israel. Thus, the Israeli response was to draw another red line in the sand by warning Saudi Arabia that basing the Tornados in the northern part of the country would be viewed as a threat to Israeli security and provoke retaliation.

The 1970s, therefore, saw both the removal of Egypt as a threat and the rise of newer threats in the form of Iraq, Iran, and potentially Saudi Arabia. By the 1980s the ability of nations like Saudi Arabia and Iraq to buy Western weaponry heightened Israel's security dilemma. As Ahron Klieman and Reuven Pedatzur argued, Israel's edge over the Arab states was obtained in part by the qualitative superiority of its Western-supplied weapons systems. By the late 1980s, however, this edge was eroded, if not eliminated, as the Arab countries were able to obtain state-of-the-art Western arms on a commercial basis. This led to the fear that in some areas, such as airborne early warning, the Arab states—more particularly Saudi Arabia—had a better capability than Israel.[99]

When this qualitative buildup was combined with ongoing defensive preparations—like Syria's efforts to continue improving its air defense system after the 1982 war and its massive ground fortifications along the Israeli border—it was feared that it would blunt the edge of Israel's deep-strike strategy in a future war.[100] By the late 1980s the Middle East arms race also entered a new dimension as Saudi Arabia and Syria had acquired surface-to-surface missiles and Iraq's own missile program had given it the capability to launch attacks on Israel.

Supplier constraints continued to pose a problem for Israel, though this concern seems to have been exaggerated. The United States, as Israel's principal weapons supplier, constricted the supply of weapons on several occasions in order to obtain Israeli compliance with U.S. political goals. Weapons transfers were restricted in 1974 to get the withdrawal of Israeli forces from the Sinai. The transfer of F-16 fighters was halted after the bombing of the Iraqi nuclear reactor in 1981. Arms deliveries were also halted or delayed after the annexation of the Golan Heights and the Israeli invasion of Lebanon.[101] These supplier restraints were used in part to justify the initiation of major weapons development projects like the Merkava, the Kfir, and later the Lavi.

These concerns are exaggerated because Israel's arsenal grew qualitatively in the period under question, as both the army and the air force were able to modernize their inventories with U.S.-supplied weapons. Further, there was a continuing lobby in the Israeli government which called for reducing costly indigenous programs and instead using the money to buy weapons abroad. These issues are discussed in the next section.

THE RISE OF DOMESTIC PRODUCTION

The growth of the arms industry continued through most of the 1970s and 1980s as economic, political, and strategic factors pushed for its development. At the same time, the Israeli government was locked in a continuing arms transfers relationship with the United States. The strategic push for the arms industry came from both the continuing arms race with the Arab states as well as from the need to avoid supplier embargoes.

The 1973 war created a need for what Zeev Bonen has called "niche filling." Bonen's argument is that gaps (shortcomings) exist in the various niches of the IDF. Such niches are different types of military conflicts—air to air, air to ground, ship to ship. There are a number of problems with niche filling. Filling the niche may evoke a response that creates a new niche.[102] Developing a standoff missile with a range of twenty kilometers may lead the enemy to buy countersystems that can operate from a greater range, thus creating a new niche. The filling of a niche may also lead to the demand for systems to support it. Purchasing an aircraft carrier requires the procurement of an expensive support fleet. For Israel, the filling of a niche in the 1970s and 1980s only led to the creation of new ones due to the modernization of the Arab armed forces.

The 1973 war exposed several gaps in the different niches. Israel's dependence on air power and armor had left it critically short in the area of field artillery and mobile infantry. Thus when the IAF started losing significant numbers of aircraft to Egyptian SAM coverage, the IDF lacked the artillery to provide support to its ground forces. Similarly, the overemphasis on armored thrusts had left the infantry without a rapid and protected means of transport. While Israel was eventually able to prevail, the high personnel and materiel costs of the war dictated changes in the Israeli force structure.

The army acquired new armored personnel carriers to provide greater mobility to the infantry. Field artillery was imported and local production also commenced. The air force sought better aircraft but also bowed to the need for electronic countermeasures (ECM) and standoff weapons. It also acquired the Grumman Hawkeye AWACS to track low-flying aircraft. The air transport wing was also expanded as a result of the problems encountered in the 1973 war. The navy shifted its strategy from coastal protection to a long-range fleet that would protect Israel's shipping lanes. As always, its status as the poor cousin of the Israeli armed forces led it to seek indigenous solutions to its demand for weaponry. It commissioned the development of the Dabur class long-range naval vessels and of the Gabriel Mk.2 antiship missile. The latter was to have a range of 40 kilometers and would thereby allow Israeli boats to remain out of the missile range of enemy vessels.[103]

As mentioned in the previous section, the United States was to use the constriction of arms sales on several occasions to pressure Israel into accepting its diplomatic goals in the region and, not surprisingly, this met with the Israeli determination to seek independence through local production. The bureaucratic battle in this area was waged between those who felt that indigenous arms production should cover the design and development of big-ticket items like tanks and aircraft, and was opposed by those who believed that Israel should import systems and improve them at home.

The indigenous production lobby was headed by Shimon Peres, who served as defense minister in the 1970s and as the prime minister in the Labor-Likud power sharing agreement of the mid-1980s. It also included Moshe Arens, who was the chief engineer for IAI in the mid-1970s and defense minister in the 1980s. Peres and Arens argued that the economic costs of indigenous production were far outweighed by the technological advantages and independence from supplier restraints such projects provided. Opposed to the development of such programs was a lobby that included, most notably, Yitzhak Rabin. Rabin had played an important role in the Israeli national security process since the mid-1960s: first as chief of staff, then as Ambassador to the United States, prime minister, defense minister, and once again prime minister. Rabin's argument was that the Israeli economy could not bear the expense of major weapons programs—tanks, aircraft—and, instead, he recommended the purchasing stripped down systems from the United States and subsequently customizing them to match Israeli requirements.[104] Such a process would have played to the Israeli arms industry's strong points of retrofitting and installing modern electronics. Rabin's stand was consistent on this issue since he opposed the development of the Merkava in the 1970s and later the Lavi in the 1980s. But it was the views of the indigenous production lobby that won out on both the Merkava and later the Lavi. The strategic factors argument is, however, insufficient to explain this decision. One needs to also look at the economic situation and the growing influence of the Israeli arms industry within the country's economy.

Klieman and Pedatzur suggest four reasons explaining the arms industry's influence and ability to continue receiving projects: (1) the extensive network of personal ties between industry managers, IDF, and MOD officials; (2) the political and economic power wielded by the industry as one of Israel's largest employers; (3) the fact that more than half of the defense industry is government owned; and (4) that the military industries have a monopoly on local project data.[105]

The process whereby retired IDF officers started moving into the arms industry gained momentum in the 1970s and 1980s. General David Ivri of the IAF, for example, was to become the head of IAI after retirement and was subsequently to be appointed in charge of weapons procurement policy at the MOD. Air force commanders Benny Peled and Mordechai Hod went on to head the computer firm Elbit and chair the IAI board respectively.[106] Klieman and Pedatzur argue that, "Given such close ties between military leaders, industry leaders and senior officers in the IDF and the MOD, decisions concerning military industrial development may not always be influenced only by 'pure' military, economic and political considerations, but also by a very specific industrial lobby."[107]

Economic and employment considerations have also driven the funding of new weapons projects. The Israeli government's investment in industry, particularly the arms industry, after the 1967 war helped to jump-start the economy from the recession of 1965-1967. Investment in this sector was continued after the 1973 war, as it was one of the most productive sources for Israeli exports; industrial exports rose from about 75 percent of total exports in 1967 to about 85 percent by 1980. It is estimated that Israeli arms exports constituted 6 percent of total industrial exports in 1967. By 1974 the share had risen to ten percent and by 1977 it had risen to twenty-five percent.[108] By the mid-1980s the arms industry had also become one of the largest employers in the country with close to 20 percent of the industrial workforce engaged in the weapons production process. For a society that had a commitment to high employment levels and social welfare such a group would be difficult to ignore.

Coupled with the economic considerations was the fact that the arms industry had become a major export earner for the country. Klieman and Pedatzur cite the following figures for Israeli weapons exports: $14 million in 1967, $68 million in 1970, $72 million in 1972, $200 million in 1974, $1200 million in 1980, $1400 million in 1984, and $1700 million in 1989.[109] Thus the arms industry was a major export earner even as Israel's import surplus continued to grow, it external debt increased and its debt servicing continued to expand.

The political economy of weapons production in Israel also dictated the channeling of funds into the defense industry. The fact that the bulk of these industries—and certainly the largest employers—were government owned meant that they had to be given contracts to maintain employment and profitability levels. Further, as is the advantage with any local arms industry, it was able to manipulate data to serve its interests. Perhaps the best case of the arms industry's capability to push through a project, and the economic crisis that developed from it, was the Lavi project.

THE LAVI

The failure of the Lavi project best exemplifies the constraints facing the Israeli arms industry and, more importantly, the constraints Israel faced as a regional power in the international system. The project was initiated not primarily with a specific threat in mind, but to forward the agenda of the largest Israeli armaments company, IAI. It was made feasible by large grants from the United States, and was later terminated due to escalating costs and other constraints.

By the mid-1970s IAI's work on the Kfir series was winding down and the company was looking for a follow-on project both to keep the assembly lines open and the company's engineering and design staff employed. In 1974, IAI proposed the development of a next-generation fighter to the then defense minister, Shimon Peres, who agreed that IAI use 200 million Israeli shekels of its discretionary funds to start research into the project. The rest of the Israeli cabinet was not informed of the project. At the same time, Israel was purchasing F-16s from the United States and seeking other aircraft for its air fleet. The IAI argument became that the country should purchase a mix of the F-16 and an indigenous fighter. By 1978, Ezer Weizman, the Likud Defense Minister, agreed to allowing 200 engineers to work on the project even though there was no cabinet approval of the project. The IAF did not lobby for the Lavi because it was "cool" toward the project. The Finance Ministry, similarly, opposed the project because of its high financial costs.[110]

The plane was originally conceived as a low cost and small aircraft which was to be powered by the General Electric F-404 engine and would be a low technology back up to Israel's fleet of F-15 and F-16 fighters.[111]   450 aircraft were to be built and would complement an air fleet spearheaded by American fighter aircraft. In February 1980 the government ratified the project but in 1981 the IAF raised objections stating that the plane did not fit its requirements. The IAF demanded substantial changes to make the plane a multi-role aircraft with longer range and a greater complement of armaments.[112]   A new and more powerful engine, the Pratt and Whitney 1120, composite materials, and state of the art avionics were added to make the plane the equivalent of the F-16.[113]

A feasibility study was ordered in 1981 by the new Defense Minister, Ariel Sharon, and based on the study the "big" Lavi was given a final go-ahead. The report was, however, written within the defense ministry rather than by independent sources. This led to an underassessment of the unit cost of the Lavi compared to the F-16 as well as an exaggeration of the absorptive capacity of the IAF. The report stated that the IAF would buy over 400 aircraft but, as the subsequent State Comptroller's investigation showed, the IAF's realistic absorptive capability was around 200 to 210 aircraft.[114]

The Lavi project was thus started without a clear assessment of the costs or of the market potential of the aircraft. Not surprisingly the project started to run into trouble very early. The first problem was the escalating cost. In 1980 the Lavi's original program estimate was around $1.06 billion. The figure rapidly escalated, as can be seen by the following figures. In October 1981 the estimate rose to $1.27 billion. One year later it was $1.77 billion. By July of 1986 the figure had reached $2.57 billion.[115]

The development of the Lavi was also heavily dependent on financial assistance from the United States. In 1984 the Reagan administration agreed to allocate $250 million from its foreign military sales (FMS) for the development of the Lavi. This commitment was to grow over the next three years: in FY 1984 the United States allocated $550 million for the development of the Lavi, in FY 1985 it was $400 million and it allocate a further $800 million for FY 1986 and FY 1987.[116] Despite the infusion of U.S. capital the Lavi was too expensive a program for the Israeli government. Continuation of the program would have required diverting funds from other projects to develop the airplane. Ambitious naval plans, for example, rested on the Lavi's developmental budget being capped. Similarly, work on the Arrow antiballistic missile would have had to be cut back to fund the Lavi.[117]

Another reason the Lavi's cost kept escalating was that the plane had to be repeatedly modified to satisfy the changing requirements of IAF pilots. In an interview the then head of IAI, Moshe Keret, explained how these demands hurt the project,

The pilots, he noted, wanted a wide range of capabilities in the Lavi and IAI tried to engineer virtually all of these into the aircraft, sometimes without regard for whether doing so significantly increased the aircraft's capability or whether the cost of incorporating the requirements was greater than desired.[118]

This led to a paradoxical situation because the Lavi was supposed to provide Israel with an advanced technological base and technological independence. In fact the reverse was happening because the program was taking away resources—both in terms of scarce capital and skilled labor—from other industries where advanced technology was being developed. Further, by the mid-1980s, Israel's comparative advantage in weapons production lay not in the manufacture of advanced platforms but in the development of the systems which had been added on to them. Thus the Israeli arms industry had become a competitive manufacturer of radars, ECM and EW equipment, missiles and military medical equipment. The Lavi's development was eating into the future growth in these areas. The plane was also heavily dependent on U.S. technological assistance. Yitzhak Rabin stated that 45 percent of the Lavi was to be built in the United States and 730 companies were to be involved in its manufacture.[119]

There was also pressure from the United States to terminate the program. The escalating costs of the Lavi worried Pentagon officials, who believed that the program was becoming infeasible and hurting Israel's defense efforts. General Accounting Office (GAO) and Pentagon studies disputed the Israeli government's estimated unit price of $14.5 million. The GAO estimated $17.8 million while the Defense and State Departments, the Office of Management and Budget, and the National Security Council put the price at $22.1 million.[120] At such prices the Lavi was significantly more expensive than the F-16, while not providing a major technological advancement over the American aircraft. Further, U.S. officials pointed out that by 1990 the Lavi would consume nearly half of the military assistance package given to Israel. They also warned that military assistance levels would not increase substantially in the future and that money would have to be taken from other military programs, or military readiness accounts, to bring the Lavi to fruition.[121]

What eventually killed the Lavi, however, was the breakdown of the bureaucratic coalition that had allowed the project to be initiated. As the Lavi became an unpromising program the American government announced that it was willing to allow the use of Lavi FMS funds for other weapons programs within Israel. This led the makers of the Merkava tank, Israel Shipyards, and the army and navy to form a coalition against the program.[122] Further, even the end user of the Lavi, the IAF, sought the aircraft's termination because of the availability of cheap F-16s from the United States. Thus the Lavi was terminated in 1987.

The failure of the Lavi program highlighted the problems Israel faced by the late 1980s in developing its military arsenal. At a time when globally the national production of arms was becoming an increasingly difficult task, Israel was seeking to develop indigenously a state-of-the-art fighter. Yet it had severe financial constraints and a limited market. As a regional power the cost of bringing a major weapons platform to fruition was beyond Israel's financial limits. The Israelis were made to learn the lesson that economic strength goes hand in glove with the development of a significant and indigenous defense capability.

The project also exemplified the dependence Israel's government and armed forces had developed on the financial largesse of the United States—an issue discussed more elaborately later in this chapter. The aircraft was dependent on both technological inputs and subsidies from the United States. The growth of the domestic arms industry was in some ways counterproductive for Israel. As a major export earner, it created a national constituency that could not be ignored for technological and employment reasons. While the failure of the Lavi terminated the development of big ticket items in the arms industry, it led to a reemphasis on the areas where Israel had acquired strengths—in the production of secondary systems like electronics and small arms and ammunition. But even the strength of the secondary areas could not counter the crisis the Israeli arms industry faced by the late 1980s.

As mentioned earlier, the Israeli arms industry became a major exporter of weapons in the 1980s with annual sales of over a billion dollars. The success of such sales mask the difficulties the arms industry faces. Despite the touted technological advances of the arms industry, the bulk of these sales were of small arms and ammunitions and the refurbishment of older systems. The Merkava and the Kfir were never export successes due to both their own shortcomings and restraints imposed by the United States, which supplied the power plants on both systems. As far as the transfer of major weapons systems goes, the stratification among international arms producers has not changed over the past two decades—the major suppliers still sell the high-technology major systems and account for over 90 percent of international arms sales. Further, Israel's success in arms exports was also the result of a successful sales strategy targeted at states which for political-military reasons could not obtain weapons from the major suppliers. It also began at a time when Israel was one of few non-western countries exporting weapons. Arms sales to South Africa were possible because of the growing resistance to apartheid in the early 1970s, which culminated in the UN arms embargo of 1977. Sales to China were possible because Beijing required a supplier who could refurbish the large amount of Soviet-origin weapons in its arsenal. Arms sales to Taiwan took place at a time when Taipei was being ostracized by the international community. Finally, the sales to authoritarian regimes such as Zaire, El Salvador, and Honduras were made at a time when these nations were being shunned internationally for their human rights policies.

In the post-Cold War international system old pariah states like South Africa and Taiwan have become full-fledged members of the global community, removing the need for a third-tier supplier like Israel. The number of weapons producers has also increased, and with it competition for the low technology systems Israel provides has grown. Israeli arms companies complain that while in the past they faced two to three international competitors for the weapons they produced, they now have to deal with twenty odd firms.[123]

Even as the international arms market is becoming difficult to sell in, the Israeli arms industry has been put in the position where it has to depend on exports. The IDF drew up a multi-year plan in the early 1990s that called for a shift to increasingly sophisticated weapons systems. At the same time the IDF, due to Israel's economic crisis, was emerging from a decade which saw the slashing of defense expenditure. As budgets declined—with arms expenditure dropping from over 20 percent of GNP in the early 1980s to around 10 percent by the early 1990s—the IDF decided to use its sparse resources to purchase proven systems from abroad rather than depend on indigenously designed systems. Further, the quick shift in the technological balance caused by Arab weapons imports from the West led to the demand for advanced Western systems. Thus IDF purchases from the arms industry continued to decline through the 1980s. In 1985, 45 percent of the arms budget went to domestic procurement, but by 1989 the figure had fallen to 28 percent. IAI, the largest defense employer, had domestic sales of $440 million in 1987, with the figure dropping to about $260-270 million by 1989.[124] Naturally this placed crucial importance on raising export levels. These cutbacks in spending affected employment in the arms industry. The Lavi cancellation led to the laying off of approximately 22,000 defense industry workers in the country. Similarly, IMI, Israel's second largest defense employer, was to shrink its workforce from a 1985 high of 14,600 to 9,000 by 1991.[125] From both a military and an employment perspective such cutbacks created vulnerability in the Israeli system.

The changes in the global arms market have not only led to cutbacks in the Israeli arms industry but also to a shift in what is being produced and being purchased. Israel's arms industry has moved toward the manufacture of subcomponents and refurbishment of older systems because there is a thriving market of cash starved countries which require such products and services. Israeli defense contractors are now providing upgrades for ex-Soviet aircraft, particularly MiGs. India is one country which has sought Israeli assistance to upgrade both its MiGs and its T-72 tanks.[126]

US AID AND THE DOMESTIC ECONOMY

In the 1970s and 1980s Israel, despite its success on the battlefield and growth in indigenous weapons production, became increasingly dependent on the United States for military assistance. U.S. assistance took four forms: the transfer of modern weapons systems and the signing of technology transfer agreements; subsidizing Israeli defense production efforts by allowing FMS money to be spent on the development of Israeli weapons systems; offsets and purchases from the arms industry helped raise Israel's defense exports; and the provision of grants to subsidize Israeli defense expenditure and allow for the utilization of domestically generated capital for indigenous programs. What this section will try to show, however, is that the inflow of American military assistance could not stop Israel's economic crisis—and the role high militarization levels played in it—from worsening. In fact, Israel, through the 1970s and 1980s, had to shoulder a high militarization burden which in part led to a worsening external debt, spiraling inflation, and lower economic standards.

The United States's primary role since the early 1970s has been that of a weapons supplier for Israel. The extent of U.S. military assistance can be seen in the large number of U.S. weapons in the Israeli inventory, despite the existence of an indigenous arms industry. By early 1993, the IAF inventory included 112 McDonnell-Douglas Phantoms, 47 MD F-15 Eagles, 149 General Dynamics F16 Falcons, 121 MD A-4 Skyhawks and 95 Kfirs (another 75 Kfirs were estimated to be in storage). Its fleet of nearly 100 attack helicopters were entirely of U.S. origin.[127] U.S. weapons supplies, therefore, accounted for over 80 percent of the air force's arsenal. Thus, the Kfir, which most Israeli accounts describe as a successful combat proven aircraft, was at best a second-line aircraft in the Israeli arsenal with the IAF depending heavily on American imports.

Also, Israel's AEW capability was significantly enhanced through the import of Grumman E-2C Hawkeyes.

In the army the position was better because successful Israeli upgrades of the British Centurion and the domestic production of the Merkava composed about one-third of Israel's 4,500 tanks of non-American origin. But in the areas of air defense and armored personnel carriers the dependence on the U.S. was heavy—with Israel possessing around 5,900 U.S. made APCs. Israel was successfully able to reduce the dependence in field artillery, mortars, and antitank weapons with both indigenous and captured weaponry.

The navy as the poor cousin of the armed forces—because of the lower level of threat emanating from the maritime front—was paradoxically in the best position since the bulk of its missile craft was locally produced. But the weapons systems on these vessels as well as the naval electronics depended on U.S. supplies. By the 1990s Israel had a powerful military arsenal, but it was largely American in origin.

Equally useful to Israel was a series of agreements signed since the early 1970s which allowed it to enter into technology transfer and collaboration agreements with the U.S. and permitted the use of American military assistance for the purchase of domestically manufactured systems. These included:

1. A 1971 agreement to allow production of American weapons in Israel.
2. The granting of permission in 1979 to Israeli companies to bid on Pentagon projects.
3. The establishment in 1981 of a Defense Trade Initiative to enhance Israel's defense production.
4. A 1983 agreement whereby Israel was allowed to use up to 15 percent of FMS funds to purchase Israeli-produced systems and Jerusalem to obtain offsets for the purchases made with FMS funds.[128]

Such agreements were beneficial to Israel in a number of ways. The infusion of U.S. capital permitted the initiation and development of major programs like the Lavi and the Merkava. The fact that Israeli firms were allowed to bid on Pentagon contracts not only gave the arms industry access to the lucrative U.S. market but also permitted the establishment of joint ventures with U.S. firms—the latter allowing Israel greater access to modern U.S. technology. An increasing number of Israeli firms are setting up such joint companies with U.S. firms in order to survive in the adverse international arms market.[129]

But despite the infusion of external capital Israel's militarization has been excessive for the country, leading to cutbacks in spending in the mid-1980s. The 1973 war and its political consequences imposed a heavy economic burden on the nation. The war resulted in the Arab oil embargo and the fourfold increase in oil prices. For Israel the oil shock imposed a heavy economic burden on the country and by 1980 it had to spend about 10 to 11 percent of its GNP annually on oil. Coupled with the rise in oil prices was the escalation in defense expenditure with Israel spending approximately 25 percent of its GNP on defense in the 1970s (Table 3.1).

Table 3.1
Israeli Defense Expenditure as a Percentage of GNP, 1964–92

Year(s)	Total	Domestic
1964-66	10	6
1967	18	10
1968-69	19	12
1970	25	14
1971-72	22	14
1973-75	33	17
1976-78	27	15
1979-80	24	15
1980-84	19.9	14.3
1985-87	16.6	11.7
1988	16.2	10.4
1989	13.6	10.2
1990	13.5	9.9
1991	13	8.9
1992	11.5	8.5

Source: Bank of Israel Annual Reports, 1980, p. 92, 1987, p. 63, and 1992, p. 107. (Total includes loans, grants, and available hard currency).

Table 3.2
Israel: Annual Rise in Rate of Inflation, 1970–92

Year	Rise in %
1970-73	15.4
1974-78	41.2
1979-82	118.9
1983	190.7
1984	444.9
1985	185.2
1986	19.7
1987-89	18.8
1990-92	16

Source: Bank of Israel Annual Reports, 1987 p. 31, and 1992 p. 6.

Commenting on these twin pressures the Bank of Israel said in its annual report that even though Israel received grants and loans from the United States to help finance the defense budget, "Even excluding such aid, the defense share of GNP that is financed by the domestic economy is extremely large and

has no equal in other Western countries."[130] The report went on to say that the
heavy burden placed by the oil import bill,

has rendered the defense burden more onerous than in the past. *It is difficult for the
Israeli economy to renew its growth, reduce its dependence on American aid, and at the
same time maintain the current trend in military spending* (emphasis added).[131]

The Israeli government was acknowledging that guns and butter were
competing claims in the economy and that economic growth had to be
regenerated. There were obvious indicators for concern about this in the 1970s
and 1980s. Inflation started spiraling in the 1980s, reaching a high of 444
percent in 1985 (See Table 3.2). Israel's external debt also started to rise going
from $6.4 billion in 1975 to a high of $19.7 billion in 1984 (See Table 3.3).

Table 3.3
Israel's External Debt and Annual Debt Service Amount, 1975–92
($ billion)

Year	Net Debt	Debt Service Amount
1975	6.4	n.a.
1976	8.1	1.03
1977	9.5	1.1
1978	10.9	1.3
1979	12.8	1.4
1980	14.1	1.7
1981	n.a.	n.a.
1982	15.6	2.02
1983	18.3	2.02
1984	19.7	2.8
1985	19.3	2.9
1986	19.2	3.2
1987	19.2	3.2
1988	18.6	3.4
1989	16.3	2.9
1990	15.7	3.3
1991	15.5	2.6
1992	15.1	2.9

Source: Bank of Israel Annual Reports, 1980 p. 219, 1987 p. 2, and 1992
p. 112. (n.a. is not available)

From the mid-1980s the external debt did not fall below $15 billion,
and debt accounted for over 50 percent of the GNP between 1984–1987 (See
Table 3.4). Israel was reaching such high levels of military spending and debt
even while the U.S. was continuing to generously fund the Israeli militarization
effort. Moshe Efrat's study of the US-Israeli military link shows that between

1970-85 Israel's total defense expenditure was $60.8 billion. Of this $17.6 billion was in non-repayable grants from the United States. So over 25 percent of Israel's defense expenditure was subsidized by the United States, yet this did not soften the domestic impact of defense spending.[132] Clearly there had to be cutbacks. The Israeli government took the first steps in 1985 when it introduced an anti-inflation program, and for the latter part of the 1980s defense expenditure was cut, going down from about 14 percent of the GNP (for domestic defense expenditure) between 1980-84 to 8.5 percent of the GNP in 1992 (Table 3.1).

Table 3.4
Israel's External Debt and Debt Service as a % of GNP

Year	Net Debt as % of GNP	Net Debt Service as % of GNP
1977-81	61	n.a.
1982-83	64	8.5
1984	77	12
1985	81	13
1986	65	12
1987	55	9
1988	43	8
1989	37	7
1990	29	6
1991	26	5
1992	23	5

Source: Bank of Israel Annual Reports, 1987 p. 207, 1988 p. 182, and 1992 p. 113.

As mentioned earlier, such cutbacks led to slashing orders on domestic weaponry. It also led to U.S. military assistance being invested in current defense costs rather than in research and development. Over 50 percent of the money saved from the Lavi's termination, for instance, was not reallocated to other defense projects. Instead it was spent on the combating the Intifada and other current defense costs.[133] Not surprisingly, large scale retrenchment in the arms industry also took place, as by the early 1990s massive layoffs of defense industry workers were carried out. Israeli experts reckon that the country will be unable to invest as much in the defense industry and in the development of high technology in the 1990s.[134] This scale-back, therefore, has led to consequences for both the Israeli arsenal and its indigenous defense production capability. More importantly, it has also raised questions about Israel's security and status as an emerging power.

During this phase resistance to the nuclear program in the Israeli political leadership lessened and Israel embarked on the development of a full-scale weapons capability. By the early 1990s this included the development of

Command, Control, Communications, and Intelligence (C^3 I) facilities and a second-strike capability.

ISRAEL'S NUCLEAR PROGRAM

Resistance to the Israeli nuclear program started dying out in the late 1960s and was certainly no longer a constraint after the 1973 war. There were bureaucratic and military reasons for this. The size of the Dimona project, in terms of the financial and human investment, made it a difficult program to slow down. Hersh cites sources to show that by the mid-1960s Dimona accounted for over 10 percent of the Israeli defense budget and the program had swallowed some of Israel's best technological and scientific manpower.[135] The size of the project, therefore, made it difficult to be terminated. The Israeli cabinet had, in fact, decided to veto the building of a separation plant, but Dayan went ahead with the program secretly. When Eshkol found out about it he could only rubber stamp a project already under way.[136] Militarily and politically, the breakdown of the French alliance in 1967 once again proved the inability to depend on allies, while the military successes of Egypt and Syria in the 1973 war made the need for a nuclear deterrent all the more necessary.

Israel, consequently, has followed a policy of retaining nuclear ambiguity while enhancing its option. The option was enhanced through the development of delivery systems, the acquisition of some C^3 I capability, and reportedly the creation of a second-strike capability. Israel took over production of the Jericho from Dassault, modified the missile, and significantly improved its range. The improved Jericho I, which was operational by 1974, had a 700-mile range and the Jericho II, which was tested in the late 1980s, had a range of 1,100 miles.[137] The improvements on the Jericho were reportedly made with contraband as well as dual-purpose U.S. technology.[138] Israel also improved the yield of its nuclear weapons by building boosted fission weapons. According to Mordechai Vanunu, a disgruntled technician at the Dimona plant, the Israelis had been working with lithium and tritium to boost the yield of their nuclear weapons. In fact, the Vanunu revelations led experts to state that Israel had up to 200 nuclear weapons.[139]

Israel's C^3 I capability was enhanced through a successful space program. The Israel Space Agency was established in 1983 and in 1988 it had used a modified Jericho II (called the Shavit) to put the Offeq-1 satellite into space. In 1990, the Offeq-2 satellite was put into orbit.[140] The lowest altitude of the Offeq-2 was 129 miles, making it suitable for taking pictures. According to one source the resolution of the satellite cameras was supposed to improve and would be used for, "real-time intelligence gathering, early warning, and targeting." In April 1995 Israel put the Offeq-3 satellite into orbit with the mission of covering both Iran and Iraq. The Offeq-3 was to "increase Israel's ability to monitor developments in the military infrastructure and nuclear programs of neighboring countries." Observers also pointed to the military application of the Shavit rocket that put the satellite into orbit. Due to the fact that Israel has to launch its rockets westward to avoid the impression of an attack on the Arab states, the rocket was supposed to be "very strong" and therefore could "appear in other versions."[141] Further, Israel is to use the French Ariane launch vehicle to put a $300 million communications satellite, Amos, into geosynchronus orbit 22,300 miles above Zaire. Amos will relay military and communication traffic to Israeli ground and air forces and to its cruise-missile carrying submarines.[142]

The enhancement of nuclear capability also included creating a nuclear war-fighting capability. During the 1973 war the Israeli government had readied its nuclear weapons with a mutual assured destruction-type of scenario in mind. If Israel was to be overrun then it would inflict heavy casualties on the Arab world in the process. After the 1973 war, however, the Israeli government started creating the capability for nuclear war fighting, that is building a series of weapons that could be used for any contingency—from limited nuclear attacks to all-out strikes of medium- and long-range missiles. Thus a range of nuclear weapons from land mines to counter Syrian tank columns in the Golan Heights to warheads for ballistic missiles were to be built. The Israelis also reportedly wanted nuclear artillery shells and air-to-ground missiles. Finally, like the superpowers, the Israeli government wanted a nuclear triad of attack aircraft, ballistic missiles, and cruise missile submarines.[143] Yet while trying to build up such a force Israel continued its earlier policy of nuclear ambiguity.

Ambiguity, or as Cohen and Frankel prefer, opaqueness, in the nuclear area requires the following conditions: (1) no test of nuclear weapons because this is the most visible sign of having crossed the nuclear threshold; (2) denial of the possession of nuclear weapons while acknowledging the capability to build such weapons quickly; (3) no direct nuclear threats to one's enemies; (4) no official military doctrine integrating nuclear forces into the country's force structure—such a doctrine would involve debate on the issue within the national security system and would lower secrecy; (5) no military deployment should take place because it is detectable; (6) there should be no open debate, in most Western countries, once open deployment took place it was followed by acrimonious public debate on the role of nuclear weapons in national security; and (7) under opacity, a "rigid insulation of nuclear weapons activities from the routine foreign and defense policy activities."[144]

Israel has followed all of these conditions in its nuclear policy. No weapons test has taken place on Israeli soil. The one test attributed to Israel was the mysterious flash in the Indian Ocean near the Prince Edward Islands in 1979. Occasional claims have been made about Israeli capabilities such as, for example, Moshe Dayan's claim in 1976 that Israel was capable of producing nuclear weapons, but the existence of such weapons has never been openly acknowledged. Israel has never directly issued nuclear threats to its enemies. Even during the Gulf War, the Israeli response to Scud attacks was to claim the right to retaliation but not state what form it would take.[145] Nor has Israel espoused a stated nuclear doctrine, be it deterrence or war-fighting, for its nuclear force.

Cohen and Frankel also argue that such a force should not be militarily deployed because it would be detectable. The extent to which this argument applies in the Israeli case needs to be discussed. By the early 1990s, Israel had a standing force of Jericho missiles, as well as the C^3 I and the bomber forces to deliver nuclear weapons. Further, the 1986 disclosure by Mordechai Vanunu of the extent of the Israeli nuclear program also provided evidence that was hard to ignore. Yet Israel continues to enjoy the status of an opaque nuclear power rather than a public one. The reason for this is that proliferation lies in the eye of the beholder.

Both the United States and the former Soviet Union did not treat Israel as an errant proliferator in the 1970s and 1980s, even though evidence continued to mount about the Israeli weapons program. There were compelling reasons why the United States did not call Jerusalem on its nuclear program. As a major sponsor of the NPT, the United States would have been forced to take action against a country that had openly violated the regime. The acknowledgment of the Israeli nuclear program would also have led to domestic laws being applied against Israel, particularly the cut-off of foreign assistance. Israeli analysts also believe that forcing Israel to renounce its nuclear capability would have had adverse implications for U.S. foreign policy. Given the U.S. commitment to Israel's existence, taking such a step would have meant that Washington would have to have provided a nuclear commitment to Israel—something the United States was unwilling to do. As for the former Soviet Union, if it had challenged Israel's nuclear posture it would have faced pressure from the Arab states to help them acquire nuclear weapons, or at least to provide nuclear guarantees—something Moscow was unwilling to do. In the Soviet case, however, warnings were issued to Israel after successful test launches of the Jericho II in 1987 and 1988 because the missile had the capability of hitting targets in the southern Soviet Union.[146]

The last two conditions of opacity are the lack of a public debate and the insulation of nuclear issues from both foreign policy and defense activities. In Israel the nuclear issue has been insulated from public debate and has been treated as a "non-public issue that both proponents and opponents would rather not talk openly about."[147] In a country where most issues are subject to a vigorous public debate, the nuclear issue is not discussed because of the "sacredness of security" aspect of the program (i.e., it is not in the interest of national security to discuss the issue). Cohen and Frankel also attribute this view to the general public's discomfort with nuclear weapons. The leadership similarly has refused to engage on an open debate on the subject because of a continuing cultural unease in the Israeli leadership about the role of nuclear weapons. Given the Jewish experience with the Holocaust there is a natural distaste for weapons of mass destruction. Yet at the same time there is the need to prepare for a worst-case scenario, which requires the use of nuclear weapons to prevent another Holocaust. This contradiction of the Holocaust experience and the need for nuclear deterrence has " brought about a certain inhibition in the way Israel handles nuclear weapons. The grounds for the evolution of Israel's opaque stance can be found to be both moral and prudential."[148]   As a consequence there has been no serious debate questioning the role of nuclear weapons, or even the costs of such a program.

The second aspect of the Israeli nuclear policy was the use of preemptive strikes to remove potential threats. This was the case with Iraq's quest for nuclear weapons. Israeli agents destroyed Iraq's first reactor just before it was shipped from France and took out the second reactor in an air strike code named Operation Babylon in 1981.[149]   After the strike the then prime minister, Menachim Begin, issued a statement that the reactor was meant to produce bombs which were intended to be used against Israel. Further, these weapons would be used against Israeli population centers. The Israeli government therefore "decided to act without further delay to ensure the safety of our people." The statement concluded that: "On no account shall we permit an enemy to develop weapons of mass destruction against the people of Israel."[150]

Thus under Begin Israel became committed to using the preemptive strike, which had been used so successfully in the past in conventional warfare, to prevent nuclear threats. The threat posed by Iraq again became an issue in April 1990 when Iraq threatened to respond with chemical weapons to a possible Israeli attack of Iraq's nuclear infrastructure.[151]   But despite the public posturing by both countries, there were secret talks between Israeli and Iraqi officials, mediated by Egyptian president Hosni Mubarak, to pursue plans for chemical and nuclear disarmament in the region. The talks reportedly continued until the end of August 1990, even after the Iraqi invasion of Kuwait.[152]

After the Iraqi invasion of Kuwait the situation changed, as Iraq threatened that in the event of a war it would possibly broaden the conflict with chemical weapons strikes against Israel. Despite its nuclear arsenal and the possibility of using a preemptive strike, Israel, mindful of U.S. interests, had to follow a more graduated response. In trips to Israel before and during the war, U.S. Deputy Secretary of State Lawrence Eagleberger had made it clear that the United States wanted Israel to "stay out of the war, to keep its nuclear weapons sheathed, and to trust Washington to control the means and conduct of the battle."[153]   The Israeli leadership's response was to signal Iraq that they would enter the war only if Iraq crossed the nonconventional threshold.[154]   While attacking Israel, Iraq did refrain from using chemical weapons. Thus there were limits to Israel's use of a preemptive strategy in the nuclear field. Where its interests clashed with that of its main ally it had to modify its tactics even if it meant facing attacks on its civilian population.

A third aspect of the Israeli nuclear strategy was the country's approach to arms control and disarmament. Israel did not sign the NPT but had to respond to Arab efforts at arms control in the region. The Arab governments had demanded in the past that Israel sign the NPT and submit its facilities to IAEA inspections. Israel's response was to call first for conventional arms control, because it was the one way for the Arab states to successfully confront Israel, and then seek nuclear disarmament. But in 1975 Israel dropped this demand and instead called for a nuclear weapons free zone (NWFZ) of the type proposed for Latin America in the Treaty of Tlatelolco. The negotiations for the treaty were to be held face to face and the Israeli government expanded the region to be covered by the treaty by including India and Pakistan in the proposed NWFZ.[155] Unlike India, where the official policy on disarmament and arms control emerged from the moral distaste of the leadership for weapons of mass destruction, the Israeli policy arose from the more practical concerns of establishing a regional military balance that would ensure Israeli security.

THE PRESENT, THE FUTURE

Since independence, Israel's security doctrine was based on a mix of internal self-sufficiency and external dependence. Its quest for self-sufficiency was moored in Zionist economic philosophy, which saw the end result of independence overriding the economic costs of programs. Further, like other newly independent countries it sought to achieve technological advancement and saw the arms industry as a primary vehicle to achieve this goal. At the same time, Israel existed within a high-threat environment that fueled the desire for imported weapons and an external alliance. One of the ways to attain such an alliance was to project the nation as a strong and powerful ally within the region. Israel's military prowess and its indigenous military capability were seen as tools to achieve this end. The alliances with the external powers which followed resulted in the inflow of modern weapons systems and allowed Israel to maintain its qualitative edge over its opponents.

Yet, at the same time, Israel was a nation of immigrants. People had come there to achieve a more secure or materially better life. Providing the infrastructure and services to satisfy these needs were also priorities. It should be remembered that both in 1952 and 1965-1967, when economic conditions declined, emigration from Israel increased. Being a nation of immigrants, Israel also received a well-educated population with diverse skills, thus creating the need to find employment to utilize these talents. This combination of external and internal compulsions, therefore, drove Israel's militarization process.

During the 1990s, these assumptions that drove the building of Israel's military arsenal have weakened. Since the 1980s, Israel has had to make a clear choice between guns and butter, and the government has responded by curbing defense spending. Further, the Zionist dream of self-sufficiency is not a credible objective in the international political economy of the 1990s. As discussed in chapter 2, even the major powers no longer view arms production as an exercise in national sovereignty. Instead, the economic rationalization of consumer products has hit the arms industry as well. Questions of sovereignty in arms production have been replaced with the demand for cost effectiveness. Consequently, arms production has become an internationalized endeavor. Israeli companies have recognized this trend and in the 1990s moved to set up an increasing number of joint ventures with firms in the U.S.

Codevelopment and coproduction of systems are seen as creating an interdependent relationship and, therefore, moving Israel away from a dangerous dependency on the United States. Klieman and Pedatzur show that Israeli military sales to the Pentagon rose from only $9 million in 1983 to over $250 million in 1987.[156] But this is a minuscule amount to a country that has a $270 billion-plus defense budget. Moreover, defense collaboration plays only a small part in the relationships of interdependent countries. European interdependence does not come from the European fighter aircraft. It comes from strong political, economic, and, increasingly, cultural links.[157] Collaboration in arms production was only grafted on to this process later.

The death of the Cold War and the Gulf War of 1991 have also reshaped Israel's view of its security dilemma. First, the post-Gulf War peace treaties with such as Jordan, Morocco, and Saudi Arabia have created hopes for a more secure Middle East. The 1993 peace treaty with the PLO and the subsequent creation of a Palestinian Authority have led to the first important steps to resolving Israel's internal security dilemma. Second, doubts remain about whether the peace process can be broadened to accommodate currently hostile states such as Iran, Syria, and Iraq. This leads to the need for a continued and expensive military capability. Third, some Israelis argue that the demise of the Cold War has lessened Israel's significance to the United States as an ally in the Middle East. The events of the 1991 war saw both radical (Syria) and conservative (Saudi Arabia, Egypt) regimes recognizing that they had to accommodate the interests of the United States in the region. As the Arab states move toward such an accommodation, Israel's value as an ally is necessarily lessened. Israeli analysts now talk of Israel as a small state and believe there will be a "normalization" of relations with the United States—more in the pattern of the United States's relations with other small states. The insistence on the part of the United States that Israel become a signatory to the Missile Technology Control Regime (MTCR) is a case in point. Nor does Israel expect a growth in U.S. assistance; in fact, the Israelis believe that such assistance will decline over a period of time.

This "normalization," however, comes at a time when the continued militarization of the Middle East is taking place. Iran's military buildup, the U.S. decision to sell $23 billion worth of arms to Saudi Arabia, the continued dispute over the Golan Heights with Syria, and the possible threat of post sanctions Iraq all cause unease within the Israeli security framework.

With the benefits of interdependence being as yet unproven, the possible answer for Israel's security dilemma may lie in the development of a declared nuclear capability. It is argued that if Israel were to openly declare its nuclear option, it would act as a permanent deterrent to the Arab states. Israel has taken the steps to make its deterrent more effective by building an advanced Jericho missile and acquiring a satellite capability.[158] The attainment of this capability was possible both because there were no external options available for import and because an internal consensus existed in Israel's national security system about the need to have such a system—given the missile acquisitions of other states.

But Avner Yaniv makes a convincing argument against the declaration of a nuclear capability, and indeed against the declining value of the Israeli policy of nuclear ambivalence. Israel's policy of nuclear ambivalence has rested on developing all of the systems needed for a nuclear force without openly declaring the existence of such a capability. Yaniv argues that such strategy has paid dividends in that it has deterred the Arab states. Egypt, believing Israel had nuclear weapons in 1973, did not seriously try to recapture the entire Sinai and the Syrians stopped their assault on Israel's borders. Similarly, Saddam Hussein's decision to use conventional warheads rather than chemical ones in his Scud attacks on Israel is seen by Israeli observers as proof that the undeclared nuclear deterrent worked.[159]

Yaniv believes that the declaration of a nuclear capability would actually work against Israel because it would be impossible to deny its opponents access to such weapons. If the Middle East were to be nuclearized there could be for Israel two disastrous consequences. One is that both the Israelis and the Arabs would have a first-strike capability, thereby encouraging one side or the other to preempt. The other is that both sides would develop a stable nuclear balance—a second-strike capability. This too would work against Israel because the ongoing buildup of Arab forces is eroding Israel's conventional edge. In a future conventional war, therefore, the Arab states would have an inherent advantage because the threat of Israeli nuclear retaliation would not be credible.[160] Yaniv's conclusion is that only major-power-guaranteed arms control and a multilateral settlement among the Middle East disputants would guarantee Israel's long-term security. In fact the changed regional and international environment seems to be pushing Israel in this direction.

ATTEMPTS AT REGIONAL ARMS CONTROL

As part of the 1991 Madrid Middle East Peace Conference, Israel agreed to include a section on Arms Control and Regional Security (ACRS). A number of subgroups were created to develop confidence-building measures in the areas of information exchange and prenotification, communications, incidents at sea and search and rescue, and to discuss long-term objectives.[161] Subsequently, the Rabin government signed the Chemical Weapons Convention without any conditions. While these were promising signs for peace in the region, there is continued disagreement over how to deal with the nuclear issue.

The Arab states, led by Egypt, have been pushing for Israel to sign the NPT and accept international inspection of its installations. The Egyptian foreign minister, 'Amr Musa, in a statement said that Israel's refusal to place nuclear installations under international supervision was an obstacle to a comprehensive peace in the Middle East.[162] The Egyptian approach would seem to be based on a recognition of regional power realities and changed international circumstances. Within the region Israel's nuclear superiority cannot be matched without a major effort by one of the Arab states or Iran. To apply pressure on Israel regionally, therefore, would be difficult. At the same time, the changed international climate could make the United States and Russia more likely to put pressure on Israel to restrict its nuclear efforts.

The Israeli stand on nuclear arms control and verification is a continued preference for a regional approach. In an interview with the Egyptian newspaper *Al-Ahram*, Prime Minister Rabin articulated Israel's concerns about the NPT and his view on how regional nuclear arms control should be conducted. Rabin stated that there were flaws with the NPT verification process because a signatory, Iraq, had not complied with its provisions. The fact that the NPT does not cover conventional weapons is also seen as flaw. Instead, Rabin suggested bilateral peace talks and, once peace was established, bilateral arms control arrangements with "mutual bilateral control and there would be a supervision system between each two countries (Israel and Egypt, Israel and Syria, etc.) rather than international control.[163] The Israeli government subsequently modified its stand on international inspection of its nuclear installations. Shimon Peres agreed in principle to talks on submitting Israeli installations to international inspection two years after peace treaties had been signed with the entire region—including Iran, Iraq, and Libya.[164]

While these are negotiating positions, it is unlikely that Israel would renounce its nuclear capability as South Africa has done. As Ze'ev Schiff has argued: "No Israeli government, even the most moderate, will agree to make peace and simultaneously to weaken, in fact, dismantle its chief deterring power."[165] But what *is* likely is that Israel may have to agree to confidence-building measures in this area. These could include making its force public and agreeing to reductions in force levels. Israel would have to take such steps because countries like Iran and Iraq are unlikely to enter into a regional nuclear arrangement without Israel as a cosignatory. The willingness to take such a step is important given Israel's concern with the growth of the Iranian nuclear program. Rabin believed that Iran was on the path to develop nuclear weapons and his successor, Shimon Peres, has said that Iran's refusal to sign the NPT is an issue with that country. There has been some concern that the Israelis will launch an Osirak-type raid on the Iranian nuclear facility.[166] But calling for Iran to sign the NPT while Israel itself has not put its own nuclear force on the table will not be acceptable to Tehran. Further, an Osirak-type strike would not make sense in the new Middle East. The 1981 strike took place in a Cold War setting, and in one where, with the exception of Egypt, every Arab state was Israel's enemy. In the new Middle East in which Israel has a peace treaty with Jordan, is negotiating with Syria, and is moving toward discussing issues of cooperation with Saudi Arabia, such a preemptive strike would only hurt the peace process. And, as the Iraqi experience showed, it would only temporarily delay the Iranian quest for nuclear weapons, not halt it.

CONCLUSION

What becomes clear from the preceding discussion is that the development of Israel's military arsenal was heavily dependent on the existence of external suppliers and the availability of resources. First France, and later the United States, provided Israel with the weaponry and technology to build up its arsenal. In the U.S. case it also included the heavy subsidization of Israeli military production efforts. Ambitious programs like the Lavi and the Merkava could not have been undertaken without external assistance. Similarly, the decision to terminate the Lavi was also partially driven by U.S. reluctance to fund a unpromising program.

The establishment of such an arms acquisition system also made the influence of organizational politics inevitable. The existence of an arms industry that had to compete with an advanced external supplier of weapons meant that some of the programs being conceived were unrealistic and beyond the nation's capabilities. The existence of the external supplier also meant that the armed forces could turn to imported weapons whenever they saw an immediate threat or a shortfall in resources. Thus the Israeli arms industry has faced the situation of building arms for a user who may or may not purchase the system. It has also been forced to turn to an export-oriented strategy.

The political economy of Israeli arms production and acquisition also has implications for future force structures. The Lavi experience showed in the 1980s that even the production of one big-ticket item was enough to wreck havoc on the nation's defense industry and military budget. In the future, therefore, Israel is unlikely to commission the production of major weapons platforms. This means it will have to depend on external forces for the supply of such systems. The continued dependence on the United States for such systems cannot be countered by the sole means of interdependence. It also requires fitting into the United States's plans for the Middle East—in this case a broad-ranging peace process. Not working with the United States means an economically draining defense expenditure and an insecurity dilemma that will be increasingly difficult to resolve.

NOTES

1. Edward N. Luttwak, "Commentary—Defense Planning in Israel: A Brief Retrospective" in *Defense Planning in Less-Industrialized States Stephanie G. Neumann* ed. (Lexington Mass.: Lexington, 1984), 131.

2. Martin Van Creveld, "The Making of Israel's Security," in *Defense Planning in Less-Industrialized States* Stephanie G. Neumann ed., 120.

3. Ibid., 118.

4. Luttwak, "Commentary—Defense Planning in Israel," 134.

5. Ze'ev Schiff, *A History of the Israeli Army: 1874 to the Present* (New York: Macmillan, 1985), 52.

6. Shlomo Avineri, "Israel and the end of the Cold War," *The Brookings Review* (Spring 1993): 26.

7. Ritchie Ovendale, *The Origins of the Arab-Israeli Wars* (London and New York: Longman, 1992), 145.

8. Stewart Reiser, *The Israeli Arms Industry: Foreign Policy, Arms Transfers, and Military Doctrine of a Small State* (New York: Holmes and Meier, 1989), 18-21.

9. Avner Yaniv, *Deterrence Without the Bomb: The Politics of Israeli Strategy* (Lexington , Mass: Lexington, 1987), 31.

10. Ariel Levite, *Offense and Defense in Israeli Military Doctrine* (Boulder Co., Westview, 1989), 33.

11. Yaniv, *Deterrence Without the Bomb*, 34.

12. Levite, *Offense and Defense*, 49.

13. Schiff, *A History of the Israeli Army*, 58-65.

14. Yaniv, *Deterrence Without the Bomb*, 71.

15. Reiser, *The Israeli Arms Industry*, 19.

16. Ibid., 17.

17. Shimon Peres, *David's Sling* (New York: Random House, 1970), 28.

18. Reiser, *The Israeli Arms Industry*, 22.

19. Ibid., 24-25.

20. Edward Luttwak and Dan Horowitz, *The Israeli Army* (London: Allen Lane, 1975), 121-122.

21. Reiser, *The Israeli Arms Industry*, 26.

22. Ibid., 28.

23. Ibid., 19.

24. Ibid., 19.

25. Stockholm International Peace Research Institute (SIPRI), *Arms Trade Registers—The Arms Trade with the Third World* (Cambridge, Massachusetts and London: MIT Press, 1975), 52-55.

26. Yaniv, *Deterrence Without the Bomb*, 33.

27. Ibid., 53.

28. SIPRI, *The Arms Trade with the Third World*, (New York: Humanities Press, 1971), 530.

29. Avner Cohen and Marvin Miller, "Facing the Unavoidable: Israel's Nuclear Monopoly Revisited," *Journal of Strategic Studies*, 13, no. 3 (1990): 65.

30. Peter Pry, *Israel's Nuclear Arsenal* (Boulder, Colo.: Westview Press, 1984), 5.

31. Fuad Jabber, *Israel and Nuclear Weapons: Present Option and Future Strategies* (London: Chatto and Windus, 1971), 18-19.

32. Seymour M. Hersh, *The Sampson Option: Israel's Nuclear Arsenal and American Foreign Policy* (New York: Random House, 1991), 27.

33. Ibid., 28.

34. Pry, *Israel's Nuclear Arsenal*, 10.

35. Jabber, *Israel and Nuclear Weapons*, 22.

36. Hersh, *The Sampson Option*, 30.

37. SIPRI, *Arms Trade Registers—The Arms Trade with the Third World*, 44-45 and 54-55.

38. Raimo Vayrynen and Thomas Ohlson, "Egypt: Arms Production in the Transnational Context," in *Arms Production in the Third World*, Michael Brzoska and Thomas Ohlson ed., (London: Taylor and Francis, 1986), 107.

39. Ibid., 114-118.

40. Yaniv, *Deterrence Without the Bomb*, 96.

41. Reiser, *The Israeli Arms Industry*, 47- 49.

42. Ibid., 57.

43. Ibid., 53.

44. Ibid., 55.

45. Ibid., 62-63.

46. Edward A. Kolodziej, *Making and Marketing Arms: The French Experience and it Implications for the International System* (Princeton, New Jersey: Princeton University Press, 1987), 340.

47. Ibid., 340.

48. Ibid., 341.

49. Ibid., 342.

50. Ibid., 340-342. Kolodziej, however, points out that such deals were made without the permission of the U.S.

51. The nonproliferation rationale of U.S. arms sales policy is discussed in Shlomo Aronson, *Conflict and Bargaining in the Middle East* (Baltimore and London: Johns Hopkins University Press, 1978), 50-56.

52. Ibid., 51.

53. Reiser, *The Israeli Arms Industry*, 51.

54. Yaniv, *Deterrence Without the Bomb*, 80.

55. Reiser, *The Israeli Arms Industry*, 59.

56. Aaron S. Klieman, *Israel's Global Reach: Arms Sales as Diplomacy* (Washington: Pergamon-Brassey's, 1985), 21.

57. Avner Cohen, "Most Favored Nation," Bulletin of the Atomic Scientists 51, no. 1 (January/February 1995): 45.

58. Ibid., 33.

59. Steven Weismann and Herbert Krosney, The Islamic Bomb (New York: Times Books, 1981), 114.

60. Hersh, *The Samson Option*, (New York: Random House, 1991), 271.

61. Jabber, *Israel and Nuclear Weapons*, 29.

62. Ibid., 33.

63. Yair Evron, *Israel's Nuclear Dilemma* (Ithaca, New York: Cornell University Press, 1994), 4.

64. Jabber, *Israel and Nuclear Weapons*, 34.

65. Evron, *Israel's Nuclear Dilemma*, 6.

66 . Ibid., 6-7.

67. Ibid., 7.

68. Cohen, *Most Favored Nation*, 46.

69. Jabber, *Israel and Nuclear Weapons*, 96.

70. Cohen, *Most Favored Nation*, 50.

71. Ibid., 52.

72. Ibid.

73. Pry, *Israel's Nuclear Arsenal*, 15-16.

74. George H. Quester, "Nuclear Weapons and Israel," Middle East Journal 37, no. 4 (Autumn 1983): 553.

75. Avner Cohen, "Nuclear Weapons, Opacity, and Israeli Democracy," in *National Security and Democracy in Israel,* Avner Yaniv ed. (Boulder, Colo.: Lynne Rienner, 1993), 211.

76. Leonard S. Spector with Jacqueline R. Smith, *Nuclear Ambitions—The Spread of Nuclear Weapons 1989-90* (Boulder, Colo.: Westview, 1990), 153.

77. Cohen, "Nuclear Weapons, Opacity, and Israeli Democracy," 212

78. Evron, *Israel's Nuclear Dilemma*, 9.

79. Cohen, "Nuclear Weapons, Opacity, and Israeli Democracy," 213.

80. Yaniv, *Deterrence Without the Bomb*, 128.

81. Ibid., 131.

82. Naftali Blumenthal, "The Influence of Defense Industry Investment on Israel's Economy," in *Israeli Security Planning in the 1980s,* Zvi Lanir ed. (New York: Praeger, 1984), 169.

83. Klieman, *Israel's Global Reach*, 22.

84. Gerald M. Steinberg, "Indigenous Arms Industries and Dependence: The Case of Israel," Defense Analysis 2, no. 4 (December 1986): 293-294.

85. Klieman, *Israel's Global Reach*, 22.

86. Blumenthal, "The Influence of Defense Industry," 167-68.

87. Klieman, *Israel's Global Reach*, 58-66.

88. Gerald Steinberg, "Israel: High Technology Roulette," in *Arms Production in the Third World,* Michael Brzozska and Thomas Ohlson eds. (London and Philadelphia: Taylor and Francis, 1986), 166.

89. Reiser, *The Israeli Arms Industry*, 82.

90. Anne Hessing Cahn, "United States Arms to the Middle East 1967-76: A Critical Examination," in *Great Power Intervention in the Middle East,* Milton Leitenberg and Gabriel Sheffer eds. (New York and Oxford: Pergamon Press), 102.

91. Cited in, *Israel—MERI Report* (Dover, N. Hampshire: Croom Helm, 1985), 127-8.

92. Alex Mintz and Gerald Steinberg, "Coping with Supplier Control: The Israeli Experience," in *The Dilemma of Third World Defense Industries: Supplier Control or Recipient Autonomy*, Kwang-Il Baek, Ronald D. Mclaurin and Chung-in Moon eds. (Inha University, 1989), 140-41.

93. Michael Brzoska and Thomas Ohlson, *Arms Transfers to the Third World, 1971-85* (Oxford: Oxford University Press, 1987), 7.

94 . Ibid., 19.

95. Ibid., 18.

96. Ibid.

97. Ibid., 17.

98. Ibid., 20.

99. Ahron Klieman and Reuven Pedatzur, *Rearming Israel: Defense Procurement Through the 1990s* (Boulder, Colo.: Westview Press, 1991), 33-35.

100. Ibid., 37.

101. Mintz and Steinberg, "Coping with Supplier Control," 145 and Steinberg, "High Technology Roulette," 165.

102. Zeev Bonen, "The Technological Arms Race—An Economic Dead End?," in *Israeli Security Planning in the 1980s: Its Politics and Economics,* Zvi Lanir ed. (New York: Praeger, 1984), 123-25.

103. Reiser, *The Israeli Arms Industry,* 156.

104. Klieman and Pedatzur, *Rearming Israel,* 73-74.

105. Ibid., 125.

106. Ibid., 126.

107. Ibid., 127.

108. Blumenthal, "The Influence of Defense Industry," 174.

109. Klieman and Pedatzur, *Rearming Israel,* 79.

110. Reiser, *The Israeli Arms Industry,* 173-75.

111. David A. Brown, "Israel Reviews Decisions That Led to Lavi Cancellation," *Aviation Week and Space Technology* 127 (September 14, 1987): 22.

112. Galen Roger Perras, "Israel and the Lavi Fighter: The Lion Falls to Earth," in *The Defense Industrial Base and the West,* David G. Haglund ed. (London and New York: Routledge, 1989), 195.

113. Perras, "Israel and the Lavi," 195.

114. Klieman and Pedatzur, *Rearming Israel,* 98-99.

115. Ibid., 65.

116. Perras, *Israel and the Lavi,* 198.

117. *Aviation Week and Space Technology,* 126 (March 2, 1987): 22.

118. Brown, "Israel Reviews Decisions," 23.

119. *Aviation Week and Space Technology* 127 (September 14, 1987): 23.

120. *Aviation Week and Space Technology* 126 (March 2, 1987): 20.

121. Ibid.

122. Reiser, *The Israeli Arms Industry,* 180.

123. Jane's Defense Weekly (15 February, 1992): 235.

124. Klieman and Pedatzur, *Rearming Israel,* 67.

125. *Jane's Defense Weekly* (15 February, 1992): 236.

126. *Interavia: Business and Technology* 50 (October 1995): 5 and *Deccan Herald* (Bangalore), 7 August, 1996.

127. *The Military Balance 1992-93* (London: Brassey's, 1992).

128. Moshe Efrat, "The USA and the Israeli Military Economic Dimension," in *Israeli Security Planning,* Zvi Lanir ed., 135-36.

129. *Jane's Defense Weekly* (February 15, 1992): 235.

130. *Bank of Israel Annual Report 1980* (Jerusalem: Government of Israel, 1981), 79.

131. Ibid., 79.

132. Efrat, "The U.S. and the Israeli Military Economic Dimension," 131.

133. Klieman and Pedatzur, *Rearming Israel,* 95-96.

134. Ibid., 158.

135. Hersh, *The Sampson Option,* 136-137.

136. Pry, *Israel's Nuclear Arsenal,* 22.

137. William E. Burrows and Robert Windrem, *Critical Mass: The Dangerous Race for Superweapons in a Fragmenting World* (New York: Simon and Schuster, 1994), 286-287.

138. Ibid, 452.

139. Spector with Smith, *Nuclear Ambitions*, 161.

140. "Israel Orbits Offeq-2 Spacecraft," *Aviation Week and Space Technology* 132 (April 9, 1990): 20.

141. *FBIS-NES-95-079*, 25 April, 1995, 36.

142. Burrow and Windrem, *Critical Mass*, 310-311.

143. Ibid., 283-284.

144. Avner Cohen and Benjamin Frankel, "Opaque Nuclear Proliferation," *Journal of Strategic Studies* 13, no. 3, 1990, 21-22.

145. Yair Evron, "Deterrence Experience in the Arab-Israel Conflict," in *Deterrence in the Middle East, Where Theory and Practice Converge*, Ahron Klieman and Ariel Levite ed. (Boulder, Colo.: Westview Press, 1993), 114.

146. Cohen and Frankel, "Opaque Nuclear Proliferation," 26-27.

147. Ibid., 28.

148. Ibid.

149. A good discussion of Operation Babylon is provided in Stephen Green, *Living by the Sword: America and Israel in the Middle East 1968-87* (Brattleboro, Vt.: Amana, 1988), 135-152.

150. Ibid., 138.

151. *New York Times*, 3 April, 1990.

152. Geoffrey Aronson, "Hidden Agenda: U.S.-Israeli Relations and the Nuclear Question," *Middle East Journal* 46, no. 4 (Autumn 1992): 619

153. Ibid., 621.

154. See, for example, an address by Foreign Minister David Levy, Foreign Broadcast Information Service, Daily Report—Near East and South Asia (*FBIS-NES*), 5 December, 1990, 36.

155. Quester, "Nuclear Weapons and Israel," 554.

156. Klieman and Pedatzur, "Rearming Israel," 180.

157. For a discussion of the cultural aspect see Samuel Huntington, "The Clash of Civilizations", *Foreign Affairs* 72, no. 3 (Summer 1993).

158. Gerald M. Steinberg, "Israel: Case Study for International Missile Trade and Nonproliferation." in *The International Missile Bazaar—The New Suppliers Network* William Potter and Harlan W. Jencks ed. (Boulder: Westview, 1994), 235-237.

159. Avner Yaniv, "Non-Conventional Weaponry and the Future of Arab-Israeli Deterrence," in *Non-Conventional Weapons Proliferation in the Middle East*, Efraim Karsh, Martin S. Navias, and Philip Sabin eds. (Oxford: Claredon Press, 1993), 219.

160. Ibid.

161. Gerald M. Steinberg, "Time for Regional Approaches?" *Orbis* 38 no. 3 (Summer 1994) 419.

162. *FBIS-NES-94-170*, 1 September, 1994, 27.

163. *FBIS-NES-94-177*, 13 September, 1994, 43.

164. *FBIS-NES-945-038*, 27 February, 1995, 12.

165. Quoted in P. R. Kumaraswamy, "Egypt needles Israel," *Bulletin of the Atomic Scientists* 51, no. 2, (March/April 1995): 12.

166. *FBIS-NES-94-177*, 13 September, 1994, 41 and *FBIS-NES-95-078*, 24 April, 1995, 32.

4

Building an Arsenal:
The Brazilian Experience

In both the Indian and Israeli cases it became apparent that the constraints posed by the domestic political economy as well as those of international suppliers shaped the way the force structures of each nation emerged. In the third case I have chosen to discuss, Brazil, the outcome has been similar. And like India and Israel, constraints imposed by the existing political economy as well as external conditions, rather than the military objectives of the armed forces, have shaped the eventual force structure of the nation. Like India and Israel, Brazil has faced supplier restrictions on both weapons systems and technology transfers, consequently creating the rationale for an indigenous defense production capability; as with the other two countries, Brazil has a scientific-industrial base which also creates a constituency for indigenous weapons programs. Like Israel, Brazil was also able to use this base to develop a successful arms export program in the 1980s. Further, and here the comparison with India is more apt, Brazil's national leadership sees the nation as achieving major-power status in the international system. Weapons production is seen as the basis for future technological growth, with the latter goal providing development and independence from external powers.

But there are also significant differences between the Brazilian case and the Indian and Israeli ones. Unlike the latter two countries, Brazil's development of its force structure has taken place in a low-threat environment. Brazil's last major war was fought in the nineteenth century and it does not face an opponent whose arsenal is being constantly upgraded either through indigenous efforts or through transfers from external powers. Second, the Brazilian armed forces took over the reins of government from 1964–1985 and shaped not only national security doctrine but also the economic policies meant to facilitate it. This, to some extent, caused a linkage between the national leadership, the armed forces, and the arms industries and removed some of the bureaucratic tensions which existed in the Indian and Israeli cases.

Further, unlike India and Israel, Brazil's militarization effort is of relatively recent vintage and has not undergone major shifts as a consequence of external conflicts. This chapter, therefore, adopts a slightly different approach for studying the Brazilian case. While retaining the framework—threats and bureaucratic politics as demand factors and suppliers and resources as supply factors—it discusses them in two rather than several discrete historical periods. The two major periods are 1964–1985, when the military ruled Brazil, and the from 1985 to the present where we are seeing a democratic Brazilian regime trying to impose constitutional and institutional controls over the armed forces.

THE THREAT

Brazil has not fought a major war since 1870 and its armed forces have seen action only three times in the past one hundred years. It was part of the U.S.-led intervention in the Dominican Republic in the 1960s and a late entrant on the side of the Allies in both World Wars. In the 1970s its traditional rivalry with Argentina flared up and this, in part, provided the rationale for developing an indigenous nuclear capability. But the principal focus of the Brazilian armed forces after securing control of the government in the 1960s lay in the challenge posed by potential insurgencies within the country and in promoting national development.

When the Brazilian military seized power in 1964 it espoused a doctrine of national security that encompassed both military and economic issues.[1] The military regime declared that economic development was an integral part of the national security doctrine. High levels of economic growth were actually seen as legitimizing the military rule of the country.

At the military level, the military regime's preoccupation was with the internal security threat posed by the Left. By the late 1960s the military regime faced both insurgencies in the outlying regions of the countries and urban terrorism. Given that its principal threat was from internal insurgents, the Brazilian government did not find it necessary to invest large amounts in the purchase of advanced weapons systems. In fact the Brazilian defense budget did not exceed 1 percent of the GNP well into the 1980s. Further, as a signatory to the 1947 Rio Treaty, Brazil receive subsidized weaponry from the United States, thereby removing the need for an indigenous defense capability.

By the early 1970s the internal security threat was crushed and the Brazilian military, in search of a mission, began to assess threats emanating from the region as well as the international system. According to Stanley Hilton, the threat was seen as coming from Brazil's traditional regional rival, Argentina, and from Soviet-Cuban expansion in Latin America as well as in the South Atlantic. At a more abstract level the need for military modernization was also seen as being necessitated by the advances in military technology.

In the region, the revival of Peronism in Argentina was seen as a potential threat, especially since Argentina had a lead over Brazil in the progress of its nuclear program.[2] Argentina had also stated that it would not allow the economic expansion of Brazil into the La Plata Basin. Although the two countries reached an agreement over the nuclear issue in 1980, this did not prevent Argentina from announcing in November of 1983 that it had successfully enriched uranium, thereby causing greater concern in Brazil. Hilton argues that the Brazilian military was concerned that an unstable Argentina would be tempted to use nuclear weapons in the region to divert attention from the growing internal schisms in that country. Argentina's subsequent rearmament program after the 1982 Falklands War was also viewed with disquiet and seen as justifying a Brazilian conventional buildup. Brazilian military sources also pointed to the dispute with Chile over the Beagle Channel as proof that Argentina would not hesitate to use force to resolve its conflicts with other states.[3]

The expansion of Soviet and Cuban influence around the globe in the late 1970s and early 1980s was also seen as a potential threat. The Brazilian government viewed Cuba as the principal threat in the region, given its past record of supporting regional insurgencies and, by the early 1980s, its influence in consolidating the rule of socialist regimes in Nicaragua and Grenada. Cuba was also viewed as an "aircraft carrier" for Soviet expansion into the Caribbean and the Latin American region. The growth of Soviet naval power in the 1970s was viewed as posing a threat because Brazil, by the 1970s, had committed itself to the idea of a 200-mile continental shelf for national exploitation. Soviet naval expansion was seen as threatening sea lanes in the South Atlantic, particularly Brazil's supply of oil from the Middle East. Control over the sea lanes would also leave Brazil vulnerable to an attack from an external power.[4]

Finally, the advent of new military technology was seen as a threat to Brazil's security. The Yom Kippur war of 1973 and the Vietnam War had opened the Brazilian military's eyes to the advancements in military technology. This belief was reinforced with the performance of so-called smart weapons in the Falklands War. The Brazilian forces felt that the development of such weapons left the country, at the very least, vulnerable to a surprise attack by an outside power.[5]

LEADERSHIP PERCEPTIONS

While the rivalry with Argentina, the growth of Soviet-Cuban influence, and the advancements in technology may have provided potential threats, these were not the only factors that influenced the development of Brazil's force structure and arms industry. Instead, one has to look at the perceptions of the national leadership toward the defense industry and military power: its role in national development and in the fulfillment of foreign policy objectives.

After coming to power in 1964 the military regime's long-term goal became one of making Brazil achieve major-power status. The economic development of the country was central to achieving this goal. Within this context militarization—through the development of a defense industry—was seen as one of many ways to acquire advanced technology and, consequently, to propel the country into the developed world. Therefore much of Brazilian defense planning in the 1970s and 1980s was geared toward achieving these interlinked objectives. This policy of enhancing development through militarization was called the Doctrine of Security and Development.

Patrice Franko-Jones writes that Brazilian thought on national security has been in development since the World War I, when the idea of security and development was first formulated.[6] The argument was made that true political sovereignty could only come after economic development. Such development in turn could only be provided by strong state leadership. This argument was used by the Vargas government (1930–1954) to initiate policies for the establishment of a military industrial complex, but the doctrine gained true stature when it was institutionalized by the Brazilian military in the 1950s by the Superior War College (ESG). The ESG saw the development of the nation leading eventually to technological autonomy and great-power status.

The desire for technological autonomy lay not only in the role it played in enhancing the nation's status, but also, as Kapstein argues, in Brazil's experience in World War I and II. In both of these conflicts Brazil faced shortages of weapons or denials of weaponry by the major powers.[7] In World War II the Allied powers gave preference to the American and European forces in the supply of weapons and the Brazilian forces rarely received the weapons they requested. This led President Vargas to state that the first lesson Brazil had learned from the war was that, "only the countries which can really be considered military powers are those sufficiently industrialized and able to produce weapons within their own frontiers the war materials they need."[8]

Industrialization, therefore, was seen as a prerequisite for military power, and this argument found an institutional home in the ESG. The dominant concern of the ESG became one of bringing together military and civilian personnel to achieve national security through rapid economic development. In order to achieve this goal four precepts were established. First, defense policy was expanded to include economic and political security. Patrice Franko-Jones writes, "As ESG became the articulator of development policy for Brazil, this broad concept of national security often legitimized painful economic and political programs in the name of defense. This influence also mobilized financial and political support for the development of a military industrial complex in Brazil."[9]

Second, the ESG argued that Brazil's strategic location, size, and resources gave it the potential for becoming a world power.[10] Third, Brazil's lack of international status was explained by the inability of the federal government to formulate an effective development policy. Fourth, the ESG argued that to overcome these weaknesses the country needed a strong scientific establishment able to create and implement national goals.[11] What followed of course was the belief that the military, and within it the ESG, was the only institution within Brazil that had the cohesiveness, discipline, and strength to formulate and enforce these objectives.

Until the 1964 coup, the ESG and its brand of "developmental nationalism" exerted little influence on actual governmental policies, however it did create a cadre of civilian and military elites who subscribed to its security doctrine and who would later become major figures in Brazilian political, military, and economic institutions. It is estimated that by 1962 nearly 80 percent of the new general officers had been through the ESG, and at the time the 1964 coup took place nearly two-thirds of the active duty generals were ESG graduates.[12] Thus when General Castello Branco and his advisors took over they were ready to implement the ESG doctrine.

The military coup provided the impetus for greater defense industrialization in Brazil. Initially defense production was increased to occupy idle industrial capacity, but by the late 1960s, as nationalist hardliners increased their influence within the regime, "military-technological capabilities came to be viewed as an important part of a broader quest for technological autonomy."[13] The growth of these technology-intensive military industries was also viewed favorably by the regime's civilian economic planners who believed it would promote industrialization, economic expansion, and export-led growth. Thus a strong pro-militarization constituency emerged among the civilian technocratic elite, to whom management of economic policy had been entrusted. Consequently, the budding Brazilian defense industry benefited from both high-level attention and policy coordination during military rule.[14]

The development of the Brazilian military industrial complex, therefore, was possible because of the assumption of power by a military-technocratic elite that was guided by a coherent national security policy that linked economic development with future military self-sufficiency and international status. Due to such unique features operating in the Brazilian case a military-industrial complex did emerge in which the Brazilian state supplemented the efforts of the private sector to produce weaponry.

The last statement needs to be elaborated. While the post-1964 Brazilian state was to foster military industries, it did not do so through intensive state industrialization and at the expense of the private sector—as was the case in most other Third World nations. Instead, as explained in the next section, it was to do so by providing vital inputs such capital, technology, coordination, a protected market, and, eventually, international marketing skills to the nation's arms industry. The insistence on keeping the private sector involved in weapons production came from the belief that it would create greater efficiency in weapons production. Further, it also viewed multinational corporations as being important for economic development and facilitated their entry into weapons production.

WEAPONS PRODUCTION: THE MILITARY ERA

The political economy of Brazilian weapons production emerged from the recognition of certain crucial factors—the country's limitations resulting from late industrialization, the size of its domestic market, and the shortcomings of the private sector.

Until the advent of military rule, defense industrialization had been a largely private enterprise which had met with failure. During the Vargas regime the Brazilian government had set up three munitions plants and given heavy subsidies to the private defense manufacturers. It had also guaranteed an internal arms market. But, despite such incentives, private industry failed to deliver the goods. In the 1930s attempts were also made to build an aircraft industry from scratch but failed for technological and fiscal reasons.[15] Subsequently, when, in the 1960s, the government's call for the manufacture of aircraft was not responded to by the private sector, the government decided to set up a joint venture aviation company—Embraer.[16]

Another problem the infant Brazilian defense industry faced was that the nation, as a late industrializer, did not have the requisite technology to develop modern weapons systems. Thus the decision was taken at an early stage to import technology with the hope that it would provide the necessary learning skills and eventually lead to domestic advancements in science and technology. One notable area in which such technology imports took place was the computer industry. According to Emanuel Adler, the appeal to the military of such imports and their subsequent innovation by domestic R and D efforts was "that it fit with their perceptions and expectations that Brazil would soon become a world power."[17] In fact it was thanks to the Brazilian Bank of National Development and the Brazilian Navy, which required computers for its naval vessels, that the Brazilian government established Cobra S.A. in 1975 to manufacture computers under license from Ferranti.[18]

The impact of multinational corporations on the development of weapons technology was more widespread than in just the area of high technology. In the 1950s the Brazilian government established a technology park, San Jose dos Campos, in Sao Paulo and invited multinationals into the country. Both the Brazilian State and private sector companies sought close collaboration with military transnationals who could offer advanced military technology. This led to 100 joint ventures with European firms. A number of major European and American firms provided technologies to the Brazilian arms industry. Beretta and FN of Belgium entered in the area of small arms and ammunition. Northrop, Piper, Aermacchi, and Fokker were in the aircraft industry. While Ferranti Philips, AEG-Telefunken, General Electric, and Texas Instruments were the major firms involved in military electronics.[19] While the emphasis in the 1970s was on low and intermediate technologies, which were "off the shelf" (see below), by the 1980s the level of technology sought had advanced significantly as witnessed by the growth of the electronics industry and the increase in the number of informatics multinationals based in Brazil. The small size of the domestic market also dictated, from the onset, that Brazilian weapons would have to be exported in sizable numbers to keep the industry healthy. Thus Embraer, which was established in 1969, was selling aircraft on the international market as early as 1975.

The impact of these factors was to create four types of state intervention in the weapons production process: outright state ownership, joint ventures with private firms, the operation of technology centers, and fiscal promotion.[20] Outright state ownership meant that the government owned at least 50 percent of the company, appointed and controlled the top management, and the firm was established for a public purpose. The aviation firm Embraer and the munitions company IMBEL fell in this category. The crucial role of the state in developing the Brazilian arms industry can be seen in the operational histories of Brazil's big three firms—Embraer, Avibras, and Engesa—all of which gained success either domestically or internationally through focused state intervention.

THE STATE AND THE ARMS INDUSTRY

The failure of the Brazilian aircraft industry in the 1930s combined with Brazil's vulnerability to the abrupt termination of external weapons supplies, led the Brazilian Air Force to take the first steps to create the necessary human resources for a Brazilian aerospace industry. In 1949 the air force established the Institute for Aeronautical Technology (ITA) to train engineers. Later the air force established the Center for Aeronautical Technology (CTA), which was to undertake the actual design of aircraft and conduct advanced research in the field of aeronautics. The institutional impact of ITA-CTA has been crucial, as engineers trained by, and who have worked for, these institutions have gone on to occupy prominent positions in Brazilian industry and state organizations. As Dagnino and Proenca point out this placed many former "ITAns" in the position to shape public policy on industrialization and the domestic development of technology.[21]

By the late 1960s, engineers working at CTA had designed a rugged commuter aircraft with military applications and the center invited private industry to bid for the project. When private industry did not respond to the bid, the engineers at CTA took their case to the air force brass. The air force persuaded the government to establish a company, Embraer, which was 51 percent state owned, to put the CTA plane into production.[22] The plane, the Bandeirante, was put into production and sold well in both the domestic and international markets. International sales were possible because of its low price, the fact that the oil crisis created a demand for fuel-efficient commuter aircraft, and because Brazil was one of the few nations that actually had such an airplane on the market. Domestically, the requirements of the air force created a guaranteed market for eight years.[23]

Embraer was given a further boost by the government when it was decided that the air force's next strike aircraft, the Aermacchi 326, the Brazilian variant of which was named the Xavante, was to be license produced. The Xavante was a subsonic ground attack aircraft, which fitted the air force's requirement to counter perceived threats. Brazil did not face an air superiority threat from the fighter aircraft of other countries and the Xavante was a low-technology plane suitable for Brazil's counterinsurgency operations.

Embraer's approach to the development of technological skills is worth noting here because it is symptomatic of the problems Brazil faced in the future development of its arsenal. Embraer was to take its model for aircraft production from the Brazilian automobile industry. The automobile industry was established by multinational corporations that sought the highest level of technological activity—final assembly. This allowed control over the other industries that supplied components.[24] Following this example, Embraer officials decided that they would not build their aircraft from scratch. Instead they focused on the design, aerodynamics, and final manufacture of the aircraft. Crucial components like engines and avionics were left to other manufacturers, particularly transnational corporations, or were imported. Embraer's decision to not develop all of its technology from scratch was based on the belief that what mattered was to have control over the final product. Such control was only possible if Embraer was designing and later assembling the final product. Practical considerations also prevailed because as Franko-Jones points out, the Brazilian armed forces recognized from the outset that for the arms industry to sustain itself it would have to export weapons. This meant producing weapons that were marketable rather than those which were more technologically advanced but risked not coming to fruition. The Tucano trainer/counterinsurgency aircraft was a product of this philosophy and it was successfully exported to the United Kingdom in the major South-North arms deal of the 1980s.

This strategy was subsequently followed in the development of the AMX fighter. The Brazilian Air Force, as part of its modernization plan of the late 1970s, demanded a new single-seat attack aircraft. The plane was to be a follow-on to the Xavante but Embraer, despite its impressive efforts in the 1970s, did not have the capability to jump up the technological ladder and build a subsonic aircraft with next-generation electronics. Embraer therefore entered into an agreement to codevelop and produce the aircraft with the Italian companies Aermacchi and Aeritalia.[25] Embraer is responsible for making 30 percent of each unit, "including the wings, air intake, weapons pylons, jettisonable fuel tanks, landing gears and reconnaissance pallets.[26] Embraer's eventual goal is to reduce imports to about 40 percent of the AMX.

To put Embraer's efforts in perspective, both India with its LCA and Israel with the Lavi were trying to develop more advanced combat aircraft. Both planes were supposed to be comparable, or as their publicity releases claimed, superior to the General Dynamics F-16 which, by the mid-1980s had become the popular aircraft on the market for developing nations. Embraer, by laying the foundation for producing aircraft, was hoping to move up to the same technological level as India and Israel in the next decade. In 1986 it was reported that the company was studying the development of a supersonic aircraft.[27]

In the 1980s Engesa was billed as the world's largest producer of armored vehicles, but the firm's roots were in the automobile industry. The firm developed a unique suspension system—dubbed the boomerang system—which allowed vehicles to perform off-road maneuvers.[28] The Brazilian Army recognized the utility of this system as well as the advantages of securing domestically produced replacements for its aging jeeps, trucks, and Greyhound tanks. A shortage of hard currency and the unreliability of external suppliers pushed the army toward seeking a domestic replacement.[29] In 1972 Engesa began production of the EE-9 Cascavel and EE-11 Urutu for the army. The Brazilian Navy subsequently ordered an amphibious version of the Urutu. Franko-Jones adds that the idea for Engesa to develop these armored vehicles, "came not from any grand government strategy, but from good personal relations between people in the firm and those in the Army."[30] The project was seen as being mutually beneficial because it saved hard currency and promoted local industry.

Engesa was able to export its armored personnel vehicles widely throughout both Africa and the Persian Gulf. The rugged nature of the vehicles and the fact that they were technologically simple and easy to maintain made them attractive purchases. The purely commercial nature of Brazilian arms sales also appealed to nations around the world. Indeed Brazilian diplomats stressed that unlike both the Western and Eastern blocs their arms sales were purely commercial and, therefore, not subject to supplier restraints.[31]

Engesa profited from the Urutu and Cascavel because they were technologically simple and used components which were "off the shelf"—readily available in the Brazilian automobile industry. In fact Engesa saw major sales during the Iran-Iraq war with Iraq purchasing over two hundred armored cars from the company.[32] Like Embraer, however, Engesa's next project, the Osorio tank, required an increase in technological capability that the firm could not meet through indigenous efforts. Instead the tank's engine, gearbox and tracks were of German origin (GE bid to design a second gearbox and gas turbine) and Westinghouse and Vickers were the sources for the fire control system and gun. With such a high import content the tank had to find a large enough export market to recover development and production costs. The Saudi Arabian government actually invested $54 million in developing the tank and in 1985, agreed to purchase 280 Osorios and eventually build another 1,200—a deal that was estimated to be $3 billion.[33] By the early 1990s, however, the deal had fallen through despite intensive Brazilian lobbying, and this setback was largely responsible for Engesa's filing for bankruptcy in 1990 (the firm was forced into financial insolvency due to unpaid Iraqi war debts and partly due to the cash squeeze created by the high developmental cost of the Osorio).[34]

The third Brazilian giant was Avibras, a fully private industry, although, like Embraer and Engesa, it received technological support from the state. Formed in 1961, Avibras designed, developed, and produced civilian and military rockets with 100 percent national technology. The company developed an entire set of air-to-surface and surface-to-surface missiles as well as civilian rockets. Further, Avibras created subsidiaries in space research and in the electronic, chemical, aerospace, and communications sectors.[35] While the company benefited originally from CTA-derived technology, more recently it has had weak links with the Brazilian military, as 90 percent of its orders were from foreign sources.[36] The main reason for this being the limited domestic market for missiles and other armaments. The company's philosophy therefore became one of "export or die." Avibras recorded a dramatic rise in exports in the 1980s, with sales leaping from $4 million in 1980 to over $90 million by 1982 and eventually reaching $340 million in 1987.[37]

Avibras's success as an export earner lay in both the existence of favorable international conditions and the nature of technology inputs employed by the company. The Iran-Iraq war was a godsend for all Third World arms industries because of the transfer restrictions imposed by Western governments on their arms manufacturers. Consequently, twenty-eight countries ending up selling weapons to both combatants. As I have argued elsewhere, if you do not take into account exports to Iran and Iraq, total Third World arms sales in the 1980s become minuscule. This was certainly the case for the Brazilian arms industry, particularly Avibras, whose fortunes rested on the financial solvency of one customer—Iraq. The other reason for Avibras's success was that, unlike Engesa and Embraer, it did not have to depend on the import of expensive components for its weapons systems, and technology acquisition costs were minimal.[38] Avibras was also hurt by the post-Gulf War crisis in the Brazilian arms industry and shifted its production focus to the civilian sector.

EXPORTS

Brazilian exports were fueled, as noted earlier, by the recognition that the arms industry could not survive on domestic orders. Exports were also viewed as fulfilling Brazilian foreign policy aspirations of acquiring greater influence within the international system. While economic and prestige factors provided the rationale for exports, the success of Brazilian sales in the 1980s must be explained.

Brazil's success in establishing an export market lay not in the development of new products that revolutionized the market, but instead in the ability to fill a niche in the international market, and through highly effective salesmanship, which was orchestrated by the Brazilian government. Brazilian weapons were of low- to medium-technology and consequently were able to be used and maintained by armed forces that did not have the skills to maintain advanced technologies. Gouvea Neto calls this a "niche strategy" that was designed to avoid direct competition with the superpowers. Instead it sought markets through the sale of "tropicalized" technology, export credits, customizing weaponry, and maintaining flexibility in the form of payments (barters).[39] This was particularly appealing to the nations of the Middle East, and, in fact, Libya, Iraq, and Saudi Arabia accounted for the vast majority of Brazilian weapons sales outside the Latin American region in the 1980s.[40]

Further, the Brazilian policy of viewing arms as a purely commercial transaction appealed to nations that had lost their traditional suppliers due to international embargoes. Nor were restrictive conditions placed on the resale or transfer of these weapons. Consequently this "no strings" arms sales policy led to Brazilian arms sold to Libya being subsequently transferred to Iran during the

Iran-Iraq war.[41] Finally, the Brazilian government, through its diplomatic missions and, on occasion, through presidential intervention, sought to promote the sale of these weapons.

Table 4.1
Major Arms Exporters of the North and the South, 1981–91
(U.S. $ million, at 1991 prices)

	1981	1982	1983	1984	1985	1986
North						
U.S.S.R.	26570	26570	26200	25090	21580	26120
U.S.	12840	13070	15670	13710	13850	11180
U.K.	4180	4639	2566	2715	1996	4009
France	2389	1406	2837	3879	1747	1458
South						
China	597	1827	2161	2715	905	1579
Israel	552	604	284	744	905	859
N. Korea	746	879	297	744	437	304
Brazil	254	949	176	840	462	328

	1987	1988	1989	1990	1991
North					
U.S.S.R.	25790	24600	21480	14770	6600
U.S.	16720	12930	14650	10300	9600
U.K.	5652	5329	5099	4472	3700
France	3297	1928	2061	3952	1100
South					
China	2473	3288	2495	1456	925
Israel	854	522	1004	458	380
N. Korea	471	765	423	166	160
Brazil	765	709	98	104	70

Source: World Military Expenditures and Arms Transfers, 1991–1992 (Washington, D.C.: U.S. Arms Control and Disarmament Agency, 1994), pp. 97–127.

Despite such publicized sales, the actual role of the Brazilian arms industry in the international system remained fairly insignificant. Western press reports overestimated the extent of Brazilian arms sales primarily because of the high-profile nature of these sales. Another contributor to this was the publicity material of the Brazilian government, which sought to exaggerate sales to make Brazilian weapons more attractive to international customers. A good example of such exaggerations was the Brazilian sale of the Osorio tank to Saudi Arabia. The Osorio sale was supposed to be a billion dollar deal but it was never consummated, and this failure was largely responsible for the financial crisis Engesa faced in the late 1980s and early 1990s. Similarly, Iraq's inability to pay Avibras led to financial troubles for that firm.

Brazil's actual arms sales were modest in the 1980s and were not capable of making the nation into a major player in the international arms trade (see Table 4.1). One can speculate about the reasons for Brazil's notoriety as an arms exporter. It was partly due to the strictly commercial policy of arms sales, which meant that weapons would end up in the hands of unsavory regimes like Iraq. The other reason lay in the rising demonology about non-Western military capabilities that started emerging in the 1980s.

With the Indian explosion of a nuclear device in 1974, the concerns about nuclear proliferation in the Third World gathered force as Western security analysts saw unstable Third World regimes using nuclear weapons to resolve their external disputes. There was also the feeling that nuclear-armed Third World states would sell these weapons or the technology to other Third World countries. The statements of leaders like Pakistan's Zulfiqar Ali Bhutto, who called for the development of an Islamic Bomb, also provided evidence to support such concerns. By the 1980s, this concern had spread to the sale of conventional weapons as wars like the Iran-Iraq conflict became the marketplace for various third-tier arms producers.

In actual fact the Brazilian conventional military capability had a limited impact both on the international arms trade and on Brazil's own capability to emerge as a major power in the international system. Its arms sales were not significant enough, nor did they involve transfers of major technology which could have created concerns about the emergence of a new force in the international system, or of a challenge to the major powers in the system. The vulnerability of the Brazilian arms industry was exposed in the post-Cold War era when it found it difficult to compete in the emerging arms market. In an interview, the president of Avibras complained that his company was hurt by the loss of markets due to the Gulf War and the changed international arms market caused by the death of the Cold War. The major powers, he complained, were dumping arms at "disgraceful prices" and this would displace Brazil, which could only sell at market prices.[42]

Further, the type of weapons Brazil produced, low-to-medium technology with high levels of foreign input, precluded the development of a powerful military force structure. Instead Brazil ended up with a conventional armed force that was heavily dependent on external suppliers of technology. What made further development of the Brazilian armed forces difficult, however, was the resource crunch caused by the debt crisis of the 1980s.

FORCE BUILDING AND RESOURCES

For the Brazilian military the 1980s marked a period in which their regional threat environment diminished and budgetary constraints limited force development but, at the same time, saw the development of a broader military doctrine. Until the 1980s, Argentina had been Brazil's main regional competitor, even though the former was demographically a much smaller nation. The usual argument made in Argentina was that "despite Brazil's superiority in numbers, it had superior soldiers. Argentine armaments were also thought to be better."[43] The Falklands War effectively destroyed this myth, as not only were Argentinean soldiers found wanting but the military leadership itself proved to be both corrupt and inefficient. Further, Argentina's own escalating debt and its transition to democracy caused its civilian governments to focus on domestic issues in the 1980s. After the 1985 regime transition took place, "Brazil found suddenly that with the exception of the nuclear field, it no longer had a competitor for regional pre-eminence at all."[44]

While the threat had diminished, it did not stop the Brazilian military from making future plans for a conflict with Argentina. The post-Falklands land threat was seen as being a surprise attack by the enemy to grab as much territory as possible and to then negotiate a settlement.[45] It was decided that Brazilian Armored Cavalry should be moved out of Rio to the south of the country bordering Argentina. A mechanized cavalry unit was to be moved along the border with Uruguay. Further, the impact of the Falklands War was also felt in military planning. It became necessary to plan for deterring an external power from projecting military force onto the Latin American mainland. It also became apparent that the Brazilian armed forces, for so long hampered by small budgets and used to countering an internal threat, were outclassed in the event of a future conflict with a technologically advanced state.[46] All three branches, therefore, came up with plans for modernizing their arsenals.

The army, under its 1985 FT-90 modernization program, sought a better transportation infrastructure within the country, a light aviation arm, new armor and artillery, and the improvement of coastal artillery with the acquisition of antiship missiles.[47] But the resource crunch of the 1980s constrained the army's modernization efforts. Under the FT-90 plan the army was to be built up to 250,000 troops by 1990. The troop level for 1985 was supposed to be 188,000 but it the army could not draft 5,000 troops because of budgetary problems.[48] As the economic crisis of the 1980s continued, the military's share of the budget fell, going from 10 percent of the national budget in 1987 to 6 percent in 1988, to 4 percent in 1989, and finally 2.24 percent in 1990. This forced the army to release 42,000 soldiers and delay the development of FT-90.[49] Specific hardware like tanks and rocket batteries could not be purchased by the army to implement parts of the FT-90 program. The army was supposed to buy the Astros II rocket from Avibras, but the cost was too high. Similarly, World War II vintage M-3 A-1 Stuart tanks were to be replaced by Osorio tanks, provided Engesa could find an export market and, thus, subsidize the deal.[50] Engesa, as mentioned earlier, never found an external market. The army was also unable to buy the aircraft needed for an army aviation wing because of the lack of funds; nor was it able to pay for a new generation of Howitzers.

The navy sought to expand its blue water fleet. It sought two aircraft carriers, air defense frigates, and sixteen corvettes.[51] It commissioned the indigenous development of destroyers, decided to license-produce German submarines, and announced in 1983 that it was initiating a nuclear submarine project. It also sought to enhance its amphibious capability.

The navy had been moving in the direction of a blue water role since the late 1970s in reaction to the growing Soviet-Cuban presence in southwest Africa. It was argued that if communist forces had bases in that area they could launch offensives on the South American mainland. Brazil retaliated with naval diplomacy—sending vessels to visit ports in West Africa, sending an expedition to the Antarctic, and seeking to strengthen ties with Nigeria. By the 1980s, the navy obviously sought a more military deterrent to the possibility of invasion. Yet the navy's plans were also hampered by the budget crunch. The plan to build two new carriers was abandoned. The fleet was unable to purchase antiaircraft missiles and the defense of territorial waters was "entrusted to 10 tugboats, disguised as corvettes."[52]

The air force was the armed service with the most obvious regional role, as its principal missions were still those of countering an insurgency and deterring an Argentinean air attack. With the decline of Argentina as a competitor and the diminished threat of an insurgency, the air force was given the lowest priority for force modernization. In fact by 1992 it was operating at the minimum level to fulfill its role and was still under pressure from government budget cuts.[53] The service's budget had been cut so severely that crew flight time was reduced, the supply of spares had reached an all-time low, and the air force brass were resigned to upgrading existing aircraft rather than expecting new airplanes.[54] The low priority accorded to the air force meant that the only weapons available to it were those manufactured locally, and in the 1980s that was Brazil's subsonic fighter, the AMX—an aircraft that once in service was to be grounded due to technical difficulties.

The modernization plans of the Brazilian armed forces, therefore, were not uniformly funded, nor were they in response to immediate threats. Indeed, as the 1980s wore on, the armed forces faced an uphill battle in trying to push for the modernization of force structures. In this historical context, the Brazilian armed forces, unknown to the general public, decided to develop a secret nuclear program. As discussed below, the secret program was in part a reaction to the problems in the civilian nuclear program. It was also a reaction to the lack of success in acquiring conventional weaponry. The Brazilian armed forces ranked their army fourth in firepower and combat efficiency in South America—behind Argentina, Peru, and Venezuela. The air force was ranked fifth behind Peru, Argentina, Venezuela, and Chile. And the navy was ranked third behind Argentina and Peru.[55] In such a situation, obtaining nuclear weapons and the means to deliver them would have moved Brazil to the front of the line in terms of prestige and military power in the South American continent.

THE NUCLEAR PROGRAM

The Brazilian nuclear program exhibits the limitations faced by Brazil in its strategy for economic development as well as the constraints this class of countries face in moving from the league of regional powers to major powers in the international system. The Brazilian program was initially beset by both bureaucratic politics and resource constraints and, subsequently, suffered from time lags, technological difficulties, and the inability to meet established goals.

The bureaucratic politics of the Brazilian nuclear program lay in the clash between those development experts who favored high levels of external inputs in the nuclear industry and the proponents of indigenous development. The former sought quick fixes to technological shortcomings that lead, consequently, to the rapid development of the country. These experts favored alliances with American and West German companies for the transfer of technology, even though such alliances left Brazil vulnerable to external pressures counter to its quest for nuclear autonomy. The latter experts favored the indigenous development of nuclear energy and are what Emanuel Adler calls "anti-dependency guerrillas." Anti-dependency guerrillas, as Adler describes it, are a Latin American phenomenon of intellectuals and technocrats who work from within the system to undermine some of its developmental objectives and promote a more nationalistic approach to the advancement of science and technology.[56] It was the proponents of indigenous development who pursued Brazil's first attempts at nuclear development.

Between 1950 and 1955 Brazil followed a "political, institutional and scientific program aimed at developing nuclear self-sufficiency {and} formulated policies to protect uranium reserves, develop and produce nuclear power, train personnel, and undertake research and development."[57] To bring this program to fruition, its head, Admiral Alvaro Alberto, sought a uranium enrichment centrifuge from West Germany. The deal was not consummated, however, because of U.S. pressure. Efforts to obtain such technology were finally halted by 1955 when the National Security Council (CSN) decided that the pursuit of such an option would risk endangering future U.S. support for Brazil's economic development and industrialization.[58]

But while Brazil moved away from the path to nuclear autonomy, there was a group of laboratories within the country that continued nuclear research. The problem with these laboratories was that they had clashing views on the path Brazil should take in the nuclear field and therefore refused to be brought under one administrative umbrella to develop a coherent national nuclear program. The fact that these different research groups were not brought under one roof "perpetuated the division of labor and fragmentation in policy and ideology among institutions."[59] Essentially this fragmentation prevented the development of a nationalist policy on nuclear power and it also prevented the emergence of a powerful group within the country that could counter the major bureaucracies that ran nuclear affairs.

These bureaucracies did not view nuclear power and its role in the economy as a unique industry with implications for sovereignty, state security, and international status. Instead they adopted the approach of the broader macropolitical consensus and applied it to nuclear energy. This approach, Etel Solingen writes, "followed the core parameters of Brazil's industrial model: rapid growth and macroeconomic stability. State entrepreneurship and foreign technology had increasingly become the means toward that end, leaving less

room for national private industrial and technological resources."[60] Solingen
adds that the ability of the central bureaucracies to enforce the macropolitical
consensus derived from the weakness of the fragmented antidependency guerrillas:
"Macropolitical consensus in the late 1960s and 1970s was strengthened by the
considerable autonomy of state structures; that is, their ability to act
independent of social class or interest group influence."[61]

Within the macroeconomic goals of the nation, nuclear energy was
viewed as providing the high levels of energy required for rapid industrialization.
So the Brazilian government sought to import reactors for this purpose. In 1971
it signed a deal with Westinghouse for the import of a light water reactor. A
number of Brazilian nuclear scientists, who favored nuclear autonomy, criticized
the project "as a turnkey plant: no local technology development would be
fostered , and it would entail dependence on foreign enriched uranium."[62] These
scientists refused to work in the Brazilian nuclear program, but the lack of a
consolidated opposition group precluded the development of an alternative
policy.

By the mid-1970s the need to speed up the nuclear program was further
strengthened by external developments. Brazil's energy situation was deemed
critical due to rapid industrial growth and the oil crisis. Adler cites figures to
show that between 1970 and 1974 electricity consumption rose by an average of
12.9 percent annually. Similarly, between 1973 and 1975 Brazil's oil imports
increased from 11.5 percent to 23.5 percent of total imports.[63] Coupled with
the need for more energy was the attempts by other Third World states to become
nuclear powers—specifically India's 1974 nuclear explosion and Argentina's
announcement that it was building a second nuclear plant. This was seen as an
indication that the Brazilian economic miracle would not suffice to make the
nation into a major political and economic power. Instead, like other Third
World nations, Brazil would have to pursue more concrete steps toward great-
power status. Brazil, therefore, had to take rapid measures to catch up with other
would-be Third World nuclear powers. The government, therefore, in 1975,
entered into a major agreement with the West German government for the
transfer of nuclear technology. The deal was seen as filling Brazilian
shortcomings in a number of areas. "The ten-billion dollar nuclear program that
resulted from the agreement with West Germany, it was thought, would solve
Brazil's energy problems, bring about nuclear fuel autonomy, create a nuclear
plants industry, develop science and technology, provide the strategic option the
military wanted, and give a slap in the face to all American governments that had
opposed the development of independent nuclear power in Brazil. Too good to
be true for just $10 billion."[64]

The agreement was opposed by both Brazilian scientists and local
industry. The scientists argued that the agreement did not consider or use the
pool of available nuclear talent in the country. Second, Brazil's hydroelectric
capacities were not being fully utilized and the mapping of potential resources in
this area was still incomplete. Third, the agreement favored West German
commercial interests rather than the long-term economic, technological, and

scientific needs of the country.[65] Brazilian industry opposed the deal because it bypassed the domestic nuclear industry and would in fact further weaken it.

The criticisms of the Brazilian nuclear scientists were valid given the financial and technological problems the program ran into. Under the agreement, uranium enrichment was to be undertaken using the Becker jet nozzle technology—a process that had not been tested at the industrial level. It soon became apparent that the process could not be made to work economically. Neither fuel reprocessing nor uranium enrichment was ever carried out in the program even though both were to take place under the aegis of the agreement. While eight reactors were to be built, construction was started on only two and these were soon bogged down in delays.[66] The cost of the program also escalated—to somewhere between $30 and $40 billion—and this happened at a time when the nation was going through the debt crisis of the 1980s.[67] Further, it became clear that the nation's hydroelectric capability was sufficient to meet its energy needs into the early part of the twentieth century. With the German program floundering and unable to give the Brazil the nuclear autonomy it wanted, the Brazilian military moved away from this program and established a "parallel program" to develop a nuclear capability.

THE PARALLEL PROGRAM

The exact date that the parallel program was started is not clear, though most scholars put it around 1979.[68] The rationale for the program began with the desire to counter Argentinean nuclear developments, but by the mid-1980s the focus had shifted to developing a nuclear capability in order to gain prestige and "political weight" in the international community. It was argued by military officials that for Brazil to gain such prestige it had to explode at least one bomb. The rationale of technological independence was also cited by officials, who said that the developed nations were putting pressure on the less-developed to not develop the technology of the entire nuclear fuel cycle, and this would hurt the country's developmental effort.[69]

Under this program all three branches of the armed forces sought to develop nuclear technology. The navy program was run out of the Institute for Nuclear Energy Research (IPEN) at the University of Sao Paulo, and it built a centrifuge enrichment facility at the town of Aramar, outside Sao Paulo. At the Aramar facility naval officials claimed they could enrich uranium to the 20 percent level and, given more centrifuges, could reach the level necessary for nuclear-weapons-grade material.[70]

The air force developed a laser enrichment facility at the CTA. The army went with the German jet nozzle enrichment technology at its Resende facility near Rio de Janeiro, and it also established a gas graphite enrichment research project at CETEX.[71] The rationale behind having three separate paths to developing nuclear technology, conducted in three different organizations, is not clear. It could be that this was a battle to protect turf given the divisions between the branches of the armed forces . It could also have been an attempt to try different routes to developing a nuclear capability quickly, but it would seem to be an excessively wasteful way of doing so. The project's secrecy was ensured through secret bank accounts.[72]

THE NUCLEAR SUBMARINE PROJECT

Officially, the nuclear submarine program was initiated in 1979 to "master the nuclear fuel cycle and to then develop a nuclear propulsion system for submarines."[73] The threat rationale for the submarine was never really explained by the navy. One admiral claimed that its utility lay in the ability to hold position indefinitely and to shift the balance of power. The Brazilian Navy had obviously learned its lessons from the Falklands War, in which British submarines had prevented maritime resupplies of the Falklands by the Argentinean Navy.[74] This rationale, however, seemed to be an afterthought, because the program was initiated three years before the Falklands War broke out. Another explanation was that it was to counter Soviet maritime presence in the South Atlantic.

A more likely explanation lay in the statement that "a nuclear submarine is a common objective among navies of the world and Brazil cannot neglect the quest for this technology which involves technological development and manpower training."[75] Another navy minister, Henrique Saboia, stated that, "Brazil would not be as great as we want, unless it masters the most modern technologies in the world, including those necessary to produce nuclear submarines."[76] The logic would seem to be that the Brazilian Navy was looking for a way to enhance its own status—and for a little navy (like Brazil's) to become a big navy it needed a nuclear submarine. More recently the Brazilian newspaper, Jornal do Brasil, argued that if Brazil wanted a real navy and not a coast guard, it should fund the continued development of a nuclear submarine. It continued that a modern navy was an undersea navy, and that, "A country at our stage of technology with an 8000 kilometer coastline, 70% of its population concentrated in the 200 kilometer wide coastal strip, and practically all its petroleum reserves located on the continental shelf must guarantee its own military defense."[77] Mastering the fuel cycle may also have been an explanation because the 1975 agreement with the FRG did little to train Brazilian scientists in the field.[78]

The nuclear submarine was conceived as a hunter-killer submarine carrying out the role of the Soviet Alfa and French Rubis class vessels. The Brazilian boat was initially supposed to have eight tubes to launch torpedoes and antiship missiles. It was to have a crew of sixty and was to weigh 4,000 tons.[79] The program had three parts: 1) to enrich uranium, 2) to build a reactor small enough to fit in a submarine, and 3) to design and build the boat itself. All three were ambitious projects, and while the navy succeeded in the first it has had problems in the area of reactor design and boat building. The cost estimates of the boat were also somewhat optimistic because Admiral Fonseca saw it coming to $200 million.[80]

The parallel program was unveiled publicly by President Jose Sarney in 1987 when he revealed that gas centrifuges at IPEN had succeeded in enriching uranium fuel to 1.2 percent Uranium-235. In 1986, it was also revealed that the air force had built a possible test site for nuclear weapons at its Cachimbo air base.[81] But while the 1980s saw Brazil's parallel program enhance its capability to produce nuclear technology for submarine propulsion and possibly develop a nuclear weapon, the economy, political changes, and regional constraints pushed Brazil into taking steps to constrain the parallel program.

Brazil's huge external debt and continuing economic crisis made it difficult for the government to continue funding such research efforts. With annual inflation running at 900 percent and an hourly minimum wage of $0.64, criticisms arose about the unnecessary waste of resources on a nuclear program.[82] Moreover, Brazil's ability to pull itself out of the debt crisis was dependent on continued U.S. support, something that would be imperiled if the Brazilian armed forces moved the nation toward an open nuclear capability.[83] Politically, the restoration of democracy brought in a civilian government that not only sought to dismantle some of these programs but also to put greater constitutional control on the military (an issue that is dealt with in greater detail in the next section).

At the regional level, the Brazilian nuclear program was playing catch-up with the Argentinean one and there was a real danger that the two nations would get involved in a debilitating nuclear rivalry. The Argentinean program had not been subjected to the infighting that marked the Brazilian program and, therefore, was able to make greater technological strides.[84] This led Brazil's military-approved president, Jose Sarney, to suggest in 1985 that the two nations open up their nuclear facilities to visits by the other.[85] Subsequent negotiations between the two countries resulted in the 1991 signing of a nuclear safeguards agreement between the two countries and the International Atomic Energy Agency (IAEA)—the so-called Quadripartite Agreement. The four parties to this agreement are Argentina, Brazil, the IAEA, and the Brazilian-Argentinean Agency for the Accounting of Nuclear Materials (ABACC). The ABACC is to work with the IAEA to establish a joint system of on-site inspections and for the safeguarding of nuclear materials.[86] Thus Brazil, while seeking to develop the nuclear option, did not make the mistake of precipitating a serious nuclear rivalry with Argentina.

THE SPACE PROGRAM

Along with the nuclear submarine program the Brazilian armed services were also seeking to develop a space program. In the 1970s, Avibras had made a series of sounding rockets (Sonda series) for the armed forces and the last of the series, the Sonda-4, was big enough to lift an 1,100-pound payload to an altitude of 200 miles.[87] In the 1980s, the armed forces decided to develop a satellite launch vehicle (VLS) and a data collection satellite (SCD-1) by 1990. The VLS was to be a liquid fueled rocket with the payload and range to be used for military purposes. The space program would have fit the nuclear needs of both the army and the air force. The army's nuclear program was originally conceived around developing nuclear artillery shells, but eventually the decision was taken to make ballistic missiles. The air force similarly wanted ballistic missiles rather than nuclear armed aircraft.[88] To get the VLS project off the ground Brazil entered into a technology agreement with France and a space cooperation agreement with China whereby Beijing was to supply Brazil with liquid fuel technology.

The VLS project did not progress smoothly because of international pressure and internal funding problems. According to the former head of the CTA, Brigadier Piva, the success of the Sonda-4 raised alarms around the world about the potential military applications of the program and subsequently led to a technological boycott of Brazil's space program. Piva recounted:

Each technological triumph caused concern. The first was when we managed to make solid propellant. In the beginning they exported the raw materials to us, almost free, because they could not believe we would get there. When they saw we had developed the propellant they began restricting the supply of raw materials to make the propellant.[89]

In fact, by 1991, the VLS program faced a multinational embargo and France reneged on its space cooperation agreement with Brazil.[90] The embargo prevented Brazil from purchasing an inertial guidance system for the VLS and this paralyzed the program.[91] Thus, by the early 1990s, the Brazilian space program was being effectively slowed down by international sanctions. Insufficient funding also hurt the program as it led to a People's Republic of China-Brazil agreement temporarily being put on hold, and it also led to the flight of skilled personnel from the program. The net result was that while the SCD (a simple satellite) could be built, the VLS program languished and, in 1993, SCD-1 was launched by an American rocket.

THE IMPACT OF THE DEMOCRATIC TRANSITION

In 1985 the Brazilian military started its disengagement from government and put into process the transition to democracy. Its carefully screened candidate, Jose Sarney, was to run the country until 1989. In 1989 Brazil had its first free elections and Ferdinand Collor was elected president. Collor's election marked the beginning of the attempt by the new civilian government to try and reestablish control over the military and its programs—in both the conventional and nuclear spheres. As it disengaged itself from political rule the military had begun to take measures to prevent precisely such control from being imposed on it.

The return to civilian rule in Brazil was initially marked by little control over the military and its affairs. The reasons for this were twofold. One was that the military shaped the transition process and, consequently, the, "military had ample opportunity to reorganize several military-industrial programs to shield them from civilian encroachment, and a unified opposition to the military's continued control over the defense sector failed to emerge."[92] The second reason was that the opposition felt that challenging the military on this issue would create an unnecessary confrontation that was not central to the transition process. In fact one of the charges leveled at the opposition was that as part of the transition process a pact had been struck to preserve the parallel program.[93] There was also the belief that if the military-industrial programs flourished they would create greater military professionalism and thereby predispose the military to leave the political stage for their traditional mission.[94]

The military reorganized important programs to guarantee influence and shield those sectors from civilian control. The military retained control over the Brazilian Space Activities Commission even after the Constituent Assembly abolished the National Security Council. The space program oversaw the country's missile development programs.[95] The armed forces were also able to retain effective control over the nuclear program.

Once President Collor took office he set about reestablishing civilian control over the military. The secret service was dismantled and placed under a civilian secretary for strategic affairs. Attempts were also made to place limits on the military-led nuclear program. In 1990 a congressional investigatory committee (CPI) found out that the military had run a parallel nuclear program and had built a test site at Cachimbo, in the state of Para. President Collor, on September 18, 1990, had the borehole at the test site filled, thus symbolically terminating the weapons aspect of the program. President Collor told Brazilian television that as soon as he entered office he ordered the deactivation of the atomic bomb program.[96] This would suggest that the president was fundamentally opposed to nuclear weapons and had taken a political decision to dismantle the program even before he entered office. It is more likely, however, that Collor's decision was taken in response to international pressures. The Gulf crisis had just broken out and with it the news had emerged that Brazilian scientists had provided assistance to the Iraqi missile program. It is believed that the decision was taken to counter the uncomfortable position the Brazilian government had been placed in after these revelations.[97] By eschewing the nuclear option Brazil was alleviating international fears and reiterating its commitment to the status quo in the international system. Although Collor sought to dismantle the program and impose civilian control over it, the armed forces were able to extract several significant concessions in the Quadripartite Agreement of 1991. They were also able to retain some control of the development of the parallel nuclear program.

The CPI visited the navy's Aramar facility and praised the progress made at the facility. It was "impressed by the nationalist sentiment at Aramar." The CPI, therefore, recommended that the parallel program be institutionalized through legislative decree. The navy retained control of the Aramar facility.[98] The army, however, was to subsequently have its graphite reactor program terminated because it did not have a peaceful purpose.[99] The most likely explanation for the termination, however, lies in the lack of progress in the project. With rising costs and a weak economy the government of Brazil probably decided to go with the program that showed the most promise—the Aramar project.

Under the Quadripartite accord nuclear materials needed to propel vehicles, including submarines, need not be inspected. This clause was put in to the agreement because of the interest of both the Brazilian and Argentinean Navies in nuclear propulsion.[100] The military was also able, despite the opposition of the Collor government, to retain control over the enrichment of nuclear fuel.[101] But while making these concessions to the military, international pressure seemed to push the Brazilians toward accepting further safeguards. By July 1994 an IAEA team along with ABACC officials was allowed to inspect the Aramar facility, with the IAEA personnel looking to see whether nuclear materials had been diverted. It was stated at that time that while ABACC inspections now took place once a month, the IAEA inspections were to also become routine.[102]

Thus despite the fact that the program remained in military hands, it was slowly but surely coming under international oversight. The civilian governments had, therefore, started moving toward accepting international control. The rationale behind it lay in the economic crisis Brazil faced, in the negative international image such steps gave the country, and in the international constraints put on its quest for dual-purpose technology.

THE LACK OF RESOURCES

By the early 1980s Brazil's economic miracle of the late 1960s and 1970s had run out of steam and instead the nation was faced with a major economic crisis. The second oil crisis, governmental attempts to artificially control inflation, and the subsidies to state enterprises caused a downward spiral in the Brazilian economy.[103] The impact on the Brazilian military was seen in low defense spending levels (Table 4.2) and an actual reduction of manpower. Weapons acquisition programs were either delayed or put on hold for all three services. The trend worsened in 1990 when the Collor government took office as prices hit hyperinflationary levels, exceeding 50 percent per month—a first in Brazilian history.[104]

Faced with this economic crisis, the Collor government decided to privatize large parts of the public sector. Although the decision to carry out privatization was taken in 1990, it took two years to carry out the first sale. By the end of 1992, however, twenty-two of the twenty-six steel, petrochemical, fertilizer, machinery, and transportation enterprises were privatized.[105] The arms industry was not exempted from the push to privatize as Embraer, one of the big three in the Brazilian arms industry, was put up for sale. Foreign buyers were solicited for Engesa as well.

The decision to privatize the arms industry would seem to be a defeat for the military and the nationalist forces within Brazil because it signaled a move away from the philosophy of security and development. The Brazilian economy, by the early 1990s, was being pushed into a situation in which it could no longer support high levels of state intervention on behalf of local industry. Hence the Collor government's move to liberalize the economy and reduce the role of the state in the Brazilian economy. As seen in the Israeli case, a crisis in the general economy had significant repercussions on the political economy of the country, which also effected the arms industry. Traditionally, arms industries have been viewed as protected enclaves in the general economy and, therefore, not subject to the forces prevailing on the broader economy. But as in the Israeli case, the economic crisis of the 1980s and early 1990s forced the Brazilian government to dismantle this protective enclave and make the arms industry subject to the same set of forces as the macroeconomy.

Table 4.2
Brazilian Military Expenditure as a
Percentage of GNP, 1981–91

Year	% of GNP
1981	0.7
1982	0.9
1983	0.9
1984	0.8
1985	0.8
1986	0.9
1987	1.0
1988	1.4
1989	1.5
1990	1.7
1991	1.3

Source: World Military Expenditures and Arms Transfers, 1991–1992 (Washington, D.C.: U.S. Government Printing Office, 1994), p. 55.

The reasons for moving away from the policy of protected enclaves lay in the transformation of the global arms market and the vulnerability of the Brazilian arms industry to such changes. As mentioned earlier, the Brazilian arms industry was an export-oriented industry, heavily dependent on sales to the Middle East. Iraq's inability to pay for the weapons it bought in the 1980s brought some Brazilian firms like Avibras to the brink of bankruptcy. The uncertain nature of the Middle Eastern market was further brought home by the 1991 Gulf War and the subsequent breakup of the Soviet Union. In the aftermath of the Gulf War prospective Brazilian customers like Saudi Arabia, Kuwait, and Iran all moved toward first-tier suppliers for the purchase of weaponry. This decision was made in part because of the vital role advanced technology weapons played in winning the war for the United States and its allies. The decision was also influenced by political considerations such as giving the big powers a stake in the region through commercial arms sales. The breakup of the Soviet Union also removed the interbloc constraints of selling weapons and, consequently, Russia started pushing aggressively to sell its weapons in the region.

The net result of these changes has been the shutting out of the smaller suppliers like Brazil from this lucrative region. Saudi Arabia, for instance, was seen as a potential customer for Engesa's Osorio tank and, in fact, development of the weapon had proceeded with an eye toward the Saudi market. But after the Gulf War the Saudi government decided to buy tanks from the United States.[106] Kuwait was another potential customer that shifted to the major suppliers. In the 1980s Kuwait had purchased rockets from Avibras but after the Gulf War the Kuwaiti government decided to purchase weaponry from both the United States and Russia. In 1993 Kuwait signed a ten-year bilateral defense agreement with Russia and it drew up a list of weapons—surface-to-air-missiles, helicopters, and armored personnel carriers—it wanted from Moscow.[107]

Faced with a diminished international market, Brazil took the step of reducing its subsidies to the arms industry, slashing the work force, and seeking to actively privatize the industry. But despite the willingness to undertake such measures Brazil was having a tough time privatizing its arms industry. By late 1994 the government had been trying to sell its stake in Embraer for three years but there were no takers, as the deal was reportedly held back by the poor performance and the high overhead of the company. At the same time, the company's workforce was halved (stakes in the company were eventually sold to a private consortium of banks, investment firms, and pension funds, with the air force holding on to 25 percent stake in the company).[108]

THE SHIFT IN THE ATTITUDE OF THE ARMED FORCES

The Brazilian government's decision to jettison some of the country's high-profile industries could be viewed as a defeat for the Brazilian armed forces, which had invested both capital and research into these industries. It could also be viewed as an indicator to the extent to which military autonomy had been restricted after the transition to democracy. But recent trends indicate that the Brazilian armed forces in fact seem to have shifted to a acquisition pattern similar to those of other middle powers when faced with major shifts in the international system and resource constraints.

It became apparent in the Israeli and Indian cases that when resources were limited the armed services preferred to purchase systems abroad rather than waste scarce resources within the country. In the 1990s the Brazilian armed forces seem to have followed this pattern of organizational behavior. Rather than invest in costly efforts to domestically develop technology, the armed forces have decided to acquire off-the-shelf systems in as many areas as possible. All three branches of the armed services have started purchasing systems abroad and what has made this possible are the changes in the international arms market.

With the demise of the Soviet Union, Brazil has found a new supplier in Russia, which has advanced weaponry available at competitive prices. Brazil's first major deal with Russia was for the purchase of Igla SA-18 SAMs, and the contract may eventually amount to $100 million.[109] Brazil is also seeking to purchase 300 T-72 tanks from Russia, with ongoing negotiations about whether payment is to be made through barter or hard currency.[110]

Modernization of the navy and the army is also being sought through purchases from Western Europe. In addition to purchasing T-72s, Brazil is also considering developing its armored force by buying second-hand Leopard tanks from either Belgium or the Netherlands. The army has also bought light field guns and mortars from the UK and Matra Mistral SAMs from France. The navy, in an effort to build up its blue water capability, is purchasing frigates and minesweepers from Britain.[111] The air force awarded Raytheon the contract for an eco-surveillance satellite—Sivam—and is reportedly seeking new fighter aircraft from the United States.[112]

What makes all these purchases from external suppliers interesting is that Brazil seems to have jettisoned it domestic arms industry as a supplier for its modernization program. Thus Embraer, which in the 1980s was proudly mentioned as a success story of the Brazilian arms industry and a vehicle for developing technology, has faced sharp reductions in its work-force, has been privatized, and, more importantly, is basing its future on the development of commuter aircraft.[113] The company used to have a 50:50 civil-military production ration, which it now wants to change to a 30:70 civil-military ratio. Military production is to center around an upgraded version of the Tucano, the ALX, which would not be a major technological leap for the firm.[114] Engesa's future also seems to be in the production of commercial vehicles. Further, big ticket weapons programs like the Osorio tank have been sidelined as the army has sought to purchase its tank force from abroad. Avibras has diversified into civilian production, building trolley bus parts, doing auto painting, and setting up a fiber optics factory.[115]

At the same time, the two programs that the armed forces fought to preserve their control over were the nuclear and space programs. The reason for this lay in the belief, much as was the case in India, that developing a nuclear capability would raise Brazil to the status of an international power—something to which Brazil is due, given its size and potential.[116] Making Brazil a militarily strong state was also seen as being important because of the transformation of the international system. Moreover, the end of the cold war competition raised the fear among Brazilian decision makers—civilian and military alike—that Brazil's leverage in world politics would shrink even further and expose the country to concerted First World pressure on economic and environmental issues. Recent efforts by international groups to stop the burning of Brazilian rain forests is an obvious example of the sort of external mitigation of national sovereignty feared by Brazil.[117] In reaction, the Brazilian armed forces have stated that one of their missions will be to expand activities in the Amazon.[118]

The Brazilian political leadership, however, has had to impose controls on the armed forces cherished programs in order to alleviate the fears of the international community. Such restraints have also been necessary in order to secure advanced technology for the country. Brazil's space program was dealt a setback in the 1980s because of the embargo imposed by Western suppliers. Thus the Collor, Franco, and Cardoso governments have had to guarantee greater transparency in Brazilian activities in the area of sensitive technologies. Brazil signed the Chemical Weapons Convention and promised not to use biological weapons.[119]

In the fields of nuclear and space technology, successive Brazilian governments have had to allow these programs to come under greater international supervision both to alleviate fears of Brazil's intentions and to secure access to particular technologies. By July 1994 an IAEA team along with ABACC officials was allowed to inspect the Aramar facility, with the IAEA personnel looking to see whether nuclear materials had been diverted. It was stated at that time that while ABACC inspections now took place once a month, the IAEA inspections were to also become routine.[120] The Brazilian government also agreed to enrich uranium to only up to the twenty percent level which would be insufficient for making a nuclear weapon.[121]

In late 1995, however, Brazil refused to become a signatory to the Nuclear Non-Proliferation Treaty (NPT) and did not ratify its extension into perpetuity. In early 1996 Brazil signed an accord with India, another nation which refused to sign the NPT, on the production of nuclear fuel out of Thorium.[122] Both moves suggested a continued desire to maintain autonomy in the field of nuclear technology but since then Brazil has been forced to take steps to restrict its nuclear option. The country signed a cooperation agreement with the United States for the peaceful use of nuclear energy.[123] Brazil also agreed to join the nuclear supply group which prevents the sale of sensitive technologies to other countries and also restricts Brazil's ability to import some technologies for developing its own nuclear program.[124] Finally, in June 1997 President Cardoso stated that the country would sign the NPT.

At the economic level the budgetary constraints of the Brazilian government have effectively slowed down the nuclear submarine program. The Brazilian Navy has stated that in order to launch a nuclear submarine by 2006–7 it would cost $2.2 billion. So far the program has cost $800 million and will require another $500 million to complete the project. After that the Navy will require another $900 million to construct the submarine.[125] Yet the Navy has been getting insufficient funding to successfully bring the project to fruition. In 1995 it asked the government for $75 million but was allocated only $25 million for the project.[126] The nuclear submarine ranks eighteenth on the list of the Navy's budgetary priorities and, at current levels, the project is not expected to be completed for another twenty years.[127]

Supplier constraints have also effected the goals and the progress of Brazil's space program. The success of the international embargo against the military dominated space program led the Brazilian government, in 1994, to create a civilian space agency for Brazil. It was argued that the creation of civilian space agency,

would guarantee greater transparence in Brazil's activities in the area of sensitive technologies. The government has already allayed the international community's fears through its nuclear policy and its promises not to use chemical and biological weapons. In addition, it is preparing a plan for monitoring exports of sensitive products.[128]

Such steps were supposed to facilitate the transfer of sensitive technologies to Brazil. These restrictions also led the Franco government to agree to be bound by the MTCR guidelines on the export of missile related technology.[129] The Cardoso government reiterated the desire to use space technology for peaceful purposes. President Cardoso told an interviewer that Brazil was interested in U.S. missile technology not for warfighting capabilities but because it wanted to be in the "vanguard of science and technology." He further stated that Brazil was willing to participate in the MTCR and to limit the use of such technology to peaceful purposes—Brazil subsequently became an MTCR signatory.[130]

Brazil's willingness to abide with international restrictions on its space program has led, since 1994, to the opening up of avenues for space cooperation and the acquisition of space technology. Following the establishment of a civilian space agency, the United States agreed to allow Brazil to purchase the inertial guidance system for the VLS. In 1996 the United States signed a space cooperation agreement with Brazil which would put a Brazilian astronaut in space, and allow for joint use of the space shuttle.[131] Thus international pressure worked to not only constrain weapons programs which would have found a ready market in the arms bazaar of the 1990s, but to also hurt the country's quest for new technologies and its desire to use strategic weapons to acquire greater international status.

Thus, despite the fact that the nuclear and space programs initially remained in military hands, they have slowly but surely come under international technology controls. With such international oversight Brazil's plans to use its nuclear and space capabilities for military purposes and to achieve great power status have been constrained and, instead greater transparency forced on Brazil's nuclear and space research programs has moved them in the direction of civilian research.

More important, President Cardoso has espoused a view of international security that while enhancing Brazil's status, is based on a commonalty of northern and southern interests. The president stated that Brazil was ready to assume a permanent seat in the United Nations Security Council and wanted to discuss the crises in the Middle East, Africa, and Europe. President Cardoso felt this was possible because there was a broad convergence of values between the north and the south in the post-Cold War era—that human rights and free markets were the best way to ensure development. He therefore argued, "I do not see the interests of the north and the south as conflicting or as preventing cooperation. I see rather a commonalty of interests based on the values that won the Cold War. Brazil's priority in foreign policy is precisely to advance these values."[132] Brazil's policy, therefore, has come full circle from one of confrontation with the north and the quest to attain technological independence, to one pushing for cooperative security and technological cooperation. In doing so its political leadership has moved away from the more nationalistic plans that drove both conventional and strategic weapons programs in the 1980s.

CONCLUSION

The Brazilian case is dissimilar to the Israeli and Indian cases due to the difference in threat environments. Unlike Israel, and to a lesser degree India, Brazil is not locked in a qualitative and quantitative arms race with its principal regional rival. The modernization of the Argentinean armed forces over the past couple of decades has been too modest to spark the kind of technological arms race that the Israelis, and to a lesser extent the Indians, have had to face. With no immediate changes in the threat environment the Brazilian armed forces did not have to rely on the continued import of weaponry to upgrade their arsenal.

Further, unlike the Indian and Israeli armed forces, which were able to obtain greater budgetary resources when faced with threats, the Brazilian armed forces were constrained over the years by a small budget that was initially reduced when the financial crisis of the 1980s took place. Third, and again unlike India and Israel, Brazil was unable to attract external suppliers who were periodically willing to modernize its arsenal with the weapons it desired. The United States, as Brazil's principal supplier, in fact restricted the type of weaponry flowing into Brazil, tried to forestall its nuclear ambitions, and used weapons transfers as leverage in an attempt to influence Brazil's human rights policies.

The combination of these three constraints should have worked to strengthen the base of the domestic arms industry. Low financial resources and the low level of interest of external suppliers should have led to a commitment to develop indigenous technology as an alternative to these constraints. The existence of a low-threat environment should also have been an advantage because it should have permitted the gradual and evolutionary development of systems in the country. Weapons development and production could have progressed up the technological ladder without the pressures to import that are placed by an external threat that has to be countered. Thus Brazil could have obtained the technological building blocks for becoming a major power domestically. Instead, Brazil suffered the Indian and Israeli fates in the development of military technology.

Like India and Israel, Brazil's ability to produce military technology was constrained by its larger political economy and the constraint imposed by financial resources. It was also constrained by the lack of a large enough domestic market. Brazil's political economy was aimed at securing rapid development, and this required a large foreign content—in the form of MNC presence and technology—in their products. Thus the arms industry was to build weapons that were heavily reliant on imported, off-the-shelf parts and were not of an advanced nature.

A small domestic market offset the advantages of the low-threat environment because it meant that the cost of indigenously produced weapons could only be subsidized by exports. But such a policy also limited the type of weapons that could be developed. In order to sell in the international arms market the Brazilians had to produce weapons that would find an immediate market—niche filling—in this case being low-to-medium technology weapons. The export strategy of niche filling made the Brazilian arms industry vulnerable for two reasons. First, as events proved, it laid the industry vulnerable to changing market conditions. The shift in the international arms market from being a sellers market to a buyers market led to more advanced weapons from first- and second-tier suppliers being available for competitive prices—thus wiping out whatever advantages Brazil had in these areas.

Second, the small size of the Brazilian arms industry and the lack of a domestic market also increased its vulnerability. When it became difficult to export and foreign customers could not pay for weaponry the Brazilian arms industry did not have the luxury of falling back on an internal market. In fact, weapons like the Osorio were only developed with the expectation of finding foreign buyers.

Thus despite the ambitious plans and statements of the early 1980s, the Brazilian arms industry had, by the early 1990s, become of secondary importance to the country's armed forces in their plans to acquire better systems and great-power status. Instead, the Brazilian armed forces followed the course of action taken by their Indian and Israeli counterparts and sought to best use their resources by importing advanced weaponry. And the domestic arms industry, once treated as an expression of national sovereignty and a strategic asset, has been allowed to fall victim to market forces.

At the same time, because the nuclear program was insulated from such external market pressures, and because the country would not be allowed to import such technology, the Brazilian nuclear industry was able to achieve a relative degree of success. But while the armed forces, particularly the navy, were able to retain some control over the development of the nuclear program, they had to acquiesce to international pressure to bring about some degree of transparency in it.

Where do these trends then leave Brazil in its quest to become a major power? While the armed forces may still project a vague extraregional threat, the ability to match it will require a heavy financial investment which it is believed Brazil cannot meet. This is especially the case with the navy's expansion plans, which also include the desire to obtain nuclear propulsion. At the same time, the indigenous production capability has shown its limitations in achieving such ambitions. Thus Brazil could conceivably develop a bomb in the basement, but without the conventional capability to back it up it will remain an incomplete military power with some fancy pieces of weaponry, but not the sort of comprehensive military force structure that makes a nation graduate from the status of a middle power to a major power. Brazil's dreams to become a major international actor, therefore, as in the case of other middle powers, will have to come from other avenues in the international system—as President Cardoso is suggesting.

NOTES

1. Stanley Hilton, "The Brazilian Military: Changing Strategic Perceptions and the Question of Mission," *Armed Forces and Society* 13, no. 3 (Spring 1987): 329.

2. Interview with Brigadier Piva, former director of CTA, VEJA 10 March 1993, 7, in *Foreign Broadcast Information Service-Latin America (FBIS-LAT*) 93-048, 15 March 1993, 32.

3. Hilton, "The Brazilian Military," 332-33 and *FBIS-LAM*-85-17, 4 September 1985, D2.

4. Hilton, "The Brazilian Military," 334-36.

5. Hilton, "The Brazilian Military," 337.

6. Patrice Franko-Jones, *The Brazilian Defense Industry* (Boulder, Colo.: Westview Press, 1992), 56.

7. Ethan B. Kapstein, "The Brazilian Defense Industry and the International System," *Political Science Quarterly* 105, no. 4 (Winter 1990-91): 580.

8. Franko-Jones, *The Brazilian Defense Industry*, 58.

9. Ibid.

10. Maria Helena Moreira Alves, *State and Military Opposition in Brazil* (Austin: University of Texas Press, 1985), 24-25.

11. Franko-Jones, *The Brazilian Defense Industry*, 59.

12. Ronald M. Schneider, *The Political System of Brazil: Emergence of a "Modernizing Authoritarian Regime," 1964-1970* (New York, Columbia University Press, 1971), 244.

13. Ken Conca, "Technology, the Military and Democracy in Brazil," *Journal of InterAmerican Studies and World Affairs* 34, no. 1 (Spring 1992): 145.

14. Ibid.

15. Renato Dagnino and Domicio Proenca, "Arms Production and Technological Spinoffs: The Brazilian Aeronautics Industry," Unpublished Paper, 1988, 5.

16. Jose O. Maldifassi and Pier A. Abetti, Defense Industries in Latin American Countries (Westport, Connecticut and London: Praeger, 1994), 46.

17. Emanuel Adler, "State Institutions, Ideology, and Autonomous Technological Development: Computers and Nuclear Energy in Argentina and Brazil," *Latin American Research Review* 23, no. 2 (1988): 64.

18. Ibid., 65.

19. Maldifassi and Abetti, *Defense Industries in Latin American Countries*, 31, 36.

20. Franko-Jones, *The Brazilian Defense Industry*, 71.

21. Dagnino and Proenca, "Arms Production and Technological Spinoffs," 6.

22. Ibid.

23. Ibid., 8-14.

24. Ibid., 9.

25. Maldifassi and Abetti, *Defense Industries in Latin America*, 48.

26. Franko-Jones, *The Brazilian Defense Industry*, 114.

27. *FBIS-LAM*-86-11, 13 January 1986, D2.

28. Raul Gouvea-Neto, "How Brazil Competes in the Global Defense Industry," *Latin American Research Review* 26, no. 3 (1991): 97.

29. Franko-Jones, *The Brazilian Defense Industry*, 124.

30. Ibid., 124-25.

31. Kapstein, "The Brazilian Defense Industry," 587.

32. Ethan B. Kapstein, *The Political Economy of National Security, A Global Perspective* (Columbia: University South Carolina Press, 1992), 111.

33. Defense and Foreign Affairs Weekly, 18-24 November 1985; and *FBIS-LAM-86-09*, 14 January 1986, D1.

34. Technologia & Defesa, Mar-Apr 1993, 32-33, in FBIS-LAT-93-183, 23 September, 1993, pp. 44-45.

35. *Technologia & Defesa*, Mar-Apr 1993, pp. 16-18 in *FBIS-LAT*-93-183, 23 September 1993, 38-39.

36. Franko-Jones, The Brazilian Defense Industry, 2, 165.

37. Maldifassi and Abetti, *Defense Industries in Latin America*, 56.

38. Franko-Jones, *The Brazilian Defense Industry*, 166.

39. Gouvea-Neto, "How Brazil Competes," 90.

40. O Globo, 19 November, 1984, p. 14 in FBIS-LAT-84-230, 28 November, 1994, p. D1.

41. Gouvea-Neto, "How Brazil Competes," 90.

42. *FBIS-LAT*-91-018, January 28 1991, 30.

43. Ian Kemp, Hal Klepak, Charles Bickers, Dean Martins, Donald Neil, "JDW Country Survey: Brazil," Jane's Defense Weekly, 9 May 1992, 808.

44. Ibid.

45. *FBIS-LAM*-85-248, 26 December 1985, D2.

46. Hilton, *The Brazilian Military*, 337-38.

47. Kemp, et. al., "Country Survey: Brazil," 811.

48. *FBIS-LAM*-86-031,14 February, 1986, D2.

49. *FBIS-LAT*-90-223, 19 November, 1990, 44.

50. *Folha de Sao Paulo*, 26 October, 1986, 18, in *FBIS-LAM*-86-211, 31 October 1986, D4.

51. O Estado de Sao Paulo, 29 November, 1990, 24, in *FBIS-LAT*-90-237, 10 December 1990, 52.

52. *FBIS-LAT*-92-107, 3 June, 1992, 32.

53. Kemp, et. al., "Country Survey: Brazil," 816.

54. *FBIS-LAT*-92-107, 3 June, 1992, 31-32.

55. Istoe Senhor, 22 April 1992, 26-29, *FBIS-LAT*-92-107, 3 June 1992, 31.

56. Emanuel Adler, *The Power of Ideology: The Quest for Technological Autonomy in Argentina and Brazil* (Berkeley: University of California Press, 1987), 93-100.

57. Ibid., 78.

58. Ibid.

59. Ibid., 79.

60. Etel Solingen, "Macropolitical Consensus and Lateral Autonomy in Industrial Policy: the Nuclear Sector in Brazil and Argentina," *International Organization*, 47, no. 2 (Spring 1993): 284.

61. Ibid.

62. Antonio Rubens Britto de Castro, Norberto Majlis, Luiz Pinguelli Rosa, and Fernando de Souza Barros, "Brazil's Nuclear Shakeup: Military Still in Control," Bulletin of the Atomic Scientists, (May 1989): 22.

63. Adler, *The Power of Ideology*, 316.

64. Ibid.

65. Castro et. al., "Brazil's Nuclear Shakeup," 23.

66. Ibid.

67. Adler, "State Institutions," 81.

68. Ibid., 82.

69. *Folha de Sao Paulo*, April 28 1985, 25, in *FBIS-LAT*-85-084, 1 May 1985, D1.

70. Jean Krasno, "Brazil's Secret Nuclear Program," *Orbis* 38, no. 3 (Summer 1994): 430.

71. *FBIS-LAT*-85-083, 30 April 1985, D1; *FBIS-LAT*-90-161, 20 August 1990, 39; and *FBIS-LAT*- 90-181, 13 September 1990, 29.

72. FBIS-LAM-87-090, 11 May 1987, D1-D2.

73. Interview with Admiral Maximiano de Fonseca, navy minister 1979-1984, Folha de Sao Paulo, September 1990, A5, in *FBIS-LAT*-90-188, 10 September 1990, 18.

74. *FBIS-LAM*-83-241, 14 December 1983, D3.

75. Ibid.

76. FBIS-LAT-89-075, 20 April 1989, 34.

77. *Jornal do Brasil*, 13 November 1995, 8, in *FBIS-LAT*-95-229, 29 November 1995, p. 35.

78. *FBIS-LAM*-87-090, 11 May 1987, D2.

79. *FBIS-LAM*-87-077, 22 April 1987, D3.

80. *FBIS-LAM*-84-017, 25 January 1984, D1.

81. Castro et. al., "Brazil's Nuclear Shakeup," 23-24.

82. Ibid., 24.

83. Krasno, "Brazil's Secret Nuclear Program," 434.

84. For details, see Solingen, "Macropolitical Consensus and Lateral Autonomy," 289-291.

85. Richard Kessler, "Peronists Seek Nuclear Greatness," *Bulletin of the Atomic Scientists* (May 1989): 15.

86. Krasno, "Brazil's Secret Nuclear Program," 427.

87. Leonard S. Spector with Jacqueline R. Smith, *Nuclear Ambitions: The Spread of Nuclear Weapons 1989-1990* (Boulder, Colo: Westview Press, 1990), 254.

88. *O Estado de Sao Paulo*, 12 April 1987, 9, in *FBIS-LAM*-87-077, 22 April 1987, D4.

89. *Veja*, 10 March 1993, 7-9, in *FBIS-LAT*-93-048, 15 March 1993, 32.

90. *FBIS-LAT*-91-214, 5 November 1991, 32.

91. Jayne Brener and Helio Contreiras, "A Secret Weapon," Istoe, 8 December 1993, 96, 98, in *FBIS-LAT*-93-246, 27 December 1996, 38.

92. Conca, "Technology, the Military," 148.

93. Folha de Sao Paulo, 22 March 1987, A5, in FBIS-LAM-87-057, 25 March 1987, D2.

94. Conca, "Technology, the Military," 149.

95. Ibid., 150.

96. *FBIS-LAT*-90-188, 27 September 1990, 17.

97. *Folha De Sao Paulo*, 25 October 1990, A3, in *FBIS-LAT*-90-211, 31 October 1990, 24.

98. *FBIS-LAT*-90-219, 13 November 1990, 64.

99. *FBIS-LAT*-92-023, 4 February 1992, 28.

100. Krasno, "Brazil's Secret Nuclear Program," 428.

101. Ibid., 433

102. *FBIS-LAT*-94-131, 8 July 1994, 40.

103. For a discussion of the causes of the Brazilian economic crisis of the 1980s, see, Antonio Barros de Castro, "Renegade Development: Rise and Demise of State-Led Development in Brazil," in *Democracy, Markets, and Structural Reform in Latin America: Argentina, Bolivia, Brazil, Chile, and Mexico*, William C. Smith, Carlos H. Acuna and Eduardo A. Gamarra eds. (New Brunswick and London: Transaction, 1994), 201-4.

104. Ibid., 204.

105. Lourdes Sola, "The State, Structural Reform, and Democratization in Brazil," in Smith et. al., *Democracy, Markets, and Structural Reform*, 157.

106. Christopher F. Foss, "Ground Forces—Who is Buying What?," *Jane's Defense Weekly*, 30 July 1994, 34-35.

107. *Jane's Defense Weekly*, 9 July 1994, 1.

108. *Jane's Defense Weekly*, 26 November 1994, 9.

109. *Jane's Defense Weekly*, 11 June 1994. 3.

110. *Jane's Defense Weekly*, 24 September, 1994, 1.

111. *Jane's Defense Weekly*, 22 January 1995, 4.

112. *The Wall Street Journal*, 31 May 1995, C20, and *Jane's Defense Weekly*, 11 June 1994, 1.

113. *Jane's Defense Weekly*, 26 November 1994, 9.

114. *Jane's Defense Weekly*, 6 March 1996, 35.

115. *FBIS-LAT*-93-183, 23 September 1993, 36.

116. Krasno, "Brazil's Secret Nuclear Program," 434-35.

117. Ibid., 433-34.

118. *FBIS-93-042*, 5 March 1993, 29.

119. *Gazeta Mercantil*, 13 December 1991, 11, in *FBIS-LAT*-92-002, 3 January 1992, 21.

120. *FBIS-LAT*-94-131, 8 July 1994, 40.

121. *Jornal do Brasil*, 13 November 1995, 8, in *FBIS-LAT*-95-229, 29 November 1995, 35.

122. *O Estado de Sao Paulo*, 30 January 1996, A 3, in *FBIS-LAT*-96-022, 1 February 1996, 20.

123. *FBIS-LAT*-96-043, 4 March 1996, 25.

124. *Jornal do Brasil*, 31 March 1996, 16, in *FBIS-LAT*-96-065, 3 April 1996, 30.

125. *Agencia Estado Sao Paulo*, 9 November 1995, in *FBIS-LAT*-95-218, 13 November 1995, 36.

126. *O Estado do Sao Paulo*, 7 February 1996, A-15, in *FBIS-LAT*-96-028, 9 February 1996, 12.

127. *Jornal do Brasil*, 13 November 1995, 8, in *FBIS-LAT*-95-229, 29 November 1995, 35.

128. *Gazeta Mercantil*, 13 December 1991, 11, in *FBIS-LAT*-92-002, 3 January 1992, 21.

129. *The Wall Street Journal*, 14 February 1994, 7C.

130. James F. Hoge Jr., "Fulfilling Brazil's Promise: A Conversation with President Cardoso," Foreign Affairs 74, no. 4 (July-August 1995): 68.

131. *FBIS-LAT*-96-043, 4 March 1996, 24.

132. Hoge, "Fulfilling Brazil's Promise," 68-69.

5

Regional Powers and Militarization

The three cases discussed in this study have examined the militarization efforts of three regional powers—Brazil, Israel, and India—two with a similar threat level and one with a dissimilar one, all of which saw military strength as enhancing their role within the international system. Militarization, as defined here, is a country's development of its military force in order to assert its foreign policy and security interests. In order to understand why these states saw such a buildup as being necessary, their militarization efforts should be placed within the context of bipolarity and the political and economic pressures it placed on these nations.

Politically, the Cold War both set the tone for the militarization efforts of these nations as well as led to the pursuit of particular strategies for militarization. The early militarization efforts of these countries were made possible by the Cold War, which saw the provision of weapons and technology—often at subsidized rates or in the form of grants—by the Western and Eastern blocs. The restrictive nature of such transfers soon became apparent for all three countries. Most of the weapons transferred were obsolete, specific systems were denied to these nations, and arms transfers were subject to abrupt halts due to the political objectives of the supplier states. The inability to acquire new systems also adversely impacted the development of military doctrine in these countries. Consequently these constraints were seen as increasing the insecurity dilemma of these states.

Due to the limitations imposed by this form of dependent militarization, these regional powers moved first modestly and then, when greater resources became available, far more comprehensively to create indigenous weapons production capabilities. State sovereignty in the bipolar system was seen as necessitating the ability to produce weaponry to maintain one's independence. It also involved committing resources to development of both conventional and strategic weapons systems.

The Cold War also created doctrines of economic development that had implications for the militarization process in these countries. Both the Liberal and Socialist models viewed rapid economic development as possible through the infusion of capital-intensive technologies. This was particularly the case with the arms industries of the developing world, where expensive and advanced weapons programs were seen as having technological and developmental spin-offs. Thus, both politically and economically these countries sought to move from dependent to independent militarization.

But the move toward independent militarization in all three countries was marred by the limitation of resources, the functioning of the domestic political economy, and the bureaucratic politics of the players in their national security systems. Resource limitations led to doctrine and force modernization acquiring an on-again, off-again character, with doctrinal shifts and force development being linked to the availability of hard currency and the willingness of external suppliers to provide advanced weaponry. This was particularly the case with the Indian Navy, whose attempts to put together a carrier force spanned three decades.

The domestic political economy in all three nations also served to constrain force development. The creation of state-supported or state-run industries did have the positive influence of initially shielding these industries from market pressures and allowing for the establishment of a domestic military industry, the creation of a defense science work-force, and the formulation of ambitious weapons programs. But these factors also had their negative and ultimately debilitating effects on the militarization processes of these regional powers.

The pressures of sovereign militarization led to defense industries seeking increasingly ambitious projects of weapons development, and the shielding of these industries from market forces committed these governments to putting their scarce resources into the development of such programs. Some of these projects failed due to their technological complexity, high cost, and the fact that the countries did not have the needed infrastructure to bring these programs to fruition. Thus India's early flirtation with a supersonic fighter, the HF-24 Marut, and later with the LCA and Arjun MBT showed the limits of such militarization efforts. The Israeli attempt to develop the Lavi, despite significant technological and financial inputs from the United States, met with a similar fate.

Moreover the attempt to shield these industries from outside pressures did not work because the bureaucratic politics of these countries' national security systems led the armed forces to seek weapons from abroad, putting them into competition with the indigenous arms industries. Thus weapons development was always under the potential threat of being undermined by imports. If these circumstances characterize the armament processes of regional powers, what does it say about the generalizations that were to be tested in this study?

The first generalization stated that building a complete force structure depended on both the continued availability of resources and the presence of an external supplier. This would seem to be true for India and Israel, as they were both able to maintain a certain degree of autonomy in weapons acquisition when they had the resources to purchase weapons from alternative suppliers. Israel's ability to secure weapons from alternative sources in the 1960s reduced its dependence on the French, and indeed allowed the country to make the successful transition to U.S. supplies when the French imposed an arms embargo after the 1967 war.

Similarly, India's hard currency reserves in the late 1970s and early 1980s allowed it to buy weaponry from the West that the former Soviet Union, it principal supplier, was either unable or unwilling to provide. Thus Indian naval expansion was restricted until the early 1980s because India's principal supplier could not provide aircraft carriers. The Indian Air Force's attempts to get a deep-penetration-strike aircraft, the Jaguar, also rested on the availability of hard currency because of Soviet unwillingness to release aircraft like the Su-24. Further, once India was able to get weapons from alternative sources it put pressure on the Soviet Union to try and preserve its role as primary supplier to India. This led to systems like the Charlie I nuclear submarine and the Tu-142 maritime reconnaissance Bear aircraft being given to India. In turn, the supply of such systems allowed the Indian armed forces to revise doctrine and move toward an extraregional presence.

In the Brazilian case the unwillingness of the United States to provide advanced weapons hindered the development of the force structure and slowed attempts at doctrinal change. The United States's supply of obsolescent equipment and its efforts to try and create an artificial military balance in the region—as Jimmy Carter did with his decision in the late 1970s that the United States would not be the first country to introduce supersonic fighters in the region—hurt Brazil's efforts to modernize its armed forces. The lack of an external threat and the fact that the region was largely free from the pressures of the East-West rivalry constrained the possibilities Brazil had for external suppliers to provide weapons on a subsidized basis. Thus, the external suppliers that Brazil was able to attract were not the superpowers nor the second-tier suppliers but instead came from the transnational corporations of the West. This, however, dictated the type of weapons to be built. Instead of seeking to develop advanced weaponry, Brazil, heavily dependent as it was on the technology provided by the transnational corporations, had to design and develop low-to-medium-technology weaponry. The problem with this approach was that when the international market for Brazilian arms collapsed, these weapons also became economically and technologically unattractive to the Brazilian armed forces themselves. As seen in the case of the Osorio tank, once sales fell through, the Brazilian Army decided to go with an imported system.

The lack of hard currency resources also dictated the nature of Brazilian militarization. Once indigenous militarization efforts were terminated in the early 1990s, Brazil began to look for external suppliers. But rather than go in for the balanced and comprehensive development of its armed forces, the nation had to focus on those systems that could match perceived threats. Thus force modernization in the 1990s favored the navy and the army while the air force had to make do with obsolescent systems.

The role suppliers and hard currency play is interesting in terms of the limitations they place on regional power militarization. Suppliers alone may allow for the acquisition of weapons in sufficient quantity, but, that does not mean that the quality levels are up to what the recipient nation would like them to be. India's dependence on the Soviet Union did allow it to build a sufficiently large inventory of weapons to successfully defeat its principal regional rival, Pakistan. In the 1960s it was the large-scale transfer of weapons from the Soviet Union to India that led to a permanent shift in the military balance in South Asia. The existence of a compliant external supplier also led to the relatively quick acquisition of weapons that could fill holes in the Indian force structure. The import of the Sukhoi-7 ground attack aircraft in the late 1960s was an example of this trend. But as mentioned earlier, the fact that India could not import weapons from other sources allowed the Soviets to restrict the type and quality of systems India could acquire. This situation changed of course in the early 1980s when the availability of hard currency allowed India to play the Soviet Union off of other suppliers.

The second generalization declared that resource availability and suppliers determine whether procurement or production take place. The trend in the past was that when resources and suppliers were available weapons were imported. When they were unavailable, there were attempts to indigenously develop these systems. Israel's decision to build the Nesher and Kfir aircraft was a result of the French arms embargo. The decision to build the Merkava tank also resulted in part from the problems emanating from the Challenger deal with the UK. In the Indian case, supplier and resource restrictions in the early 1970s provided the impetus for the development of the Chetak, later Arjun, tank. As for Brazil, the development of its arms industry was principally determined by the unwillingness of the U.S. to supply more advanced weapons and in the quantities Brazil required.

This simple trend, however, was to change over time. When India went in for the Chetak, Israel for the Merkava, and Brazil for the Osorio—to take three comparable systems—their arms industries were relatively new and did not have a track record that could be used to gauge future performance. The Indian arms industry had undergone a major expansion as recently as the mid-1960s, with the Chetak project being conceived in the mid-1970s. The Israeli arms industry made its first move toward building larger and more advanced systems in the late 1960s and Merkava was on the drawing board by the early 1970s. The Brazilian plans for the Osorio came after less than a decade of systematic defense production in the country. Thus the defense science communities in these countries were able to convince their respective national leaderships that such projects were feasible. But as the production of these new weapons systems ran into snags a second trend developed. The armed forces and the national leadership were willing to sanction indigenous production when resources were available and procurement from external sources was possible. When the resource levels were low, however, the armed forces put pressure on the national leadership for either the termination of indigenous programs or for low priority being accorded to them.

The Lavi was a classic example of this trend. The aircraft project was formulated at a time when Israel was getting funds from the United States to subsidize the development of the aircraft, and the Israeli armed forces had no real bones to pick about the aircraft's development. But as the costs of the Lavi escalated and it began to eat into the general defense budget of the nation, the Israeli armed forces pushed to have the program terminated. Further, although the program was terminated with the claim that the funds designated for the Lavi project would be earmarked for other defense R&D projects, this did not happen. Instead, the savings from the Lavi's termination were used to cover the costs of combating the Palestinian Intifada. As the resource crunch grew, the Israeli government down-sized the Israeli arms industry, moving away from the production of complete systems and instead focusing on the production of specialized components. Major systems were to be imported and in fact the reduction of the Israeli defense industry continues. Recent reports indicate calls for further cutbacks—of up to 5,000–6,000 additional workers—in the defense sector because the bill for rescuing them has risen to $2.5 billion.[1]

The Indian case has similar examples. The big push toward ambitious projects and indigenous production in the early 1980s occurred at a time when India had the hard currency resources to continue obtaining weaponry from the West and when the Soviet Union was an eager supplier of conventional weaponry. At that point in time air force officials overcame their objections about the LCA and gave the green light for its development. One can argue that the reason the air force agreed to the program, with its relatively modest technological goals, was that it had already conducted the bulk of its modernization effort and, subsequently, was going to get the MiG-29 from the Soviet Union. The Air Force also agreed to the development of an Airborne Early Warning Radar because it was unable to procure one externally on satisfactory terms. But once the resource crunch came in the Indian case, the military and the government decided to invest their limited resources in imports, and programs like the LCA, ALH, and MBT were pushed into the background, with efforts being made to kill off some of them.

The difference between these cases lies in that while Brazil and Israel were forced to terminate programs, the Indian government has taken the step of allowing indigenous programs to die a slow death. This difference may lie in the constituency of the Indian arms industry in governmental circles, which allows it to continue receiving funding for questionable defense programs. It is more likely that as a larger economy, India has the capability to sustain programs that nations with less cash flow cannot afford. Further, India's DPSUs are dual-purpose industries with successful line's of civilian products. Earth-moving equipment made by Bharat Earthmovers, a DPSU, has been successfully exported.[2] And the reactors for the Indian nuclear submarine are being built by Bharart Heavy Electrics Limited, a DPSU whose primary work is in the civilian sector.[3] This largely civilian and dual-purpose role allows the defense side of production to continue.

The third generalization was that intermittent resources lead to the opening and closing of doctrine. The intermittent availability of suppliers and resources has not only shaped the way these nations force structures develop, but has also led to the opening and closing of military doctrine. Doctrinal shifts tend to require the development of a commensurate force structure, especially in the case of regional powers that have had to largely import their hardware. When such hardware is available, doctrinal shifts take place. When the hardware is unavailable, these shifts are either put on hold or there may even be a reversion to an earlier doctrine.

In the Israeli case, the willingness of the United States to transfer advanced weapons, defense electronics, and defense technology enhanced their own technological capabilities and allowed the Israeli Defense Forces to shift toward the high-tech-oriented military strategy that paid such rich dividends in the Bekaa Valley conflict of 1982. As mentioned earlier, Brazil's plans to modernize its force structure also took a beating in the 1980s because of the economic crisis, and it was only in the early 1990s that the Brazilian armed forces started receiving the new weapons they required for their plans for power projection.

In the Indian case the navy's quest for an aircraft carrier best exemplifies the impact of resources on doctrine. As mentioned above, the navy sought an aircraft carrier for its fleet in the immediate years after independence. The lack of resources and a compelling threat made it difficult, however, for the navy to secure the carrier. The first carrier was inducted into the Indian fleet in 1961, before the Sino-Indian war and because the navy was able to convince Nehru of the need for naval aviation. At the risk of digressing, the reported story behind the acquisition of the Vikrant needs to be documented. According to Vice Admiral Roy, the navy got the carrier at the personal intervention of Lord Mountbatten. Nehru was unconvinced of the need for an aircraft carrier but Mountbatten used the following story to convince him. Mountbatten said that when he was in Burma his aide de camp had a wife in Britain. After a few months the aide received a "Dear John" letter from his wife which named her new lover. The aide wrote back saying that he knew the new lover and that he, the husband, was a much better person. The wife wrote back saying, "Yes, but he is here and you are there." Lord Mountbatten argued that was the advantage of carrier aviation—it was here. Nehru agreed.[4] To put this purchase in perspective, it was a one-shot purchase of surplus equipment from Britain and it did not lead to a rise in the naval budget or in the immediate development of a blue water force.

While the first carrier was obtained in 1961, the navy still faced an uphill battle to obtain a carrier fleet, and the proposal of the then naval chief of staff in 1968, for the creation of a blue water carrier fleet to take over from the

British in the Indian Ocean was also rejected by the Indian leadership. Subsequently in the early 1970s the navy actually scrapped plans to replace Vikrant and instead decided to use it as a helicopter carrier until the end of its life. But once funds became available again in the 1980s and there was the added pressure provided by the success of carrier aviation in the Falklands War, the navy was able to procure a second aircraft carrier.

The fourth generalization was that strategic programs survive better than conventional ones. Strategic weapons—ballistic missiles, nuclear bombs, chemical and biological weapons—are considered high-value systems, and, at least in the case of nuclear bombs and ballistic missiles, a sign of technological advancement. The production of these systems is also an expensive and destabilizing process. But, paradoxically, one can argue that it is easier to sustain such programs and bring them to fruition than to develop advanced conventional weapons. The reason for this paradox lies in that conventional programs have to compete with external suppliers for markets within the country and, consequently, can be easily put on the back burner or even terminated.

Militaries operate in a global context. They compare their force structure and its technological level with those of other nations. They read the doctrinal literature of other countries and learn from it. Certainly this was the case with the Brazilians in the early 1980s.[5] Thus, indigenous conventional weapons are always competing with external programs and there are several consequences of this competition. First, it leads to ridiculously high sights being set for indigenous production—what I call the F-16 syndrome. Being late developers, the arms industries of these countries should have worked to produce what was technologically feasible given their own inexperience, lack of infrastructure, and limited resources. What should follow is the development of low to medium technology or the attempt to fill certain niches with the appropriate skills.

Instead the arms industries of these nations opted to produce weapons that were advanced and, therefore, both costly and beyond their technological capabilities. The reason for such a move lies both in the demands of the users of these systems and in the perceptions of the producers. The users would like domestically produced systems comparable to those produced in the First World so as to stand the test of battle. The producers are driven by similar passions because they would like to design and develop systems comparable to systems produced by the best arms industries. Dr. Arunachalam, for instance, argued that continuing to develop low-technology weaponry was simply perpetuating a technological dependence.[6] It is this sort of viewpoint that leads to the F-16 syndrome because in the 1980s both Israel and India touted their expensive and ambitious fighter projects as being superior to the F-16. That such programs eat into budgets and are plagued by delays has been discussed in both cases. Further, the need to compete with outside forces leads to the desire on the part of the armed forces to repeatedly modify the specifications on these programs. Thus both the LCA and the Lavi were modified despite already being in the developmental stage, with costly results.

Second, given the competition from external suppliers it is easy to put indigenous weapons programs on the back burner or to even terminate them when the resources or political conditions become opportune to buy from abroad. The conventional programs of all three nations have suffered such a fate.

The third problem with conventional systems lies in their tendency to quickly face technological obsolescence. As K. Subrahmanyam points out, major weapons programs require a long lead time to come to fruition, usually ten to fifteen years. This long lead time means that such weapons can easily become dated. The Marut project began in the mid-1950s and continued until the early 1970s, but the plane was technologically obsolescent by the late 1960s and did not fit into the mission profiles of the Indian Air Force in the 1971 war. Thus conventional programs always face the danger of either being replaced or becoming technologically obsolescent.

Even where a nation has tried to follow the step-by-step learning approach—graduating from low, to medium, to high technology—the results have been equally unpromising. The Brazilian arms industry sought to follow this approach, and because economic and security conditions favored it—low defense budgets and a low-threat environment—it was able to supply the armed forces with a range of weapons that met its requirements. But as the technological needs of the Brazilian armed forces changed, the Brazilian arms industry was not seen as worth preserving for this purpose.

Strategic programs tend to succeed, however, because it is possible to insulate them from the conditions that prevail against conventional programs. First, strategic weapons are generally not available from external suppliers. The Soviet lease of the Charlie I submarine to India not withstanding, the first-tier arms suppliers have been reluctant to transfer strategic systems to other countries. They have, however, been willing to transfer crucial technologies for systems development. Thus India's nuclear program was able to succeed because of U.S. and Canadian assistance in the civilian field. Its future missile program may well depend on continued Russian assistance. Israel's program owed its success to French and later American assistance, while the Brazilian parallel program borrowed from the West Germany-Brazil deal of 1975. Due to the fact that complete systems could not be transferred, the armed forces had to depend on the indigenous producers of such systems.

Second, the question of obsolescence is far less important in this area. As weapons technologies, strategic weapons have been around for a long time without age having reduced their effectiveness. Thus chemical weapons developed for use in World War II can still kill effectively in the Japanese subway system. The first British biological weapons test left Guinard Island uninhabitable for forty years. And the Hiroshima and Nagasaki bombs would still increase the killing power of virtually every nation's arsenal. Unlike conventional programs, strategic programs do not face technological obsolescence and therefore would seem to justify the expenditure on them.

Third, it is comparatively easier to shield these weapons from public scrutiny and bureaucratic pressures. Due to the international pressure on potential nuclear states to not exercise their nuclear option, all of these programs have been conducted in secrecy. The national security implications of these programs have led to little public scrutiny or governmental control of the agencies concerned with the development of a nuclear capability. In India, the functioning of the atomic energy program has not been inspected by an independent body like the Indian parliament's Public Accounts Committee— unlike conventional weapons programs like the Jaguar and the Ajeet aircraft. Instead, regulation of the program is done in-house, thus removing any possibility of checks and balances in the exercise of authority or any independent regulation of the nature and focus of this program. This is something that goes completely against the spirit of the Indian constitution.

In Israel, the country's nuclear program does not come under scrutiny of the Israeli parliament and there is little public debate about the utility of nuclear weapons or about the need for an Israeli nuclear doctrine. In Brazil, as mentioned above, the parallel program remained a secret for nearly a decade, and despite attempts at civilian control, the military was able to successfully establish autonomy over the program.

It is also important to remember that the budget for the development of strategic weapons often does not come out of the budgets of the armed forces, and this removes military resistance to these programs. Instead these programs are paid for through the supposedly civilian nuclear, space, and other high-technology programs. Thus the development of such systems does not face the same pressures that conventional programs that have to be paid for out of the armed forces budgets do. Once such programs do come to fruition there is the potential, however, for bureaucratic infighting because the cost of making an operational force structure is likely to come out of the budget of the armed forces. The hard evidence on this claim is admittedly scarce. In the Israeli case, for example, even though defense spending is well documented it is difficult to figure out under which headings the nuclear weapons program is hidden. So it is difficult to discuss this issue. On the other hand the development of the Jericho missile—a potential delivery system—did come out of the defense budget. In the Indian case, however, there are writings that suggest that the development of a strategic air command should come from a budget separate from that of the Indian Air Force. Similarly, once the Indian Army had to foot the bill for the induction of the Prithvi missile, resistance to its induction arose.

Lastly, strategic programs tend to garner greater political support because of the implications they have for the nation's political status and survival in the international system. India's leading strategic analyst, K. Subrahmanyam, has argued that nuclear weapons are currency of international power and it is this aspect that makes them attractive to the political leadership of regional powers.[7] In the Brazilian case, the political and military leadership thought that nuclear weapons, or at least a nuclear capability, would compensate for the economic problems that had seemingly consigned Brazil to a secondary status in the international system.

In the Israeli case, the demand for nuclear weapons came primarily from the need to overcome the numerical superiority of the Arab states and to possess a credible deterrent. The desire to be a strong state in the international system also influenced the decision. The Israeli leadership was split on the development of nuclear weapons, but it was the nationalistic section that prevailed with the argument that nuclearization was both the path to independence from external pressures and the state's insurance of ultimate survival. It would also indirectly fulfill Ben-Gurion's desire to make Israel a strong state in the eyes of the West, and therefore worth wooing.

In the Indian case, political support for the nuclear option started because of the threat posed by a hostile and newly nuclear China in the 1960s. But as P. R. Chari argues, what started as a reaction to a threat in the Bhabha years became by the early 1970s a program driven by bureaucratic pressures to the explosion of a nuclear bomb. Political support rather than a military rationale led India down the path to nuclearization.

The fifth generalization stated that as threats die, organizational pressures sustain weapons development. Weapons programs can be initiated both as a response to a threat and as a result of organizational pressures. The latter may be couched in terms of technological autonomy or the need to retain skilled personnel by providing employment in a sufficiently advanced weapons program. Once the threat that justified the initiation of a system dies or lessens, continuation of the program depends on the organizational skills of interested groups in a country's national security system. The ability of groups within the national security system to perpetuate such programs cannot be underestimated.

In the Indian case, the missile program was initiated in the 1970s—the Devil project—with the idea of making a missile that was meant to counter the Chinese threat.[8] But as concerns over China lessened so to did any real interest in the program, and by the early 1980s not only was the program being wound down but personnel were also going to be reassigned. But in 1983 Dr. Arunachalam and Dr. Ramanna were able to successfully convince the political leadership, as well as the military, of the need for a missile program. At the same time, MBT and the ALH were revived and the LCA was given the signal. Further, despite a poor track record these programs continue. The MBT, for example, has failed to meet operational deadlines, is plagued with technological difficulties, and may not be able to function in India's principal theater of operation.[9] Yet the program continues. Similarly, the nuclear submarine program evolved out of some notion of naval strength being part and parcel of a broader maritime policy. The program continues in a post-Cold War environment where superpower conflict in the Indian Ocean and the Chinese maritime threat are no longer issues of major concern. In fact the Chinese terminated their aircraft carrier program and their nuclear submarine program has had its share of technological difficulties.

While in the Indian case organizational pressures have sustained weapons programs, in the Brazilian and Israeli cases the lack of organizational support was responsible for killing some of them. The Lavi came out of a organizational demand of Israel Aircraft Industry (IAI) to have a follow-up project to the Kfir in order to prevent a brain drain of aircraft designers and engineers. But IAI was never able to build a constituency within the Israeli national security system that would provide continued support for the airplane's development. The fact that the plane was not an advance over the F-16 as well as the large amount of resources it chewed up led to opposition building up against it. Similarly, the Brazilian armed forces were unwilling to provide the organizational support that would have saved parts of the conventional arms industry when no real threat existed to help retain them.

According to the sixth generalization, from an arms control perspective it would be easier to kill weapons that are the product of organizational desires than those that are built to counter threats. Weapons built to counter threats are likely to receive continued funding and have a constituency willing to support their development. Further, to disband them would require the removal of the threat from a country's main enemies. Thus in the Israeli case any substantive measure to bring about a reduction in its nuclear arsenal would be part of a more comprehensive reduction of forces in the Middle East. Similarly, Pakistan has consistently argued that its willingness to sign the Nuclear Non-Proliferation Treaty, was contingent on India's willingness to do so. The Indian argument remains that nuclear disarmament has to take place in a broader context that includes the major powers, especially China.

Organizationally driven programs, by contrast, survive because of the bureaucratic skills of the group that wishes to preserve the program. In order to sell these programs, the interested groups use arguments like the long-term threat, the need for technological independence, and the employment of defense science personnel within the country to prevent their migration to more conducive research climes. Such programs, however, are most vulnerable to cutbacks because the government is committing scarce resources to the development of systems that have marginal utility in the nation's immediate threat environment and are therefore difficult to justify. Thus China was to cut its expensive carrier program because the threat environment did not exist to justify the development of such a force structure. If this is the case, then programs that come out of organizational pressures should, from a regional arms control perspective, be the easier to eliminate or control.

There is one major problem with this generalization: how do you operationalize it? How does one identify a program as being driven by organizational pressures rather than threats? This is a difficult problem because the official line on any major weapons system is likely to be that it is required to meet the defensive needs of a country. The problem becomes more complex with dual-purpose research like that of space and nuclear energy where nations are likely to argue, as India does, that technological research in these areas is necessary for the economic development of the country.

Second, what starts as a organizational program may become a threat program as other nations respond to it. The Indian Navy's development and the response of the Indian Ocean littoral states is a classic example. When India started its naval buildup in the 1980s it was with no real threat in mind. Pakistan, its principal rival, had a modest brown water fleet and deterring it did not require the type of naval expansion that the Indian Navy sought. Despite vague claims about deterring the superpowers, it was unlikely that the Indian Navy would have to actually enter into a confrontation with either of the then superpowers. Yet once the Indian naval buildup began, both the southeast Asian countries and Australia became concerned about India's maritime goals. What followed was the expansion of these countries' fleets to counter, among other factors, the growing Indian naval capability. An organizational program could conceivably have become a threat-based one.

One could make the argument that while it is not easy to determine whether a weapons program is organization or threat based when it is initiated, it is more likely that such an identification can be made once the program is terminated. Termination would mean that the nation concerned believed that such a program was either not feasible or that developing it left a low cost-benefit analysis relative the threat it was supposed to match. Classic deterrence literature states that threats have to be matched—or balance has to be achieved—in order for deterrence to be in place. But in actual fact countries are able to live in military asymmetry: Pakistan vis-a-vis India; and China vis-a-vis both the United States and the Soviet Union. Instead, issues like the cost of an arms race seem to determine their decision making on these subjects. Another indication would be the lack of a follow-up program. If a conventional or strategic program was not followed up it would indicate lack of interest at the governmental level, or lack of ability at the scientific level to bring it to fruition.

Thus arms control may be best sought after a program has failed, or once it becomes clear that the project is not worth the investment put into it— cheaper alternatives and decline of the threat environment can be likely sources of such a decision. At that point in time there is low governmental support for renewing the effort, and consequently there would be a willingness to sit down and work out tangible arms control measures. The reason for initiating such talks when a program fails lies in the fact that its temporary failure does not mean that there will be no further attempts to carry out such a program. In fact, as one saw in the Indian Navy's case, bureaucratic agendas have remarkable longevity and can be restarted when the conditions become conducive. Or, as one saw in the Israeli case with the Lavi, a program may be terminated at home but the interested organization takes the effort to relocate the program, in this case to South Africa, so as to allow for the subsequent continuation of the program when the situation permits.

The systemic and structural constraints under which regional power militarization takes places not only affects the behavior of these states, but also propels them along certain standard paths. This study examined three dissimilar cases, yet militarization in all three states was driven by similar pressures that led to the reduction in significance of these nations conventional military programs. These factors also created the opportunities for the advancement of these nations' strategic programs. It also led to fairly set patterns emerging for the acquisition and production of weapons, as well as—where evidence was available—for doctrinal shifts. These characteristics about regional power militarization then bring about the following question: where do they stand in the emerging international system?

At the conventional level, these states remain dependent militarizers. At the same time, their advancement in the development of strategic weapons does not give them the ability to achieve a higher standing in the emerging international system—one where the currencies of power, as Stanley Hoffman argues, have become more diverse and consequently less dependent on military capability. The concluding chapter looks at this issue as well as what potential U.S. policy could be toward these regional powers.

NOTES

1. *Financial Times*, 6 January 1995.

2. N. Vasuki Rao, "Where Are the Arms to Export?" *Indian Express*, (New Delhi) 22 February 1989.

3. Interview with Vice Admiral Mehir Roy, Indian Navy Retd., New Delhi, August 3, 1991. Vice Admiral Roy is in charge of developing the Indian nuclear submarine program.

4. Interview with Vice Admiral Mehir Roy, Indian Navy Retd., October 22, 1990, Urbana, Illinois.

5. Stanley Hilton, "The Brazilian Military: Changing Strategic Perceptions and the Question of Mission," *Armed Forces and Society*, 13, no. 3, (Spring 1987): 337-38.

6. Interview with Dr. V. Arunachalam, Scientific Advisor to the Defense Minster, New Delhi, 8 August 1991.

7. For a critique of Subrahmanyam's argument see Amit Gupta, "Fire in the Sky: The Indian Missile Program," *Defense and Diplomacy*, 8, no. 10 (October 1990): 44-48.

8. Ibid., 46.

9. For a discussion of the MBT program, see Amit Gupta, "How India's Force Structure and Military Doctrine are Determined: I Want my MIG" *Asian Survey*, 35, no. 5 (May 1995).

6

Regional Powers in the Emerging International System

The preceding analysis of regional power capability has important policy implications, both for such states and for the larger international system. They are the following: the role of such powers in the emerging international system given their ambitions, security concerns, and the constraints on the development of their force structures; the implications this has for the United States's attempts to create new security arrangements in the emerging international system; and, the prospects for arms control in the regions in which these powers are located. These issues are important because they address the broader problem of trying to create international order in a post-bipolar international system. What I argue is that while current U.S. policy is geared toward countering a threat from the South, there can be cooperative security endeavors between the nations of the West and South. What is required is a redefinition of what constitutes systemic security in the new international system.

THE POSITION OF REGIONAL POWERS

In the emerging international system three elements drive the conventional militarization efforts of militarized regional powers. First, there is a continued dependency on the major powers for the supply of advanced conventional military systems; a dependency that stems, as discussed in earlier chapters, from the structural constraints imposed by these nations' national security systems as well as from the political economy. Second, arms production has become internationalized to the extent that the major powers themselves are pooling their resources for the development of new weapons programs such as the Eurofighter. Within such a system the attempt to individually develop advanced weapons systems increasingly lacks economic rationale.

Both of these facts are reflected in the weapons acquisition efforts of other southern states. While India, Israel, and Brazil initiated both conventional and strategic weapons programs, the same is not true for other states of the South. Iraq, North Korea, and Pakistan, for instance, did not pursue the development of advanced conventional weapons but, instead, concentrated primarily on the development of a WMD capability. It would seem that these "late-late" defense industrializers were kept from significant conventional programs by constraints of resources, suppliers, and technology. Instead, they concentrated their resources and efforts on obtaining a WMD capability to compensate for the lack of a conventional program. Iraq was certainly the richest of these states, but the Iran-Iraq war pushed it into a large debt. It also lacked the infrastructure to develop modern conventional battle systems. At the same time, the development of nuclear, biological, and chemical (NBC) weapons was both technologically feasible and allowed it to compete with the regionally predominant power—Israel.[1] Egypt, Israel's principal rival until the late 1970s, has not tried to weaponize its nuclear program, and since the plans for the Arab Organization of Industrialization were put on hold, has not really tried to produce conventional military systems.

North Korea has depended for conventional military supplies on its former communist allies and essentially ended up with an army equipped with obsolescent weaponry. But it made itself the subject of regional concern in east Asia because of its nuclear and missile programs. Pakistan, similarly, had not invested its resources in risky and expensive conventional weapons projects. It has preferred to depend on external suppliers for weaponry even though it has meant getting obsolescent arms from China and facing repeated cutoffs of military supplies from the United States. Pakistan has taken the shortcut to creating a military standoff with India by developing nuclear weapons.

Advanced non-Western states like Singapore have sought to fill certain niches in arms production rather than pursue the entire gamut of weapons production. Others, like South Korea, have restricted themselves, for the time being, to the licensed production of big-ticket items like fighter aircraft. The internationalization of defense production has also entered the South. The member states of the Association of South-East Asian Nations have gotten together to try and rationalize defense industrialization. It would seem that attempts in the South to go it alone in producing big-ticket conventional items will increasingly become the exception.

Third, conventional warfare is now faced with a new set of constraints and opportunities. During the Cold War the pursuit of conventional wars in different regions of the world was possible through superpower support, as in the Arab-Israeli case. It was also possible through the lack of interest on part of either superpower, as was the case when Tanzania invaded Uganda in the late 1970s. Further, even when a superpower was in conflict with another country—the United States in Vietnam or the Soviet Union in Afghanistan—the fact that the other superpower helped the smaller nation constrained the options of the major warring power.

In relation to regional wars, the death of bipolarity has had several consequences. The lack of superpower competition has reduced the flow of subsidized weaponry to regional powers and removed the political support and threat of military intervention that constrained the superpowers in their own interventionary attempts—Afghanistan and Vietnam. This would seem to leave a regional power vulnerable to superpower or major-power coercion (although admittedly the death of the Cold War has also removed the need for containment and thus reduced the likelihood of such coercion). This vulnerability is also heightened by the lack of a conventional capability to deter an interventionary power, or least make the cost of intervention very high.

Further, the changed nature of thinking on war in the developed nations, particularly the United States, has imposed constraints on the use of force by major powers. Both of these issues are discussed in the following section but suffice it to say that such forces place limits on the conventional capabilities of militarized regional powers.

The following question then arises: what advantages such states accrue from the possession of nuclear weapons? In the bipolar system, nuclear weapons were viewed by Brazil and Israel as being the currency of international power that permitted a move up to great-power status. They were also seen as addressing the security dilemmas of states faced with asymmetrical conventional military balances—Israel, South Africa, and Pakistan. Such a development of nuclear weapons, as seen in earlier chapters, had to be clandestine so the currency of nuclear power argument was never viable. Bharat Wariawalla, an Indian security analyst, makes the argument that in order for nuclear weapons to be the currency of international power, that currency has to be visible. Policies of nuclear ambivalence or opacity, as followed by India and Israel, make it impossible to display these currencies and therefore do not confer the prestige status that these nations may desire.[2] Nor did the development of nuclear arsenals ease these nations' conventional military burden or successfully address their security dilemmas.

In the post-Cold War world what little thinking has taken place on the role of nuclear weapons has come from those concerned with the prospects for potential proliferation. These writings take two broad approaches. One group argues that proliferation is inherently destabilizing and should be either countered or stabilized through regional and global arms control regimes.[3] The other opinion is best exemplified in the writings of Kenneth N. Waltz, who makes the argument that the proliferation of nuclear weapons can have a stabilizing influence in the international system.[4] Waltz argues that once two warring sides have acquired nuclear weapons the ability to achieve a surprise attack is gone, as is the ability to achieve technological breakthrough in weaponry. Consequently, the military balance between two rivals is stabilized. The proliferation of nuclear weapons would therefore help stabilize regional rivalries around the world. More recently Waltz has examined the role nuclear weapons can play in the emerging international system.

In discussing the role of nuclear weapons in the emerging international system, Waltz makes the following points. First, despite the shifts in the international system that seem to indicate that there are other sources of power and the belief that nuclear weapons play a diminished role in the international system, Waltz still sees nuclear weapons as being a requisite for power. He argues that a great power's panoply includes nuclear weapons. This is because in a self-help international system, and here Waltz continues to echo the Realist paradigm, "the possession of most but not all of the capabilities of a great power leaves a state dependent on others and vulnerable to those who have the instruments that the lesser states lack."[5]

Second, Waltz states that in the international system nuclear weapons allow for a loosening of the connection between a nation's economic and technological capabilities, as well as between its technological and military capabilities. Discussing the latter issue first, Waltz writes: " With conventional weapons, rapid technological change intensifies competition and makes estimating the military strengths of different countries difficult."[6]   Waltz continues that unless there is a breakthrough that would give the United States either a first-strike capability or an effective defense, Russia need not keep pace militarily with American technology. He concludes, therefore, "As Bernard Brodie put it: Weapons that do not have to fight their like do not become useless because of the advent of newer and superior type." Since America's nuclear weapons are not able to fight Russia's, the strategies of the two countries are decoupled. Each country can safely follow a deterrent strategy no matter what the other may do.[7]

Third, Waltz argues that nuclear weapons alter the relationship between economic capability and military power by making it possible for states to have varying economic capability yet still compete as major military powers. Further, if these nations are status quo powers—those not seeking to revise the structure of the international system—nuclear weapons guarantee them the security to "concentrate attention on their economies rather than their military forces."[8]   He writes: Because nuclear weapons alter the relation between economic capability and military power, a country with well less than half of the economic capability of the leading producer can easily compete militarily if it adopts a status quo policy and a deterrent strategy. Conversely the leading country cannot use its economic superiority to establish military dominance, or to gain strategic advantage over its great power rivals.[9] To what extent does the Waltz argument apply to the regional powers of the South?

Waltz's argument about the utility of nuclear weapons applies only partly to regional powers. The political situation of the regional powers of the South is different from that of the great powers in four ways. In the case of the great powers, territorial bones of contention have either been settled—the reunification of Germany—or do not assume the central position that they do in the security dilemma of regional powers, for example the territorial dispute between Japan and Russia over the Sakhalin Islands. Further, there is still doubt about what the formal territorial structure of some of these regional powers will be. In the case of India, Israel, and Brazil there is no doubt that they have the type of state legitimacy that characterizes the great powers, but, at least in the case of India and Israel, the final territorial boundaries of the state still have to be resolved. Secessionist calls in India and the issue of a Palestinian state still muddy these nations' security agendas. Also, the sort of command and control features and the confidence-building measures that the superpowers were able to develop during the Cold War—largely through a process of trial and error— have yet to be achieved in the South.

Given these facts, the sort of security that nuclear weapons offer a great power are not automatically transferred to a regional power. In the case of both India and Israel, while nuclear weapons have secured their external borders, they have not helped resolve the turmoil within. India's nuclear capability does not help it to resolve insurgencies in Punjab, Kashmir, and Assam. And a nuclear arsenal was irrelevant to Israel's attempts to counter the Palestinian Intifada. Nor did the possession of a nuclear capability prevent external support for these internal crises. As Waltz correctly argues, the possession of nuclear weapons favors status quo states but only to the extent of preventing external invasion. Even this utility of nuclear weapons has to be discussed in terms of the changed nature of the international system.

What the possession of nuclear weaponry by regional powers does is to ensure the preservation of their territorial integrity from external threats within the region. As Yaniv argues, the possession of nuclear weapons deterred military thrusts by the Arab states and possibly the use of chemical warheads by the Iraqis on their Scud missiles during the Gulf War. India's nuclear capability provides a comforting backup to its conventional superiority within the region, while within Latin America, the Brazilian nuclear program allows Brazil to counter its primary regional rival, Argentina. Yet what role does the possession of nuclear weapons provide these countries in their efforts to deter the great powers?

In the bipolar system the nuclear umbrella of one superpower could be used by the regional powers to counter the nuclear and military pressures of the other superpower. Thus when the Soviets increased military supplies to the Arab states in the 1973 Arab-Israel war, the United States responded with a level three nuclear alert. Similarly, India was given protection under the U.S. nuclear umbrella after the Sino-Indian war of 1962. In the new international system, a rival nuclear umbrella, in most cases, does not exist. Thus if a regional power is in a confrontation with a great power it will have to depend on its own nuclear arsenal to serve as a deterrent.

The problem here is that compared to the great powers the regional powers still have relatively small nuclear arsenals. So the question arises, How do you maintain asymmetric deterrence in the new international system? On the face of it an asymmetric military balance should preclude the maintenance of deterrence. But deterrence is as much about psychological conditions as it is about a military balance. An asymmetric military balance would actually remove the need for a first strike by a great power. For a regional power to launch such a strike against the heartland of a great power would invite retaliation in kind which, given the asymmetric balance of forces, would devastate the regional power. As long as an asymmetric balance remained, the great power would not fear a first strike and, to use Waltz's argument, the lack of a credible first-strike capability would make a regional power less threatening to a great power. Thus the need to make a preemptive strike against a regional power's nuclear capability is removed. This asymmetric military balance is likely to continue both quantitatively and qualitatively. It would require an enormous commitment of economic resources to catch up both quantitatively and qualitatively with the nuclear arsenals of the great powers. And any attempt to do so, especially if relations with the great powers are in a hostile setting, could invite preemptive countermeasures.

Further, in a changed international system a regional power can actually achieve asymmetric deterrence because the stakes in the system have changed. In the Cold War era, Ted Galen Carpenter argues, "a persuasive case could be made that the United States had no choice but to accept that risk [of becoming involved in a nuclear conflict] in order to prevent Soviet global hegemony. But the argument that America must continue accepting similar risks merely to discourage regional conflicts is considerably less compelling."[10] The reasons why the United States would find it difficult to accept such risks are discussed below.

For Russia, even more so than for the United States, the stakes have changed dramatically in the international system and have therefore reduced the need for getting involved in regional conflicts. The jettisoning of former Soviet allies—from Cuba to Vietnam—has effectively reduced the sphere of potential Russian intervention in the world. Instead Russia is preoccupied with events in the "near abroad" as well as with those of historical allies like Serbia. Russia's continued economic travails also limit its capacity to get involved in a conflict in far-off regions.

To sum up, these regional powers have a conditional deterrent capability thanks to their nuclear weapons programs. At the same time, however, their conventional military capabilities remain dependent on the availability of external suppliers as well as hard currency resources. Consequently they are not militarily strong enough currently to be competitors of the great powers in the new international system; nor are they economically powerful enough to be contenders in other ways. Yet this class of nations have sought an enhanced status in the international system for reasons of security and political prestige. This quest has not died with the Cold War. The question then arises, How can these nations seek greater status in the new international system?

STATUS QUO STATES

Given the constraints mentioned above, a regional power's ability to influence events in the new international system lies in presenting itself as a status quo state: a country that accepts the underlying security and economic assumptions of the new international system. The security assumptions of the new international system begin with the belief that the system is a legitimate one that does not need to be revised through global revolution. Thus, status quo states would not follow the policies of revolutionary states like the Soviet Union (1917–1939), the People's Republic of China (1949–1976), or the current polices of the Islamic government in Iran. As status quo states these countries also must agree with the consensus on what constitutes security in the international system. This would include support to multilateral institutions that seek to preserve international or regional security. It could also include the creation of new multilateral institutions or peacekeeping arrangements to fit the changed regional and international circumstances.

Being a status quo state also requires a restrictive policy on the supply of strategic weapons. There is a recognition that peace in the international system would be enhanced by restricting the transfer of conventional and strategic weapons technologies. The establishment of a United Nations conventional weapons register, the attempts to limit conventional arms sales in the Middle East, and the indefinite extension of the Nuclear Non-Proliferation Treaty (NPT), are indications of this. The proliferation policies of the major powers in the post-World War II era, however, have included both supply and restraint. Nuclear proliferation took place in the Cold War because the major powers were willing, in selective cases, to transfer critical technologies to friendly states. But overall the policy was a restrictive one, and this can be seen in the fact that once the NPT went into effect no nation has openly declared itself as a nuclear weapons state. India used up the last fig leaf when it stated that its nuclear blast was a peaceful nuclear explosion.

Such views are either tacitly or openly endorsed by status quo regional powers. Continued stability in the international system does require the nonproliferation of strategic weapons, and despite the reluctance of states like India and Israel to sign the NPT, their own policies have been those of trying to prevent the proliferation of strategic weapons. India, despite its continued opposition to the NPT, remains consistent in its efforts to slow down the Pakistani nuclear weapons and missile program. It was also one of the first nations to be concerned about the political-military implications of a so-called Islamic Bomb. Israel has pursued an activist nonproliferation policy, twice destroying Iraq's nuclear reactors—once before it was shipped from France, and again when Israeli F-16s destroyed the Osirak reactor in 1981.

Another aspect of being a status quo power is to support the political and economic underpinnings of the new international system. In the political sphere this would include a commitment to democracy and free elections. Some, like U.S. National Security Advisor Anthony Lake, would also argue that it involves a commitment to human rights. One would argue that while human rights need to be promoted, they still do not fall within the primary concerns of the major powers, and therefore it is unlikely that regional powers have to qualify in this area to be called status quo states. The Clinton administration, for example, effectively delinked human rights and trade in its China policy. As status quo states these countries also have to support the economic underpinnings of the international system—in this case the growth of a free-market system. In fact all three states in this study have made moves to privatize and liberalize their economies.

WEST VS. SOUTH?

While these nations are *de facto* status quo states, the policies of the United States—which is now the leader of the Western bloc—have yet to take this into account in trying to establish a new security order. Instead, U.S. policy makers now seems to view the South as a threat that needs to be militarily and politically countered. At the United Nations in 1993, President Clinton stated that nonproliferation would be an urgent priority of his administration's foreign policy. More specifically, the Pentagon is restructuring its forces and doctrine under its counterproliferation policy to combat a nuclear-armed southern state. Anthony Lake, in a *Foreign Affairs* 1994 article, has branded several southern states as "backlash states"—states that want to stay outside the new family of democratic, free-market nations—and has called for their containment. A policy which has subsequently been implemented against Iran and Iraq.[11]

The problem with taking such view of the South as a threat is that it precludes the option of partnership with these nations for the establishment of a more secure international system. Yet such a partnership would be beneficial to the United States given its own political, military, and economic constraints. In order to understand why such a partnership would be beneficial one needs to examine 1) what is the United States's conception of security in the emerging international system; 2) what constraints are on the United States's capability to enforce such a vision; and 3) what sort of options this provides for west-south security in a new international system.

THE ATTITUDE OF THE UNITED STATES

The attitude of the United States is based on a number of factors, the most important of which is its proven military superiority. The Gulf War showed that despite the major advances made by the South in weapons production, the United States had the capability to prevail in a set-piece conventional battle. This conventional superiority is unlikely to change in coming decades since no single southern country, or even collection of countries, has the necessary scientific base or financial resources to build up a conventional military machine.

It was this proven military superiority that led to the hope after the Gulf War that a "new world order" could be created. In this world order the hitherto defunct concept of collective security was to be revived—under the aegis of the United Nations—to maintain peace and international security. Military superiority and the new consensus among the Western powers, it was believed, could rejuvenate a mission that the UN had virtually given up after the Korean War and only revived under unique circumstances in the Gulf War in 1990. But in translating this military superiority into political power the United States was being even more ambitious than the great powers that had sat down at Dumbarton Oaks to construct the United Nations Charter. Not only was collective security and peacekeeping going to be the agenda of the new U.S.-led United Nations, but it was also going to take on new tasks—peacemaking and peace-building.

Under the rubric of peacemaking the military preponderance of the U.S.- led Western coalition was to be used for such ambitious tasks as trying to rebuild a Somali nation and restoring democracy in Haiti. Military power was going beyond the conquest of territory or the deterrence of aggression to the actual reshaping of societies—again something that had not been successfully achieved since the 1940s by the United States in Germany and Japan, and by the former Soviet Union in Eastern Europe.

The United States's attitude toward the South was also shaped by the belief that there was now a consensus in the "New West." The West in the post-Cold War era is seen by a scholar like Samuel Huntington as being one civilization, encompassing Eastern Europe and the European states of the former Soviet Union.[12] These nations temporarily had a consensus on such issues as restricting arms sales to the South, and on cooperation in the United Nations on international security issues. This consensus was supposed to make the United Nations into a viable instrument for enforcing Western will and to facilitate drawing together military capabilities to enforce order in the international system.

Additionally, while attitudes toward the former communist nations have changed in the new international system, they still remain the same where the South is concerned. In the Cold War era, the South was seen as being poor, unstable, and heavily militarized. Now the South is still considered poor, unstable, and heavily militarized. Due to such an attitude, no serious attempt has been made to bring the regional powers of the South, which do not fit this perception, into the emerging security framework. President Bush used to talk about Partners in Leadership, and he meant the United States, Germany, and Japan. President Clinton has pushed through the North American Free Trade Agreement and the Asia-Pacific Economic Cooperation. But what this really boils down to is a search for markets. No real attempt has been made to bring Southern countries in as partners in a common security framework. Brazil and India, for instance, are not included as partners in this new security framework. What follows from such attitudes is that the West is seeking to militarily defang the South and impose political solutions on it that are seen as being conducive to the "new world order."

Militarily, the primary concerns are to halt the spread of weapons of mass destruction and the means to deliver them (nuclear, biological, and chemical weapons and ballistic missile delivery systems). This includes setting up force structures to actually fight in conflicts where such weapons are used, as well as to create a Western military force which can be used for peacekeeping and peacemaking missions. The United States has been seeking to develop ties with both Russia and possibly China—the one Southern state to be solicited— to fulfill the peacekeeping function.

CONSTRAINTS

Yet while the general post-Gulf War attitude was to establish an international order—by either the use or show of force—it has broken down because of a number of constraints. Money is a major constraint. At a time when most nations in the West, particularly the United States and Russia, are faced with budgetary pressures, it is difficult to find financial resources to fund a major war effort like the Gulf War. The United States had to pass the hat around in order to get the money to fund the Gulf War. While the Western nations were willing to contribute to that effort because of the threat to world energy supplies, they may not be willing to contribute large amounts for future conflicts in the world. The reason for this reluctance is that the Western consensus on the use of force, which was fragile to begin with, is breaking down.

The Western consensus is breaking down both on the use of force and on who the precise members of the Western alliance itself are. To answer the latter question first, the "New West" was conceived as including both Eastern Europe and the European parts of the former Soviet Union under one civilizational package. In fact there are three Wests: the United States, Western Europe and Japan, and Eastern Europe. Each of these, however, has different views on the utility of force in the new international system. The West Europeans and the Japanese are less than enthusiastic about playing the international policeman, and certainly are not willing to make major financial or human commitments to do this. West European reluctance to get involved in the Yugoslavian civil war without an American commitment is an example of this. The Russians and East Europeans, unless bankrolled by other countries, are so strapped for finances that they will find it difficult to regularly send military contingents abroad for peacekeeping and peacemaking duties. Further, Russia is going through a nationalistic revival that is also creating a break in the consensus. Both the Russian government and the political opposition are arguing that Russia should play a more active role in international affairs in order to regain its lost standing as a major power. This has led to a Russian push to increase arms sales to the South. It also led Russia to declare in the UN Security Council that it would vote against stronger economic sanctions against Libya. It may also see the Russians fomenting civil unrest in the former republics of the Soviet Union. In fact, as Alexei Arbatov points out, there is already a move in the West to give Russia a free hand in dealing with the former republics, with the possible exception of the Baltics.[13] If this happens the Russians will be so preoccupied with events in their own backyard that it will be difficult for them to commit troops elsewhere. Further, Russia's ability to project military power is questionable. Russia's misadventure in Chechnya is indicative of its general military decline and while Moscow is able to involve itself in proxy wars (in former republics like Georgia, Moldova, and Tajikistan) it is not in a position to engage in a major military effort in its own right.[14]

A related constraint is the will to fight. It is becoming increasingly difficult to motivate people to go overseas and fight in wars that do not involve the vital interests of the Western nations. A number of West European nations have opposed committing troops beyond the confines of Europe. In the United States there is still a will to fight but only under specific conditions: that there be a clear cut mission, that it be ended quickly, and that it involve a low loss of life. These conditions are particularly important given the changing composition of the U.S. armed forces. Close to 30 percent of the U.S. armed forces are minorities, and increasingly the well-to-do are not entering the military. Thus the U.S. national security system is being shaped along class lines. Those making the decisions to send young Americans out to fight are the well-to-do who themselves have not seen combat. Those actually dying in different parts of the world come either from the minorities or from less well-to-do whites. As John Lewis Gaddis points out, "Resentment over this pattern—when it develops—is likely to undermine whatever foreign policy consensus may yet remain."[15]

If such constraints exist, under what situations could American military power be mobilized and used? Three types of missions may drive American intervention in the South: the resource mission, the peacemaking mission, and the punitive mission. The resource mission is to counter threats to natural resources that are badly needed by the West and fluctuations in the supply of which could hurt Western economies. At present oil seems to be the only major natural resource that falls in this category. This is also the one mission where the Western nations are most likely to agree that military action needs to be taken and will therefore provide both the monetary resources and the personnel to fulfill it.

The peacemaking mission combines humanitarian assistance—as in the case of Bosnia, Somalia, and Rwanda—with the attempt to bring about a peaceful and just society in a country—as in Haiti and Somalia. In the initial euphoria of a changed international system it was assumed that United Nations troops would be able to create strong governments that supported democracy in the South, and in the former communist world. The justification for such a mission came from the increasing number of nations that started moving toward a process that has been called the Third wave of democracy—where significant numbers of nations start the transition to democracy.[16]

The problem with this approach was that it underestimated the costs of peacemaking. Putting troops into a civil war or internal anarchy situation is not a short-term process, even if the troops have an overwhelming military preponderance. Such a process involves establishing workable governments— Lebanon and Haiti—and, in some cases, restoring civil society—Uganda and Somalia. These are long-term processes that require a continued military presence.

This was the case with the American military occupation of West Germany and Japan after World War II. In both cases the United States went through a lengthy process of military occupation: it demilitarized these societies, eradicated the institutions of Fascism, and laid the foundations for democracy. Both nations militaries were restricted in their development, with German militarization being allowed only in 1954 and Japan's rebuilding of its armed forces taking place only in the 1960s. The institutions of Fascism were eradicated through such public steps as the Nuremberg and Tokyo war crimes trials. Japan's democratic constitution was written by General MacArthur, and in Germany it was Allied support to democratic groups that led to the reesetablishment of democracy. Such a reshaping of societies was possible because these nations had lost the war, were occupied, and could not aggressively challenge the occupation by the Allied powers. Further, the Cold War demanded a long-term military and economic commitment to Germany and Japan.

Few of the conditions that facilitated the democratization of Germany and Japan in the 1940s and 1950s apply in the "new world order." The U.S. and the rest of the West do not have the military will and economic capability to enforce democratic systems in the South. Unlike in Germany and Japan, there has been aggressive resistance to the Western efforts to impose civil societies and governmental structures in the South. Lebanon in the 1980s and Somalia in the early 1990s are examples of this. Peacemaking in such situations requires the willingness to take casualties in order to enforce a particular governmental system.

This willingness is severely circumscribed by Western public opinion's distaste for casualties and is further heightened by the media. In the last few years European public opinion has been against extraregional military intervention. American public opinion has been more complex. While the average American may support the external use of military force, he/she would like such intervention to have a finite timetable and to have very low casualty rates. The Pentagon has recognized these opinions and in the Gulf War imposed military censorship to ensure that the wrong type of press coverage did not take place. There was also the drive to bring the Gulf War to a swift conclusion and bring the "boys and girls" home.

Censorship and swift conclusions, however, are not possible in peacemaking situations. Being a more long-term commitment, it is difficult to prevent independent coverage of events within a society. It was difficult to censor media coverage in the Congo and Vietnam in the 1960s, just as it has been impossible to halt media coverage in Lebanon in the 1980s and in Somalia in the 1990s. In fact when U.S. special forces landed on the beach in Somalia there were more reporters there than soldiers. Thus once casualty rates start going up and the media highlights it there is a discernible drop in public support for such operations and a clamoring to bring the boys and girls back home.

Peacemaking, therefore, is the least likely area where the U.S.-led West is willing to use force in the South. Yet situations requiring peacemaking are on the increase around the world. The breakup of multiethnic states and the consequent increase in civil wars create the need for multinational peacekeeping and peacemaking forces. Such forces, however, are unlikely to come for the reasons mentioned above. Thus in the one area where intervention is needed it will be least available.

PUNITIVE MISSION

The "punitive mission" will be aimed against terrorist groups, guerrilla movements, and "backlash" states. It could involve coming to the aid of an ally who is being threatened by one of these "backlash" states. The threat posed by these "backlash" states need to be discussed because attacks against them could lead to a full-scale war. One of the fallouts of the Gulf War was the belief that in the future no militarized southern state would be allowed to become a threat to international peace and security. Such states would be branded as rogue states, isolated in the international community and militarily neutralized. Iraq was the first rogue state to be neutralized, and Iran, Libya, and North Korea could be possible targets for future action. In such a case the West need not act in unison, since the conventional military capability of the United States would be sufficient to initiate such a war or to defend an ally who is threatened by such a state. Consensus, therefore, would appear not to be a problem. Neither, it is believed, would there be a need for a prolonged military involvement or long-term troop commitment. What would be a problem is the possession of weapons of mass destruction and the means to deliver them by the nations of the South.

The possession of nuclear and chemical weapons by the regional powers of the South, as well as ballistic missiles that could be used to deliver them, complicates the security agenda of the U.S. in the emerging international system. These weapons pose as a deterrent to the use of American military power because they severely raise the costs of intervention.[17] Former Secretary of Defense Les Aspin acknowledged this fact in a public speech when he declared: "Weapons of mass destruction may threaten our forces in the field, and in a more subtle way threaten the effective use of those forces."[18] Zbigniew Brzezinski put it more bluntly when he wrote that the existence of weapons of mass destruction in unstable nations of the world would dissuade Western public opinion from intervening in conflicts in these regions.[19] The crucial problem for the United States here would be the willingness to bear casualties. If dragging a dead soldier through the streets of Mogadishu can trigger a timetable for withdrawal, the death of large numbers of U.S. troops in a confrontation would dampen enthusiasm for such military actions in the future.

This unwillingness to bear casualties has major implications for U.S. policy on nonproliferation and intervention. As Ted Galen Carpenter argues, to discourage nuclear proliferation "U.S. policymakers have been willing to continue the Cold War era bargain: if Washington's allies and clients renounce ambitions to acquire independent deterrents, the United States will help protect their security, including in many cases extending the protection of the U.S.

nuclear arsenal."[20]   The Cold War policy was one of extended deterrence, but the nuclearization of the South leads to what Carpenter calls distended deterrence: where the United States is unwilling to get entangled in nuclear conflicts because of the problems associated with facing a nuclearized regional power;   and because U.S. clients themselves would find a guarantee from Washington less credible.[21]

Not only will the United States and the other Western countries be dissuaded from intervening because of public opinion, but the actual use of such weapons in the field of conflict could have devastating effects for the very allies that the West seeks to protect through intervention. In a North Korea-South Korea conflict the use of a nuclear weapon by the North over the South would not only kill American troops but also devastate large parts of South Korea. Similarly, if a southern nation were to use biological weapons in its opponent's territory it would make the land uninhabitable for an entire generation. Britain tested biological weapons on Guinard Island during World War II and the island remained uninhabitable until the mid-1980s. Destroying an ally you seek to save is not the ideal political outcome.

What the United States sees as its primary threat, therefore, is not the acquisition of an offensive capability by the South. The acquisition of weapons of mass destruction is not going to alter the global military balance. The United States and Russia will remain the principal nuclear powers. China, France, Britain, and possibly Ukraine (if it does not adhere to its plan to disarm) will be second-tier nuclear powers, and the nations of the South will be a distant third. It is a threat in a negative sense because it restricts Western interventionary capability. Consequently it will constrain the West's ability to create its notion of a "new world order." It is in order to counter this potential threat that the United States is reconfiguring its armed forces to deal with the challenge posed by the South. The problem with this approach is that it is essentially an adversarial one that ignores the possibility of partnership with the nations of the South in maintaining systemic security.

SYSTEMIC SECURITY

Part of the problem with this adversarial approach is the solution it seeks for Southern militarization—to accept the West's demands for arms control and eventual disarmament on Western terms. This would involve the three remaining nuclear-capable nations in the South—India, Pakistan, and Israel—giving up their nuclear options and signing the NPT. It would also involve placing limits on conventional weapons programs and the sale of weaponry to other nations. The problem with this approach is twofold. At the more obvious level it would leave regional conflicts unresolved and at the same time remove the security that weapons of mass destruction provide to the nations locked in these enduring regional rivalries. At a more fundamental level it condemns the nations of the South to a second-class status in the emerging international system. The other part of the problem comes from the current view of systemic security in the United States.

The American view of insecurity in the new international system can be divided into two approaches, state-centric and non-state-centric. Neither of these sets of writings really seeks to positively incorporate the South into the security structure of the new international system. The state-centric view is most coherently discussed by the post-Cold War realists who see the insecurity dilemma of the new international system arising from the decline of bipolarity and the subsequent transformation of the international system.

As bipolarity ended the state centric debate shifted to one of just how dangerous a multipolar system was.[22] Bipolarity was seen as having introduced systemic stability, while multipolarity was seen as causing instability because the increased number of major powers meant a greater chance of conflict. The real issue, however, was not the relative merits of bipolarity and multipolarity in creating systemic stability, but what the underlying assumptions behind the new multipolarity were. Here, sadly, the discussion rested on the assumption that multipolarity meant a return to the classic multipolar systems of Western Europe. Thus Mearsheimer, for instance, used examples from the past European systems to show how unstable multipolarity was.

What should have been discussed instead was whether multipolarity created a new world order. Classical multipolarity was marked by colonialism, spheres of influence, lack of self-determination, economic rapaciousness, and a scant regard for human rights. Further, the have-nots of the system were pawns, whose territories could be carved up to suit the demands of systemic stability. The 1884 Congress of Berlin, where Africa was carved up over a conference table, is a case in point. The post-Cold War literature does not question these characteristics of multipolarity. Mearsheimer is worried about stability, Krauthammer about[23] whether multipolarity has actually come about or whether the United States is still the only superpower. Nye, while rejecting these conceptions of world order, makes the same mistake of concentrating on the great powers. He argues, for example, that the new order is marked by transnational interdependence which leads to a diffusion of power. Nye supports his argument by indicating, among other examples, how private actors in the global capital markets constrain the way interest rates can be used to manage the U.S. economy.[24] Such interdependence, however, only exists among the major powers—Brazilians, Fijians and Rwandans do not constrain U.S. interest rates— so Nye too ends up discussing a great power-centric international system. Since the American perception is that the new international system is multipolar rather than multilateral and that it is governed by power politics it does not make sense for the nations of the South to give up their last bargaining chip. The fact is that the new international system looks very much the same from the South—by the big powers, for the big powers, of the big powers.

The non-state-centric literature is obsessed with the notion of a megadisaster in the South. Thus Thomas Homer-Dixon is worried about the environmental disaster that is about to hit the world.[25] Robert D. Kaplan sees the poverty, pestilence, and environmental degradation in the Third World causing problems for the West.[26] Benjamin R. Barber believes the twin forces of a McWorld and Jihad are leading to a disintegration of states and a reverse wave of democracy.[27]

What is needed instead of such views of Western-centric concepts of security, is the recognition that for systemic security to be achieved it has to be conceived as being all-inclusive—including all the nations of the world rather than just some states. In such a system the major nations of the South would be included in attempting to bring about a more stable international system. For this to happen the United States would have to divide the South into two groups, "status quo" and "backlash" states, and work with the former to achieve greater stability within the international system. Cooperation with status quo states would help in a range of areas, most notably peacekeeping, peacemaking, and in the area of the non-proliferation strategic weapons. Both in Brazil and India there has been talk about restricting the South-South transfer of WMD technologies. There has also been a willingness to commit troops for peacekeeping, as was the case in Somalia. Such cooperation is possible because many of the structural constraints which prohibited North-South security cooperation in these areas have either been removed or reduced in significance.

THE SOUTH'S OPTIONS

The regional powers of the South need to recognize that the end of bipolarity has provided the means to restructure the international system so that the South has a greater say in international outcomes. Part of the early Indian debate on nuclear weapons, for instance, argued what kind of role a nuclear India would play in an international system. At that point in time some Indian scholars argued that Indian possession of nuclear weapons would most likely lead that country to become a status quo power within the international system.[28] The regional powers of the South need to make the same argument now. Most southern nations that still have nuclear programs have stakes in the continuation of the present international order because of the growing economic linkages around the world. Israel, India, Pakistan, and North Korea all need Western economic assistance and, more importantly, investments, to continue to transform their economies.

Further, the death of the Cold War resolves some of the early concerns of the nonaligned movement: the prospects of global Armageddon are now negligible; the United States and the former Soviet Union states are reducing their nuclear arsenals; and most of the nations of the world—developed and underdeveloped—are concerned about the fate of their economies. Indeed, Jawaharlal Nehru saw future global security lying in such a shift of emphasis. What the South needs to do, therefore, is to prevent Western attention from being diverted to future militarization while at the same time retaining its capability for self-defense. It is in this context that declaring oneself a status quo power makes sense. Becoming a status quo nation does not mean disarmament. Instead it requires taking initiatives that convince the major powers that the regional powers of the South are willing to preserve certain common security norms.

One such proposal could entail a Southern guarantee to prevent the transfer of weapons of mass destruction and the technologies associated with it. Such a step does not endanger the security of Southern states but rather fits into the ongoing policies of some of the Southern states. While Brazil, China, and North Korea in the 1980s were willing to transfer missile technology to Middle Eastern nations, India in the 1980s, according to Dr. V. Arunachalam the then Director of Defense Research and Development, turned down $200 million worth of sales to Iraq. Pakistan, similarly, despite its rhetoric about the Islamic Bomb, refused to transfer nuclear technology to Libya. Such a guarantee would not harm southern interests yet it would assuage Western concerns about the proliferation of weaponry.

Southern states have also to come up with their own proposals for peacekeeping forces both in a regional as well as in a UN context. The need for such missions is becoming all the more widespread, even as the Western powers are weakening in their will to carry out such missions. Internationally, southern states could permanently earmark military units within their armed forces to the United Nations for potential deployment around the world. These nations could also specify in what situations and what geographic regions they were willing to allow their forces to serve. Another aspect of such a policy is that it would shift the debate on the use of such force from the great-power-dominated Security Council to the more democratic General Assembly—something that has not really happened since the 1960s. Repeated use of the UN General Assembly for proposing such operations would increase the effectiveness and the democratic nature of that international organization.

Regionally, the existence of peacekeeping organizations would allow for humanitarian intervention, extending support to democratic regimes, effectively precluding great-power intervention, and increasing regional cooperation. There is some basis for optimism in these spheres. The Indian Ocean littoral, for instance, was a hub of superpower rivalry during the Cold War as well an area full of regional tensions. Now, in the naval sphere, there is increased cooperation between the littoral states and the Indian Ocean Rim initiative may lead to broader cooperation.

Another step would be to collaborate with the arms industries of the northern countries to build new weapons systems. The major cutbacks in northern defense spending have left these nations' arms industries struggling to find new markets. At the same time, southern arms industries have run into bottlenecks while trying to produce new systems. If the southern states were to actively seek collaboration it would create an interdependence in the arms market, which would have favorable implications for both the North and the South. The North would benefit in terms of higher employment levels and the survival of key industries. The South would acquire new systems. More importantly, such collaboration would create linkages that would stress the value of the South to the North. Israel, for instance, is already pursuing such a strategy.

In conclusion, the security of regional powers lies in trying to create a meaningful role for themselves in international affairs; a role that breaks the outdated conception of multipolarity and shifts it toward a more democratic international system. Tough bargaining and the willingness to work with the major powers are the first steps in this process.

NOTES

1. Kathleen C. Bailey provides a good survey of Iraqi NBC and delivery vehicle programs and the extent to which they had progressed in *The UN Inspections in Iraq: Lessons for On-Site Verification* (Boulder, Colo.: Westview Press, 1995).

2. Wariawalla's argument is cited in Amit Gupta, "Fire in the Sky: The Indian Missile Program," *Defense and Diplomacy* 8, no. 10 (October 1990): 46.

3. For example, Scott D. Sagan, "The Perils of Proliferation: Organization Theory, Deterrence Theory, and the Spread of Nuclear Weapons," *International Security* 18, no. 4 (spring 1994): 66-107. See Seth Cropsey, "The Only Credible Deterrent," *Foreign Affairs* 73, no. 2 (March/April 1994): 14-20; Ted Galen Carpenter, "Closing the Nuclear Umbrella," *Foreign Affairs* 73, no. 2 (March/ April 1994): 8-13.

4. Kenneth N. Waltz, "The Spread of Nuclear Weapons: More May Be Better," *Adelphi Paper* No. 171 (London: International Institute of Strategic Studies, 1981).

5. Kenneth N. Waltz, "The Emerging Structure of International Politics," *International Security* 18, no. 2 (fall 1993): 64.

6. Ibid., 51.

7. Ibid. The Brodie citation is Bernard Brodie, *War and Politics* (New York: Macmillan, 1973), 321.

8. Waltz, "Emerging Structure," 52.

9. Ibid., 53.

10. Carpenter, "Closing the Nuclear Umbrella," 11.

11. Anthony Lake, "Confronting Backlash States," *Foreign Affairs* 73, no. 2 (March-April 1994): 45. Lake lists Cuba, North Korea, Iran, Iraq and Libya in this category. Such states, he argues, suppress human rights, promote radical ideologies and procure weapons of mass destruction.

12. The role of civilizational consciousness in international relations is discussed in, Samuel Huntington, "The Clash of Civilizations," *Foreign Affairs* 73, no. 2 (summer 1993): 22-49.

13. Alexi G. Arbatov, "Russia's Foreign Policy Alternatives," *International Security* 18, no. 2 (fall 1993): 42.

14. Anatol Lieven, "Russia's Military Nadir," *The National Interest*, Summer 1996, p. 25.

15. John Lewis Gaddis, "Towards the Post-Cold War World," *Foreign Affairs* 70, no. 2 (spring 1991), reprinted in *At Issue—Politics in the World Arena*, 7th, Steven L. Spiegel and David J. Pervin eds. (New York: St. Martin's Press, 1994), 35.

16. For a discussion of the Third Wave see Samuel P. Huntington, *The Third Wave, Democratization in the Late Twentieth Century* (Norman and London: University of Oklahoma Press, 1991).

17. Amit Gupta, "Third World Militaries: New Suppliers, Deadlier Weapons," *Orbis* 37, no. 1 (winter 1993): 67.

18. Remarks by Honorable Les Aspin, Secretary of Defense, National Academy of Sciences Committee on International Security and Arms Control, 7 December 1993.

19. Zbigniew Brzezinski, *Out of Control: Global Turmoil on the Eve of the 21st Century* (New York: Maxwell Macmillan, 1993), 165-66.

20. Carpenter, "Closing the Nuclear Umbrella," 10.

21. Ibid., 11.

22. See, for example John Mearsheimer, "Why We Will Miss the Cold War," *Atlantic Monthly*, August 1990, 35-47.

23. Charles Krauthammer, "The Unipolar Moment," *Foreign Affairs* 70, no. 1 (winter 1990-1991): 24-25.

24. Joseph S. Nye Jr., "What New World Order?," *Foreign Affairs* 71, no. 1 (spring 1992): 88.

25. See Thomas F. Homer Dixon, "On the Threshold: Environmental Changes as Causes of Acute Conflict," *International Security* 16, no. 2 (fall 1991): 76-116.

26. Robert D. Kaplan, "The Coming Anarchy," *Atlantic Monthly*, February 1994, 44-76.

27. Benjamin R. Barber, "Jihad v. McWorld," *Atlantic Monthly*, March 1992, 53-63.

28. An excellent overview of the early Indian debate is provided in Sisir Gupta, "The Indian Dilemma," in *A World of Nuclear Powers?*, Alastair Buchan ed. (Englewood Cliffs, N.J.: Prentice Hall, 1966), 55-67.

Bibliography

REPORTS

Aspin, Les. *Report on the Bottom-Up Review.* Washington, D.C.: Department of Defense, 1993.

Bank of Israel Annual Report. Jerusalem: Government of Israel, 1981-1992.

Blackett, P.M.S. *The Scientific Problem of Defense in Relation to the Needs of the Indian Armed Forces, Report to the Honorable Defense Minister of India,* 10 September 1948.

Eighty-Second Report Estimates Committee, Seventh Lok Sabha 1983-84. *Department of Atomic Energy—Generation of Electricity.* New Delhi: Lok Sabha Secretariat, 1984.

Public Accounts Committee, Seventh Lok Sabha. *Delay in Development and Manufacture of an Aircraft.* New Delhi: Government of India, 1982.

U.S. Department of Defense. *The National Military Strategy 1992.* Washington, D.C.: U.S. Department of Defense Publication, 1992.

Report on Nonproliferation and Counterproliferation Activities and Programs. Washington, D.C.: U.S. Department of Defense Publication, 1994.

U.S. Department of State. *Report to Congress on the Progress toward Regional Nonproliferation in South Asia.* Washington, D.C.: U.S. Department of State, 1993.

ANNUAL PUBLICATIONS

Indian Defense Review
The Military Balance
World Armament and Disarmament, Stockholm International Peace Research Institute Yearbook
World Military Expenditures and Arms Transfers

NEWSPAPERS AND MAGAZINES

Aviation Week and Space Technology
Financial Times
Foreign Broadcast Information Service, Latin America
Foreign Broadcast Information Service, Near East and South Asia
Hindu
Hindustan Times
Indian Express
India Today
Jane's Defense Weekly
New York Times
Times of India
Wall Street Journal

BOOKS

Adler, Emanuel. *The Power of Ideology: The Quest for Technological Autonomy in Argentina and Brazil.* Berkeley: University of California Press, 1987

Ali, Akhtar. *Pakistan's Nuclear Dilemma.* New Delhi: ABC, 1984.

Allison, Graham T. *Essence of Decision: Explaining the Cuban Missile Crisis.* Boston: Little, Brown and Company, 1971.

Alves, Maria Helena Moreira. *State and Military Opposition in Brazil.* Austin: University of Texas Press, 1985.

Andreski, Stanislav. *Military Organization and Society.* Berkeley and Los Angeles: University of California Press, 1968.

Aronson, Shlomo. *Conflict and Bargaining in the Middle East.* Baltimore and London: Johns Hopkins University Press, 1978.

Baek, Kwang-Il, Ronald D. Mclaurin and Chung-in Moon, eds. *The Dilemma of Third World Defense Industries: Supplier Control or Recipient Autonomy.* Boulder, Colo.: Westview Press, 1989..

Bailey, Kathleen C. *The UN Inspections in Iraq: Lessons for on-site Verification.* Boulder, Colo.: Westview Press, 1995.

Brzezinski, Zbigniew. *Out of Control: Global Turmoil on the Eve of the 21st Century.* New York: Maxwell Macmillan, 1993.

Brzoska, Michael, and Thomas Ohlson, eds. *Arms Production in the Third World.* London: Taylor and Francis, 1986.

_____. *Arms Transfers to the Third World, 1971-85.* Oxford: Oxford University Press, 1987.

Buchan, Alastair, ed. *A World of Nuclear Powers.* Englewood Cliffs, N.J.: Prentice Hall, 1966

Burrows, William E., and Robert Windrem. *Critical Mass: The Dangerous Race for Superweapons in a Fragmenting World.* New York: Simon and Schuster, 1994.

Buzan, Barry. *People, States and Fear: The National Security Problem in International Relations.* Chapel Hill: University of North Carolina Press, 1983.

Catrina, Christian. *Arms Transfers and Dependence.* New York: Taylor and Francis, 1988.

Cohen, Stephen P. *The Indian Army: Its Contribution to the Development of a Nation.* New Delhi: Oxford University Press, 1990.

Evron, Yair. *Israel's Nuclear Dilemma.* Ithaca, N.Y.: Cornell University Press, 1994.

Ferrari, Paul, Raul Madrid, and Jeff Knopf. *US Arms Exports: Policies and Contractors.* Cambridge: Ballinger, 1988.

Franko-Jones, Patrice. *The Brazilian Defense Industry.* Boulder, Colo.: Westview Press, 1992.

Gordon, Sandy. *India's Rise to Power in the Twentieth Century and Beyond.* New York: St. Martin's Press, 1995.

Green, Stephen. *Living by the Sword:—America and Israel in the Middle East 1968-87.* Brattleboro, Vt: Amana, 1988.

Gupta, Sisir. *India and Regional Integration in Asia.* Bombay: Asia Publishing House, 1964.

Haglund, David G. ed. *The Defense Industrial Base and the West.* London and New York: Routledge, 1989.

Hersh, Seymour. 1991. *The Samson Option: Israel's Nuclear Option and American Foreign Policy.* New York: Random House, 1991.

Huntington, Samuel P. *The Third Wave: Democratization in the Late Twentieth Century.* Norman and London: University of Oklahoma Press, 1991.

Jabber. Fuad. *Israel and Nuclear Weapons: Present Option and Future Strategies.* London, Chatto and Windus, 1971.

Jay, Anthony, and Jonathan Lynn. *The Yes Minister Diaries.* London: Andre Deutch, 1986.

Job, Brian, ed. *The Insecurity Dilemma. National Security of Third World States.* Boulder, Colo.: Lynne Rienner, 1992.

Kaldor, Mary, and Asborn Eide. *The World Military Order: The Impact of Military Technology on the Third World.* London: Macmillan, 1979.

Kapstein, Ethan B. *The Political Economy of National Security, A Global Perspective.* Columbia: University of South Carolina Press, 1992.

Kapur, Ashok. *India's Nuclear Option: Atomic Diplomacy and Decision Making.* New York: Praeger, 1976.

Karsh, Efraim, Martin S. Navias, and Philip Sabin, eds. *Non-Conventional Weapons Proliferation in the Middle East.* Oxford: Clarendon Press, 1993.

Katz, James Everett, ed. *Arms Production in Developing Countries: An Analysis of Decision Making.* Lexington, Mass.: Lexington Books, 1984.

_____. ed. The *Implications of Third World Military Industrialization: Sowing the Serpent's Teeth.* Lexington, Mass.: Lexington Books, 1986.

Klare, Michael, and Daniel Thomas, eds. *World Security: Trends and Challenges at Century's End.* New York: St. Martin's Press, 1991.

Klieman, Aaron. *Israel's Global Reach: Arms Sales as Diplomacy.* Washington: Pergamon-Brassey's, 1985.

Klieman, Ahron, and Ariel Levite, eds. *Deterrence in the Middle East, Where Theory and Practice Converge.* Boulder, Colo.: Westview Press, 1993.

Klieman, Ahron and Reuven Pedatzur. *Rearming Israel: Defense Procurement Through the 1990s.* Boulder, Colo.: Westview Press, 1991.

Kolodziej, Edward A. *Making and Marketing Arms: The French Experience and its Implications for the International System.* Princeton, N.J.: Princeton University Press, 1987.

Krepinevich, Andrew F. *The Bottom-Up Review: An Assessment*. Washington, D.C.: Defense Budget Project, 1994.

Lal, Pratap Chand. *My Years with the IAF*. New Delhi: Lancer, 1986.

Lanir, Zvi, ed. 1984. *Israeli Security Planning in the 1980s: Its Politics and Economics*. New York: Praeger, 1984.

Levite, Ariel. *Offense and Defense in Israeli Military Doctrine*. Boulder, Colo.: Westview Press, 1989.

Luttwak, Edward, and Dan Horowitz. *The Israeli Army*. London: Allen Lane, 1975.

Maldifassi, Jose O., and Pier A. Abetti. *Defense Industries in Latin American Countries*. Westport, Conn. and London: Praeger, 1994.

Mansingh, Surjit. *India's Search for Power: Indira Gandhi's Foreign Policy, 1966-82*. New Delhi, Beverly Hills, London: Sage, 1984.

Matthews, Ron. *Defense Production in India*. New Delhi: ABC, 1989.

Nair, Vijay K. 1992. *Nuclear India*. New Delhi: Lancer International, 1992.

Neumann, Stephanie G. ed. *Defense Planning in Less Industrialized States*. Lexington, Mass.: Lexington Books, 1984.

Nolan, Janne. *Trappings of Power: Ballistic Missiles in the Third World*. Washington D.C.: The Brookings Institution, 1991.

Peres, Shimon. *David's Sling*. New York, Random House, 1970.

Posen, Barry. *The Sources of Military Doctrine. France, Britain, Germany Between the World Wars*. Ithaca, N.Y.: Cornell University Press, 1984.

Potter, William, and Harlan W. Jencks eds. *The International Missile Bazaar: The New Suppliers Network*. Boulder, Colo.: Westview Press, 1994.

Pry, Peter. *Israel's Nuclear Arsenal*. Boulder, Colo.: Westview Press, 1984.

Rajan, M. S., and Shivaji Ganguly, eds. *Great Power Relations, World Order and the Third World*. New Delhi: Vikas, 1981.

Reiser, Stewart. *The Israeli Arms Industry*. New York: Holmes and Meier, 1989.

Rikhye, Ravi, *The Militarisation of Mother India*. New Delhi: Chanakya, 1990.

Schneider, Ronald M. *The Political System of Brazil: Emergence of a "Modernizing Authoritarian Regime," 1964-1970*. New York: University of Columbia Press, 1971.

Sharma, Dhirendra. *India's Nuclear Estate*. New Delhi: Lancer, 1983.

Singh, Harjinder. *Birth of an Air Force*. New Delhi: Palit and Palit, 1977

Singh, Sukhwant *India's Wars Since Independence* 2. New Delhi: Vikas, 1981.

———. *India's Wars Since Independence* 3. New Delhi: Vikas, 1981.

Smith, William C., Carlos H. Acuna, and Eduardo A. Gamarra, eds. *Democracy, Markets, and Structural Reform in Latin America: Argentina, Bolivia, Brazil, Chile, and Mexico*. New Brunswick and London: Transaction, 1994.

Spector, Leonard S., with Jacqueline R. Smith. *Nuclear Ambitions: The Spread of Nuclear Weapons 1989-1990*. Boulder, Colo.: Westview Press, 1990.

Spiegel, Steven L., and David J. Pervin, eds. *At Issue: Politics in the World Arena* 7th. New York: St. Martin's Press, 1994.

Strange, Susan. *States and Markets*. London: Pinter Publishers, 1988.

Subrahmanyam, K. *Indian Security Perspectives*. New Delhi: ABC, 1983.

Thomas, Raju G. C. *The Defense of India: A Budgetary Perspective of Strategy and Politics*. New Delhi: Macmillan, 1978.

Wainwright, A. Martin. *Inheritance of Empire: Britain, India, and the Balance of Power in Asia, 1938-55*. Westport, Conn.: Praeger, 1994.

Weismann, Steven, and Herbert Krosney. *The Islamic Bomb*. New York: Times Books, 1981.

Yaniv, Avner. *Deterrence Without the Bomb: The Politics of Israeli Strategy*. Lexington, Mass.: Lexington, 1987.

____. ed. *National Security and Democracy in Israel*. Boulder, Colo.: Lynne Rienner, 1993.

ARTICLES

Adler, Emanuel. "State Institutions, Ideology, and Autonomous Technological Development: Computers and Nuclear Energy in Argentina and Brazil." *Latin American Research Review* 23, no. 2 (1988).

Anderson, Robert S. *Building Scientific Institutions in India: Saha and Bhabha*. Occasional Paper Series, 11. Montreal: McGill University, (1975).

Arbatov, Alexi G. "Russians Foreign Policy Alternatives." *International Security* 18, no. 2 (Fall 1993).

Aronson, Geoffrey. "Hidden Agenda: U.S.-Israeli Relations and the Nuclear Question." *The Middle East Journal* 46, no. 4 (1992).

Avineri, Shlomo. "Israel and the End of the Cold War." *The Brookings Review* (spring 1993).

Barber, Benjamin R. 1992. "Jihad v. McWorld." *Atlantic Monthly*, March 1992.

Barua, Poonam Sethi. "India-Pakistan Confidence Building Measures, *International Security Digest* 2, no. 8. (May 1995).

Bedi, Rahul. "Collaboration Invited for LCA Program," *Jane's Defense Weekly*, January 29, 1994.

____. "India Stems Fall in Defense Spending." *Jane's Defense Weekly*, March 12, 1994.

Bhargava, G. S. 1978. "India's Nuclear Policy." *India Quarterly* 34, no. 2. (April-June 1978).

____. "The Nuclear Power Industry: Need for Reappraisal." *IUMDA Newsletter* 2&3 (1990).

Bidwai, Praful. 1994. "India and the NPT Review." *The Times of India* (New Delhi). September 22, 1994.

Bonen, Zeev. The Technological Arms Race—An Economic Dead End?" In *Israeli Security Planning in the 1980s: Its Politics and Economics*, Zvi Lanir ed. New York: Praeger, 1984.

Carpenter, Ted Galen. "Closing the Nuclear Umbrella." *Foreign Affairs* 73, no. 2 (March/ April 1994).

de Castro, Antonio Barros. "Renegade Development: Rise and Demise of State-Led Development in Brazil." In *Democracy, Markets, and Structural Reform in Latin America: Argentina, Bolivia, Brazil, Chile, and Mexico*, William C. Smith, Carlos H. Acuna, and Eduardo A. Gamarra, eds. New Brunswick and London: Transaction, 1994.

de Castro, Antonio Rubens Britto, Norberto Majlis, Luiz Pinguelli Rosa, and Fernando de Souza Barros. "Brazil's Nuclear Shakeup: Military Still in Control." *Bulletin of the Atomic Scientists*. (May 1989).

Chari, P. R. "India's Nuclear Choices: Some Perspectives." In *Great Power Relations, World Order and the Third World*, M. S. Rajan and Shivaji Ganguly eds. New Delhi: Vikas, 1981.

Chellany, Brahma. "An Indian Critique of U.S. Export Controls." *Orbis* 38 no. 3 (1994).

Chengappa, Raj. "LCA Project: A Testing Time." *India Today* 31 August 1988.

Chopra, Pushpindar. "Spinal Cord of the Indian Air Force." *Air International* (January 1975).

Cohen, Avner. "Most Favored Nation." *Bulletin of the Atomic Scientists* 51, no. 1. (January/February 1995).

Cohen, Avner, and Benjamin Frankel. "Opaque Nuclear Proliferation." *Journal of Strategic Studies* 13, no. 3 (1990)

Cohen, Avner, and Marvin Miller, "Facing the Unavoidable: Israel's Nuclear Monopoly Revisited." *Journal of Strategic Studies* 13, no. 3 (1990)

Conca, Ken. "Technology, the Military and Democracy in Brazil." *Journal of InterAmerican Studies and World Affairs* 34, no. 1 (Spring 1992).

Cordesman, Anthony. "Defense Planning in Saudi Arabia." In *Defense Planning in Less-Industrialized States*, Stephanie Neumann ed. Lexington Mass.: Lexington Books, 1984.

_____. "The India-Pakistan Military Balance." Unpublished Paper, 1987.

Cropsey, Seth. "The Only Credible Deterrent." *Foreign Affairs* 73, no.2 (March/April 1994).

Dagnino, Renato, and Domicio Proenca. *Arms Production and Technological Spinoffs: The Brazilian Aeronautics Industry*. Unpublished Paper, 1988.

Deshingkar, Giri. "CTBT—The State of the Debate in India." *International Security Digest* 1, no. 10. (September 1994).

Evron, Yair. "Deterrence Experience in the Arab-Israel Conflict." In *Deterrence in the Middle East, Where Theory and Practice Converge*, Ahron Klieman and Ariel Levite eds. Boulder, Colo.: Westview Press, 1993.

Foss, Christopher F. "Ground Forces—Who is Buying What?." *Jane's Defense Weekly*. 30 July, 1994.

Gaddis, John Lewis. "Towards the Post-Cold War World." Foreign Affairs, 70 no. 2 (spring 1991). Reprinted in *At Issue: Politics in the World Arena*, Steven L. Spiegel and David J. Pervin eds. 7. New York: St. Martin's Press, 1994.

Gouvea-Neto, Raul. "How Brazil Competes in the Global Defense Industry." *Latin American Research Review* 26, no. 3 (1991)

Gupta, Amit. "India's Military Buildup: To What Purpose?" *Armed Forces Journal International* (October 1989).

_____. "The Indian Arms Industry, A Lumbering Giant?" *Asian Survey* 30, no. 9. (September 1990).

_____. "Fire in the Sky: The Indian Missile Program." *Defense and Diplomacy* 8, no. 10 (October 1990).

_____. Third World Militaries: New Suppliers, Deadlier Weapons." *Orbis* 37, no. 1. (Winter 1993).

_____. "I Want my M-i-G: How India's Force Structure and Military Doctrine are Determined." *Asian Survey* 35, no. 5. (May 1995).

Gupta, Shekhar. "India Redefines its Role." *Adelphi Paper* No. 293. London: Oxford University Press, 1995.

Gupta, Sisir. "Break With the Past." *Seminar* (January 1965).

_____. "The Indian Dilemma." In *A World of Nuclear Powers*, Alastair Buchan ed. Englewood Cliffs, N.J.: Prentice Hall, 1966.

Hagerty, Devin. "India's Regional Security Doctrine." *Asian Survey* 31, no. 4 (April 1991).

Hilton, Stanley. "The Brazilian Military: Changing Strategic Perceptions and the Question of Mission." *Armed Forces and Society* 13, no. 3 (Spring 1987).

Hoge James F. Jr., "Fulfilling Brazil's Promise: A Conversation with President Cardoso." *Foreign Affairs* 74, no. 4 (July-August 1995).

Homer-Dixon, Thomas F. "On the Threshold: Environmental Changes as Causes of Acute Conflict." *International Security* 16, no. 2 (fall 1991).

Hummel, Christopher K. "Ukrainian Arms Makers Are Left on Their Own," *RFE/RL Reports* 14 August 1992.

Huntington, Samuel P. "The Clash of Civilizations." *Foreign Affairs* 72, no. 2 (summer 1993).

International Studies Newsletter 22, no. 4 (May 1995).

Kanwal, Gurmeet. "Strike Corps Offensive Operations: Imperatives for Success." *Indian Defense Review* (January 1988).

Kaplan, Robert D. "The Coming Anarchy." *Atlantic Monthly*, February 1994.

Kapstein, Ethan B. "The Brazilian Defense Industry and the International System." *Political Science Quarterly* 105, no. 4. (Winter 1990-1991).

Kemp, Ian, Hal Klepak, Charles Bickers, Dean Martins, and Donald Neil. "JDW Country Survey: Brazil." *Jane's Defense Weekly*, 9 May 1992.

Kessler, Richard. "Peronists Seek Nuclear Greatness." *Bulletin of the Atomic Scientists* 45, no. 5 (May 1989).

Klare, Michael. "The Next Great Arms Race." *Foreign Affairs* 72 no. 3 (summer 1993).

Kolodziej, Edward A. "Whither Modernization and Militarisation: Implications for International Peace and Security." In *Peace, Defense and Economic Analysis*, Christian Schmidt ed. London: Macmillan, 1987.

Krasno, Jean. "Brazil's Secret Nuclear Program." *Orbis* 38, no. 3 (summer 1994).

Krauthammer, Charles. "The Unipolar Moment." *Foreign Affairs* 70, no. 1. (winter 1990-1991).

Krishna, Raj. "India and the Bomb," *India Quarterly* 21, no. 2 (April-June 1965).

Krishnamurthi, M. "Self-Reliance: Lessons of Agni." *The Hindu* (Gurgaon), 5 July 1989..

Kumaraswamy, P. R. "Egypt needles Israel," *Bulletin of the Atomic Scientists* 51, no. 2 (March/April 1995).

Lake, Anthony. "Confronting 'Backlash' States." *Foreign Affairs* 73, no. 2. (March-April 1994).

Luttwak, Edward N. 1984. "Commentary—Defense Planning in Israel: A Brief Retrospective." In *Defense Planning in Less-Industrialized States*, Stephanie G. Neumann ed. Lexington, Mass. : Lexington Books, 1984.

Malhotra, Inder. "Hankering After the Harrier." *The Times of India.* (New Delhi) 17 July 1973.

Marwah, Onkar. 1977. "India's Nuclear and Space Programs: Intent and Policy." *International Security.* 2, no. 2. (fall 1977).

Masani, Minoo. "The Challenge of the Chinese Bomb—II." *India Quarterly* 21, no. 1 (January-March 1965).

Mearsheimer, John D. "Why We Will Miss the Cold War." *Atlantic Monthly*, August 1990.

Mintz, Alex, and Gerald Steinberg. "Coping with Supplier Control: The Israeli Experience." In *The Dilemma of Third World Defense Industries: Supplier Control or Recipient Autonomy*, Kwang-il Baek, Ronald D. Mclaurin, and Chung-in Moon eds. Boulder, Colo.: Westview Press, 1989.

Morrison, Barrie, and Donald Page. "India's Option: The Nuclear Route to Achieve Goal as World Power." *International Perspectives* (July-August 1974).

Navias, Martin. "Ballistic Missile Proliferation: The Third World," *Adelphi Paper* No. 252. London: International Institute of Strategic Studies, 1990.

Nehru, R. K. "The Challenge of the Chinese Bomb—I." *India Quarterly* 21, no. 1 (January-March 1965).

Nye Ir., Joseph S. "What New World Order?" *Foreign Affairs* 71, no. 1. (spring 1992).

Ollapally, Deepa, and Raja Ramanna. "U.S.-India Tensions—Misperceptions on Nuclear Proliferation." *Foreign Affairs* 74, no. 1 (January/February 1995).

Patel, H.M. "Arrangement with the West." *Seminar* (January 1965).

Prabhu, Rajendra. "Misgivings Over LCA Plan Changes." *Hindustan Times* (New Delhi) 24 January 1987.

Prasad, Srinivas. "Designed Delays: Advanced Light Helicopter." *India Today* 31 January 1986.

Quester, George H. "Nuclear Weapons and Israel." *The Middle East Journal* 37, no. 4 (autumn 1993).

Rao, N. Vasuki. "Where Are the Arms to Export?" *Indian Express* (New Delhi) 22 February 1989.

Rikhye, Ravi. "Rethinking Mechanized Infantry Concepts," *USI Journal* (April-June 1972).

_____. "A New Armored Force for India." *USI Journal* (April-June 1973).

Sagan, Scott D. "The Perils of Proliferation: Organization Theory, Deterrence Theory, and the spread of Nuclear Weapons." *International Security* 18, no. 4 (spring 1994).

Santhanam, K. "Indian Defense Technology and Infrastructure and Prospects of Indo-U.S. Cooperation." Paper presented at the Indo-U.S. Defense Workshop, National Defense University, Washington, D.C., September, 1989.

SenGupta, Bhabani, and Amit Gupta. 1986. "The Roots of Conflict in South Asia," in *Regional Cooperation and Development in South Asia*, 1, Bhabani SenGupta ed. New Delhi: South Asian Publishers, 1986.

Sola, Lourdes. "The State, Structural Reform, and Democratization in Brazil." In Smith et. al., *Democracy, Markets, and Structural Reform, in Latin America*.

Solingen, Etel. "Macropolitical Consensus and Lateral Autonomy in Industrial Policy: the nuclear sector in Brazil and Argentina." *International Organization* 47, no. 2 (spring 1993).

Steinberg, Gerald M. "Indigenous Arms Industries and Dependence: The Case of Israel." *Defense Analysis* 2, no. 4 (December 1986).

_____. "Time for Regional Approaches?" *Orbis* 38, no. 3 (summer 1994).

_____. "Israel: Case Study for International Missile Trade and Nonproliferation." In *The International Missile Bazaar—The New Suppliers Network*, William Potter and Harlan W. Jencks eds. Boulder Colo.: Westview Press, 1994.

Subrahmanyam, K. "The Islamic Bomb, U.S. Silence On Saudi Effort," *The Times of India* (New Delhi) 2 August 1994.

_____. "Strategy of Engagement." *The Times of India* (New Delhi) 6 December 1994.

Sundaram, Gowri, and Mike Howarth. "India: Indigenous Programs Flourish Amid Modernization." *International Defense Review* 4 (1986)

Sundarji, K. "Strategy in the Age of Nuclear Deterrence and its Application to Developing Countries." M. Phil. thesis submitted to Madras University, 11 June 1984.

Tellis, Ashley. "Securing the Barrack: The Logic, Structure and Objectives of India's Naval Expansion, Part I." *Naval War College Review* (September 1990).

____. "Securing the Barrack: The Logic, Structure and Objectives of India's Naval Expansion, Part II." *Naval War College Review* (October 1990).

Waltz, Kenneth N. "The Spread of Nuclear Weapons: More May be Better." *Adelphi Paper* No. 171. London: International Institute of Strategic Studies, 1981.

____."The Emerging Structure of International Politics." *International Security* 18, no. 2. (fall 1993).

Waslekar, Sandeep. "Abolishing Nuclear Weapons: Rajiv Gandhi Plan Revisited." *Acdis Occasional Paper* University of Illinois, Urbana, July 1994.

Yaniv, Avner. "Non-Conventional Weaponry and the Future of Arab-Israeli Deterrence." In *Non-Conventional Weapons Proliferation in the Middle East*, Efraim Karsh, Martin S. Navias, and Philip Sabin eds. Oxford: Clarendon Press, 1993.

Index

About the Author

AMIT GUPTA is Assistant Professor of Political Science at Stonehill College.

ISBN 0-275-95787-X

HARDCOVER BAR CODE